a decade later:
a follow-up
of social class
and
mental illness

By the same author:

J. K. Myers and B. H. Roberts, *Family and Class Dynamics in Mental Illness*, Wiley, 1964

a decade later: a follow-up of social class and mental illness

Jerome K. Myers and Lee L. Bean

in collaboration with
Max P. Pepper
Yale University

john wiley and sons, inc.   new york · london · sydney

to our wives

This is a report on a ten-year follow-up study of persons enumerated in the 1950 New Haven Psychiatric Census. In the original study, significant relationships were found between social class and the development, prevalence, and treatment of diagnosed mental illness. The present study focuses upon social class as a determinant of the patients' experience in the ten years following the original study. More specifically, three questions are raised: Is social class related to treatment status at follow-up in 1960? Are there social class differences in the patients' treatment and readmission experiences during the ten-year period? Are there social class differences in the adjustment of former patients in the community? Briefly, the findings indicate that there are, indeed, social class differences in what happened to the patients in the ten years following the original study, and successive chapters describe the details of these differences.

The planning for this study began nearly ten years ago when August B. Hollingshead, Fredrick C. Redlich, and Jerome K. Myers were completing the original study of social class and mental illness. Although a follow-up study was not considered at the start of the original research, such a study was given increasing consideration as the project developed. Beginning in 1953, Hollingshead served as chairman of the Committee on Follow-Up Studies in Mental Illness of the National Institute of Mental Health. His experience on this committee helped focus our attention on the need for follow-up research and the feasibility of restudying our original sample of patients.

Because of other commitments, Redlich decided not to participate as a major collaborator in the new study. Therefore, Max P. Pepper, psychiatrist, joined Hollingshead and Myers in 1958 in drafting a research proposal. In 1960, the National Institute of Mental Health, United States Public Health Service, made a research grant which supported the study to its conclusion. Before the research was actually started, Hollingshead became involved in another research project supported by the United States Public Health Service. Consequently, in May 1960, Lee L. Bean joined the project as a sociologist. Myers, Pepper, and Bean collected and analyzed the data. In 1963, Pepper assumed the position of Director of Mental Health Planning for the state of Connecticut and had to reduce his participation in the study. Therefore, Myers and Bean authored the manuscript, with Pepper serving as a regular consultant.

This book is intended for both a lay and a professional audience. It is interdisciplinary in its appeal, and (we hope) it will be of interest to social workers, psychologists, anthropologists, nurses, public health workers, and mental health volunteer workers, for example, as well as to sociologists and psychiatrists. Because of the varied audience, we have tried to keep technical discussion at a level that can be understood by all readers.

This study could never have been completed without the cooperation of the patients, their families, and the members of the nonpatient sample. We have tried our best to preserve their anonymity. Persons are identified only by initials (which are not the actual initials of their names), and details which might be identifiable have been altered without otherwise distorting the materials.

We are indebted to many persons who helped to make this research possible. The professional and administrative staffs of the psychiatric hospitals and clinics whose patients we studied were always cooperative. Dr. Wilfred Bloomberg, Commissioner of Mental Health of Connecticut, and his staff made our task considerably easier by coordinating the efforts of state agencies in Connecticut. Josef Hes, a psychiatrist, assisted in the development of the research instruments and in data collection. Connie Harris, a research assistant, was especially helpful in the analysis of the data and Lillian Smith typed the manuscript. Janet Turk was invaluable in editing this book and preparing the index. Her professional competence and skill are evident. We also express our gratitude to the many persons who assisted in the collection and analysis of the data. Their dedication and perseverance were essential to the success of the project.

Finally, we owe special thanks to August B. Hollingshead and Fredrick C. Redlich for their constant encouragement and assistance from the project's inception to its conclusion. Hollingshead's comments and criticisms after reading a draft of the entire manuscript were particularly helpful for its final preparation. Both men have been instrumental in making Yale a center for interdisciplinary research in social psychiatry and in providing the support necessary for the type of research reported in this book.

Jerome K. Myers
Lee L. Bean

New Haven, Connecticut
January, 1967

contents

part four | summary and conclusions   199

a decade later:
a follow-up
of social class
and
mental illness

introduction

part
one

Chapters One and Two describe the research problem and how the data were collected to test a series of hypotheses about social class and (1) the outcome of psychiatric treatment, and (2) the adjustment of former patients in the community. Chapter Three describes the social setting to which most patients returned after treatment. Readers who are not interested in the details of scientific procedures may wish to omit Chapter Two.

the research problem

Mental disorders continue to be one of the major medical and social problems in America today, despite increasing efforts over the past two decades to develop more effective methods of treatment and rehabilitation. Although there has been an increase in hospital discharges during recent years, it has been more than offset by a rise in admissions, particularly in readmissions. The number of patients, for example, in state, county, and private psychiatric hospitals in the United States decreased by about 11,000 (from 540,475 in 1961 to 529,396 in 1962) at the same time that the number of admissions increased by almost 21,000 (from 320,735 to 341,533).[1] This pattern of rising hospital readmissions is found in other countries as well. In a study of schizophrenics in England, for example, the number of new admissions increased by 700 between 1954 and 1959, but readmissions increased by nearly 7000 for the same period.[2]

As more patients move back and forth between the hospital and the community, it has become increasingly evident that little is known about the long-range effectiveness of psychiatric treatment, either in-

---

[1] United States Bureau of the Census, *Statistical Abstract of the United States,* 85th Edition, Washington, D.C., 1964, p. 80, and 86th Edition, Washington, D.C., 1965, p. 80.
[2] See Eileen M. Brooke, "Discussion," *Proceedings of the Royal Society of London (Series B. Biological Sciences),* 159, 217 (1963).

patient or outpatient, or of the experience of former patients in the community. Much psychiatric research has centered on the patient in treatment, especially the hospitalized patient, and the outcome of treatment has been viewed primarily in terms of discharge. But the course of a person's mental illness is generally lengthy and complex, extending in time both before and beyond treatment. Mental illness is not a discrete episode set off, on the one hand, by disease onset and, on the other, by terminal hospitalization or "cure." For this reason cross-sectional studies of mental illness at one point in time need to be supplemented by longitudinal investigations.

Research is needed on the "career" [3] of the patient after his discharge, his adjustment and life in the community, and further cycles of treatment and discharge generated by rehospitalization or further outpatient care. The study reported in this book is an example of such research—*an examination of the influence of social class upon the long-range outcome of psychiatric treatment and the adjustment of former patients in the community.*

This study also reflects the growing interest in social psychiatry which has been defined as the "exploration of social systems and culture and their impact on psychiatric phenomena." [4] Although most early psychiatric theories of etiology and treatment were primarily organic or psychological in nature, there is an increasing acceptance of the view that there are social components in mental illness as well as organic, intrapsychic, and interpersonal elements. As the focus of attention shifts from the patient undergoing treatment to the patient in the community, the importance of the social environment in psychiatric problems becomes especially clear.

The aspect of the social environment studied in this research—social class—is of central importance in sociology, and its usefulness in understanding human behavior is well documented. Theories of social stratification may differ in detail, particularly in terms of the bases for the systems of inequalities, but all agree that the various ranking systems in

---

[3] Goffman divides the career of the mental patient into three main phases: the prepatient, the inpatient, and the expatient. His insightful work focuses upon the first two phases, particularly the period of hospitalization. See Erving Goffman, *Asylums: Essays on the Social Situation of Mental Patients and Other Inmates*, Aldine Pub., Chicago, 1962.

[4] See Fredrick C. Redlich and Max P. Pepper, "Social Psychiatry," *American Journal of Psychiatry*, 116, 611 (1960); T. A. C. Rennie, "Social Psychiatry: A Definition," *International Journal of Social Psychiatry*, 1 (1955). For a review of the major issues and research in social psychiatry, see yearly summary, "Social Psychiatry," by Max P. Pepper and F. C. Redlich in the January issues of recent years of the *American Journal of Psychiatry*.

a society set limits to the range and patterns of interaction among its members.[5] Members of any society are more likely to interact with social equals than with individuals in different rank positions. Various hierarchically ranked groupings in the society, identified as social classes, tend to be distinguished from one another not only in terms of different occupational roles, educational backgrounds, and resources but also by systematic behavior patterns and styles of life. The constellation of similar behavior patterns and styles of life is elaborated and expressed in distinctive social-class subcultures.[6] Consequently, an individual's position in the status hierarchy influences his attitudes, values, behavior, the privileges he enjoys, and his very life chances.

THE RESEARCH PROBLEM

The research reported in this volume grew out of the studies of social class and mental illness begun in New Haven in 1950. The original studies demonstrated a relationship between social class and certain aspects of diagnosed mental illness, namely, its development, prevalence, type, and treatment.[7]

---

[5] Marx, for example, was primarily concerned with the economic differentiation of the population stemming from the division of labor found in any society. Weber, in contrast, argued that populations tend to become differentiated along three dimensions: class, status, and power. Later writers have refined, reexamined, and, in some cases, extended the concept almost to the point of "overconceptualization."

For a brief review of significant theoretical discussions of social class, see Reinhard Bendix and Seymour M. Lipset, "Karl Marx' Theory of Social Classes," in R. Bendix and S. M. Lipset (eds.), *Class, Status, and Power*, The Free Press, Glencoe, Ill., 1953; Max Weber, "Class, Status, Party," in H. H. Gerth and C. Wright Mills (eds. and trans.), *From Max Weber: Essays in Sociology*, Oxford University Press, New York, 1946; Talcott Parsons, "A Revised Analytical Approach to the Theory of Social Stratification," in Bendix and Lipset, *op. cit.*; Kingsley Davis and W. F. Moore, "Some Principles of Stratification," *American Sociological Review*, 10, 242 (1945); Joseph A. Kahl, *The American Class Structure*, Rinehart, New York, 1957, pp. 1–38; and Harold W. Pfautz, "The Current Literature on Social Stratification: Critique and Bibliography," *American Journal of Sociology*, LVIII, 391 (1953).

[6] See, for example, Leo Srole, Thomas S. Langner, Stanley T. Michael, Marvin K. Opler, and T. A. C. Rennie, *Mental Health in the Metropolis: The Midtown Manhattan Study*, Vol. 1, McGraw-Hill, New York, 1962, pp. 194–95; S. M. Miller and Frank Riessman, "The Working Class Subculture: A New View," in Arthur B. Shostak and William Gomberg (eds.), *Blue Collar World*, Prentice-Hall, Englewood Cliffs, N.J., 1964; Herbert H. Hyman, "The Value Systems of Different Classes: A Social Psychological Contribution to the Analysis of Stratification," in Bendix and Lipset, *op. cit.*; A. B. Hollingshead, *Elmtown's Youth*, Wiley, New York, 1949.

[7] August B. Hollingshead and Fredrick C. Redlich, *Social Class and Mental Illness*, Wiley, New York, 1958; Jerome K. Myers and Bertram H. Roberts, *Family and Class Dynamics in Mental Illness*, Wiley, New York, 1959.

The present study deals with later periods in the career of the mental patient—treatment outcome, the probability of readmission to treatment, and adjustment in the community after treatment. It focuses upon relationships between social class and what happened to the patients in the ten years following the original study. Specifically, three hypotheses are investigated:

Hypothesis One. Social class is related to treatment status in 1960 at follow-up.

Hypothesis Two. Social class is related to the patient's treatment and readmission experience during the period from 1950 to 1960.

Hypothesis Three. Social class is related to the former patient's adjustment in the community.

To answer the questions upon which this research is based, it was necessary to follow a group of patients from the period in which they received treatment to some later date. An ideal research design would be to study a community—following a cohort from the development of a mental illness and its psychiatric treatment to death and cataloging the events which are significant throughout the life cycle—but practical considerations, particularly the time needed, precluded such a study. However, a follow-up study must cover a period of sufficient length to encompass the widest possible range of events occurring during the life cycle of the patient. Since there were no hard-and-fast rules or guides available as to what would constitute an adequate follow-up period, it was decided to follow up the patient after a lapse of 10 years from the period of the original psychiatric census. Ten years probably constitute an adequate time period because patients not discharged from treatment by then probably never will be. Previous studies of hospital patients demonstrate clearly that an individual's chance for discharge is very slight, indeed, if he is not discharged within 10 years after admission.[8]

PREVIOUS RESEARCH

Although there have been many follow-up studies of psychiatric patients, there is little comprehensive knowledge about the experience of such patients *after treatment.* Generally, previous studies have been undertaken to answer very specific questions. Because they have deliberately restricted themselves, most follow-up studies are extremely limited in

---

[8] Leta M. Adler, James W. Coddington, and Donald D. Stewart, *Mental Illness in Washington County, Arkansas: Incidence, Recovery, and Posthospital Adjustment,* University of Arkansas Research Series No. 23, Fayetteville, Ark., 1952.

scope and provide only fragmentary information about the career of mental patients and the factors related to treatment outcome. Their limitations are as follows:

First, most follow-up studies include a homogeneous patient population. Frequently studies are limited—to patients of a single diagnostic category, such as schizophrenics; by demographic factors, such as sex, age, or marital status; by entrance into treatment for the first time; or by treatment for a specified period of time.[9] Such constrictions on the patient sample studied have methodological values as well as limitations. By dealing with a homogeneous population, the size of the sample needed for study can be reduced, and the effects of certain variables which might be confounding the phenomena under investigation can be controlled. For example, if in a sample of males differences in the rate of discharge are noted for certain factors, this variation obviously is not due to male-female differences. Despite such advantages, the use of a homogeneous sample makes it impossible to deal with confounding effects. If the independent variable under examination is sex-linked, for instance, it would be impossible to determine whether or not its effect is the same for males and females.

Second, most previous studies have been limited to certain aspects of the treatment process. Generally, patients from only one institution or type of institution are included in the study or patients treated by a single form of therapy, for example, psychotherapy, electroshock, insulin coma, or lobotomy.[10] Such studies have the same advantages and limitations brought into being by the use of a homogeneous sample.

---

[9] Jones, for example, restricted his study to neurotics: Maxwell Jones, *The Therapeutic Community: A New Treatment Method in Psychiatry*, Basic Books, New York, 1953. The Adler study deals only with males entering treatment in one state hospital during a specified time period: Adler, Coddington, and Stewart, *op. cit.* The Brown analysis covers male chronic schizophrenic patients only: George W. Brown, "Experiences of Discharged Chronic Schizophrenic Patients in Various Types of Living Group," *The Milbank Memorial Fund Quarterly*, XXXVII, 105 (1959). Another study is limited to discharged female patients only: Simon Dinitz, Shirley Angrist, Mark Lefton, and Benjamin Pasamanick, "Instrumental Role Expectations and Posthospital Performance of Female Mental Patients," *Social Forces*, 40, 248 (1962). A recent example is a study of patients in a psychiatric unit of a general hospital: Arnold D. Bucove and Lawrence I. Levitt, "A Seven-Year Follow-Up Study of Patients in a General Hospital Psychiatric Service," *American Journal of Psychiatry*, 122, 1088 (1966).
[10] L. B. Kalinowsky and H. J. Worthing, "Results with Electroconvulsive Treatment in 200 Cases of Schizophrenia," *Psychiatric Quarterly*, 17, 144 (1943); Alejandro Rodriguez, Maria Rodriguez, and Leon Eisenberg, "The Outcome of School Phobia: A Follow-Up Study Based on 41 Cases," *American Journal of Psychiatry*, 116, 540 (1959); W. Freeman, "Level of Achievement After Lobotomy: A Study of

A third limitation of most studies is that patients have not been followed over an extended period of time. Usually subjects are restudied within a few months to a few years after their discharge from treatment or after the original study. Therefore, it is impossible to identify long-term patterns of recurrent treatment, discharge, community adjustment, and readmission.[11] The studies of Ziegler and Paul and Bennett and Klein are unusual in following patients for 20 and 30 years respectively. However, the population followed in these studies was small and limited—66 hysterical females and 14 childhood schizophrenics.[12] Recently, some other long-term studies have appeared in the literature, but they also are extremely limited in scope.[13]

1000 Cases," *American Journal of Psychiatry*, 110, 269 (1953); Peter A. Martin, "Convulsive Therapies: Review of 511 Cases at Pontiac State Hospital," *Journal of Nervous and Mental Disease*, 109, 142 (1949); J. S. Gottlieb and P. E. Huston, "Treatment of Schizophrenia: Follow-Up Results in Cases of Insulin Shock Therapy and in Control Cases," *Archives of Neurology and Psychiatry*, 49, 266 (1943); D. W. Goodrich, E. Swengel, and G. Saslow, "The Social Adjustment of 50 Patients in a Clinic for Comprehensive Medicine," *Journal of Nervous and Mental Disease*, 120, 227 (1954); and Arthur Harris, Inge Linker, Vera Norris, and Michael Shepherd, "Schizophrenia, A Prognostic Social Study," *British Journal of Social and Preventive Medicine*, 10, 107 (1956).

[11] Among the more recent comprehensive short-term follow-up studies are: Howard E. Freeman and Ozzie G. Simmons, *The Mental Patient Comes Home*, Wiley, New York, 1963; Dinitz et al., *op. cit.*; M. Lefton, S. Angrist, S. Dinitz, and B. Pasamanick, "Social Class, Expectations, and Performance of Mental Patients," *American Journal of Sociology*, LXVIII, 79 (1962); George W. Brown, G. M. Carstairs, and G. Topping, "Posthospital Adjustment of Chronic Mental Patients," *Lancet*, 685 (Sept. 27, 1958); F. A. Freyhan, "Course and Outcome of Schizophrenia," *American Journal of Psychiatry*, 112, 161 (1955); J. S. Bockoven, A. R. Pandiscio, and H. C. Solomon, "Social Adjustment of Patients in the Community Three Years After Commitment to The Boston Psychopathic Hospital," *Mental Hygiene*, 40, 353 (1956); R. Holmboe and C. Astrup, "A Follow-Up of 255 Patients with Acute Schizophrenia and Schizophreni-form Psychoses," *Acta Psychiatrica et Neurologica Scandinavica*, 32, (Suppl. 115), (1957); Jones, *op. cit.*; and Jack F. Wilder, Gilbert Levin, and Israel Zwerling, "A Two-Year Follow-Up Evaluation of Acute Psychotic Patients Treated in a Day Hospital," *American Journal of Psychiatry*, 122, 1095 (1966).

[12] D. K. Ziegler and N. Paul, "On the Natural History of Hysteria in Women. A Follow-Up 20 Years After Hospitalization," *Diseases of the Nervous System*, 15, 301 (1954); Stephen Bennett and Henriette R. Klein, "Childhood Schizophrenia: 30 Years Later," *American Journal of Psychiatry*, 122, 1121 (1966). Other studies noted for the unusually long period of the follow-up include: Paul Errera, "A 16-Year Follow-Up of Schizophrenic Patients Seen in an Outpatient Clinic," *Archives of Neurology and Psychiatry*, 78, 84 (1957); Arthur Harris, "The Prognosis of Anxiety States," *British Medical Journal*, 2, 649 (1938); and T. A. C. Rennie, "Follow-up Study of 500 Patients with Schizophrenia Admitted to Hospital from 1913 to 1923," *Archives of Neurology and Psychiatry*, 42, 877 (1939).

[13] See, for example, *American Journal of Psychiatry*, 122 (1966), which features reports of recent follow-up studies.

A fourth limitation of most follow-up studies is the neglect of social factors in treatment outcome and posttreatment performance. Research generally deals with demographic, medical, and psychiatric variables. Variations in discharge rates, for example, are explained in terms of diagnosis, type of treatment, length of treatment, age, sex, or some similar variable.[14]

Next, few studies have attempted to follow the patient into the community or to secure information not available in institutional records. There is generally scant information concerning the performance of the patient after his discharge; patient behavior or performance in the community has seldom been studied.

Typically, follow-up studies are restricted to available medical and psychiatric records maintained by either the treatment agency or some central statistical center. Perforce, these studies deal only with the outcome of treatment for a select group of individuals who entered specified treatment agencies (generally for the first term of treatment) during some specified period of time. If the patient returns to treatment after discharge, he is usually included in the study only if he returns to the original treatment agency or a limited number of other agencies. Malzberg's detailed analyses of the discharge and readmission rates for New York state patients treated in public hospitals is one of the better examples of such work and serves to illustrate the limitations, as well as advantages, of such studies.[15] Malzberg's study is restricted to a description of the probabilities of discharge for specified diagnostic groups and for specified time periods after a first admission to a New York state psychiatric institution; no assessment of the patients' adjustment in the community after discharge is considered.

When researchers attempt to study patient behavior in the community, objective measures for the evaluation of the various dimensions of posttreatment performance are rarely included. A common practice is to use global and subjective ratings of patient adjustment by clinicians or inter-

---

[14] T. Braatøy, "The Prognosis in Schizophrenia with Some Remarks Regarding Diagnosis and Therapy," *Acta Psychiatrica et Neurologica*, 11, 63 (1936); John R. Ross et al., "The Pharmacological Shock Treatment of Schizophrenia: A Two-Year Follow-up Study from the New York State Hospitals with Some Recommendations for the Future," *American Journal of Psychiatry*, 97, 1007 (1941); and E. Frankel, "Outcome of Mental Hospital Treatment in New Jersey: A Statistical Review of State Mental Hospital Activities," *Mental Hygiene*, 32, 459 (1948).

[15] Benjamin Malzberg, "Cohort Studies of Mental Disease in New York State, 1943–1949," *Mental Hygiene* (reported in 10 parts) 40–41, (1956–1957). Other examples of such studies are B. A. Lengyel, "Remission and Mortality Rates in Schizophrenia," *American Journal of Hygiene* (Section A) 33, 16 (1941); and Charles Rupp and E. Fletcher, "A Five to Ten Year Follow-up Study of 641 Schizophrenic Cases," *American Journal of Psychiatry*, 96, 877 (1940).

viewers in the field. Thus, adjustment is categorized as "good," "fair," or "poor," or mental status as "improved," "same," or "worse." [16] Such judgments may be valuable for clinical purposes, but they are difficult to replicate for research purposes since the criteria for performance evaluation are not precise enough.

Finally, few studies have utilized effectively an adequate control group of nonpatients to provide a base line for measuring the performance of former patients in the community.[17] If only patients are studied, it is impossible to determine whether adjustment differences by some variable, such as sex or marital status, are related to factors connected with psychiatric illness and its treatment or are reflections of differences to be found within any population.

Several recent studies differ from most previous follow-up research in a number of ways. The scope of these studies has been expanded to include not only the chance of discharge from treatment but also an evaluation of patient behavior in the community after discharge. They attempt to determine how well former patients perform their community roles and what factors are associated with successful or unsuccessful adjustment. In studying the experience of the former mental patient in the community, social and psychological factors which may be related to the outcome of psychiatric treatment are examined systematically. However, these more comprehensive studies have all been concerned with the problem of the patient after hospitalization so that the former psychiatric outpatient is not included. Also, most have been limited to patients of one sex, diagnosis, or treatment agency, and the period of follow-up has been relatively short.

The Adler study of male patients admitted to the Arkansas State

---

[16] See, for example, Paul H. Hoch, J. P. Cattell, M. D. Strahl, and H. H. Pennes, "The Course and Outcome of Pseudoneurotic Schizophrenia," *American Journal of Psychiatry*, 119, 106 (1962); E. Ziskind et al., "Metrazol and Electric Convulsive Therapy of the Affective Psychoses: Control Series of Observations Covering a Period of 5 Years," *Archives of Neurology and Psychiatry*, 53, 212 (1945); and E. D. Bond and F. J. Braceland, "Prognosis in Mental Disease," *American Journal of Psychiatry*, 94, 263 (1937).

[17] Studies have been conducted with experimental and control groups of patients to determine the effectiveness of types of therapy. Jones, for example, studied two groups of neurotics after discharge from a psychiatric hospital to determine the effectiveness of an industrial-neuroses unit attended by one group. See Jones, *op. cit.* One recent study has used the neighbors of former mental patients as a comparison group for studying the community behavior of former patients. See Mark Lefton, S. Dinitz, S. S. Angrist and B. Pasamanick, "Former Mental Patients and Their Neighbors: A Comparison of Performance Levels," *Journal of Health and Human Behavior*, 7, 106 (1966).

Hospital is one of the earliest to follow the patient into the community.[18] Special attention was paid to social and economic adjustment following discharge, and quantitative scales were developed to provide precise measures of patient performance. A number of other follow-up studies have been carried out by researchers associated with The Maudsley Hospital in London, England.[19] One of the more recent, reported by George W. Brown, is representative of this research.[20] Brown studied a group of chronic male schizophrenic patients discharged from London hospitals. Using evaluations of adjustment by social workers and limiting the study to the first year after discharge, Brown related the living arrangement of the patient to his posthospital adjustment, as measured by the ability of the patient to remain out of treatment for a year.

Brown's study of the London patients is similar in some respects to the Boston studies carried out by Freeman, Simmons, and their associates.[21] In their major study, which followed a number of smaller longitudinal exploratory projects, a group of patients was followed for one year after discharge or until rehospitalization occurred. This study, which is more analytically structured than any of the other follow-up studies, finds also that specified types of living arrangements, as well as other social factors, are related to posttreatment performance in the community. Similarly, a significant study carried out by Dinitz, Pasamanick, and their associates in Ohio has demonstrated that for a selected group of female, mentally ill patients, marital status and socioeconomic status are related to posttreatment performance during the first year after discharge.[22]

Our research builds directly on these recent studies of social and psychological factors associated with the experience of former patients in the community. Ours, however, differs from these and earlier studies in several ways: we included all patients from greater New Haven who were in treatment in psychiatric hospitals and outpatient clinics in

---

[18] Adler et al., *op. cit.*

[19] For example, see Brown, *op. cit.*; Brown et al., *op. cit.*; Harris et al., *op. cit.*; and Vera Norris, *Mental Illness in London*, Chapman and Hall, London, 1959.

[20] Brown, *op. cit.*

[21] The major findings of this series of studies are reported in Freeman and Simmons, *op. cit.* and Ozzie G. Simmons, *Work and Mental Illness*, Wiley, New York, 1965.

[22] S. Angrist, S. Dinitz, M. Lefton, and B. Pasamanick, "Social and Psychological Factors in the Rehospitalization of Female Mental Patients," *Archives of General Psychiatry*, 4, 363 (1961); S. Dinitz, M. Lefton, S. Angrist, and B. Pasamanick, "Psychiatric and Social Attributes as Predictors of Case Outcome in Mental Hospitalization," *Social Problems*, 8, 322 (1961); Lefton et al., *op. cit.*; and Dinitz et al., *op. cit.*

1950 at the time of the original study. The follow-up covers a 10-year period, tracing patients through all the treatment agencies with which they had contact and all the types of therapy they experienced. Former patients living in the community in 1960 were studied intensively and their adjustment was measured by a variety of objective criteria. Moreover, a matched control group was studied to provide a basis for the evaluation of patient behavior. Finally, the study focuses on one major independent variable, social class, and investigates its influence in detail.

THEORETICAL ORIENTATION

The general theoretical position taken in this research is that there are social components in mental illness as well as organic, intrapsychic, and interpersonal elements. More specifically, the theory proposes that the social environment in which man lives and the values he holds are related to the development, manifestation, prevalence, treatment, and consequences of mental illness. Our particular interest is with one aspect of the social environment—social class.

Most research in social psychiatry has dealt with etiological and epidemiological considerations, that is with factors in the development of psychiatric disorders in the individual and the distribution of these disorders in various communities, populations, and sociocultural groups. The recent studies by Leighton and his associates in Nova Scotia and by Srole, Langner, and their associates in New York are excellent examples of the utilization of these two theoretical approaches.[23] The original New Haven studies also were of this type. The present research extends social psychiatric theory to later stages in the natural history of mental illness. Social class has been demonstrated to be related to the development, distribution, and treatment of mental illness. The outcome of treatment and its consequences for the patient, however, have been largely ignored. Does social class continue to operate at this stage of the patient's career as at the earlier stages?

---

[23] A. H. Leighton, *My Name is Legion* (The Stirling County Study of Psychiatric Disorder and Sociocultural Environment, Vol. I) Basic Books, New York, 1959; Charles C. Hughes, Marc-Adélard Tremblay, Robert N. Rapoport, and A. H. Leighton, *People of Cove and Woodlot*, (The Stirling County Study, Vol. II), Basic Books, New York, 1960; Dorothea C. Leighton, John S. Harding, David M. Macklin, Allister M. Macmillan, and A. H. Leighton, *The Character of Danger*, (The Stirling County Study, Vol. III) Basic Books, New York, 1963; Srole et al., *op. cit.*; Thomas S. Langner and Stanley T. Michael, *Life Stress and Mental Health: The Midtown Manhattan Study*, Vol. II, The Free Press of Glencoe, New York and London, 1963.

This study, as did the original New Haven research, deals with treated mental illness. Since we are studying patients and former patients, it is necessary to distinguish between disease or illness, on the one hand, and the sick or patient role, on the other. The traditional medical or psychiatric approach to mental illness has been to view it as an illness or disease. Even though only a few specific disorders, such as general paresis and the toxic and alcoholic psychoses, can be traced directly to organic causes, the general approach has been medical in nature. Mentally ill persons are regarded as sick; they are diagnosed by medical specialists—psychiatrists—as having one or another organic or functional disorder. However, the very process of diagnosis and treatment provides a social definition—that of mental patient.

Mental illness refers to a complex condition which includes subjective feelings, disturbed interpersonal and social relationships, and psychosomatic symptoms. The labeling of such conditions as mental illness depends on a variety of factors, such as the therapist's diagnosis, the patient's interpretation of his condition and his seeking of professional assistance for it, the action of his family and friends in getting him into treatment, and the action of various institutional representatives of society such as physicians, police, judges, and social workers. The decisive element in assuming the role of mental patient is not necessarily the fact of the illness itself, but the recognition by the individual and/or others that help is needed in coping with the condition.[24] The individual, having been given the label by the societal expert responsible for such matters, is then recognized as mentally ill. Regardless of the extent or severity of the individual's actual psychiatric illness, once he is labeled he becomes a mental patient and is treated as such by other members of society who can identify him as occupying this role.

From a sociological view, this research is a study of certain phases of the career of the mental patient. We are dealing with a social role—that of the mental patient—and the psychiatric illness itself is only one aspect of this role. Equally important are the social components, for other persons behave toward the patient on the basis of his label as well as of his actual illness.

Our previous research in New Haven dealt with the earlier aspects of the career of the mental patient: factors leading to the assumption of this role at different class levels, its definition, and the treatment received by persons in this role. The present research raises questions about the rela-

[24] Robert N. Wilson, "Patient-Practitioner Relationships," in Howard E. Freeman, Sol Levine, and Leo G. Reader (eds.), *Handbook of Medical Sociology*, Prentice-Hall, Englewood Cliffs, N.J., 1963, p. 275.

tionship between class and later stages in the mental patient's career. After the patient is assigned to treatment, a number of things may happen to him: He may remain in treatment until he dies. He may be discharged to the community where he is unable to adjust and therefore returns for further treatment, starting the cycle of possible outcomes again. Or, finally, he may be discharged and never return for further treatment; in that case he may become a self-supporting member of society, or he may live in a protected atmosphere, contributing little to his family or community and demanding much in terms of care and attention. Although the outcome of mental illness has not been stressed in social psychiatric theory and research, it clearly constitutes a most significant aspect of the career of psychiatric patients.

Perhaps a greater understanding of mental illness can be gained by viewing the career of the mental patient as one that is deviant in our society rather than by viewing it primarily as a medical or psychiatric problem alone. In many ways psychiatric treatment is a mechanism of social control as well as a process to "cure" the patient's illness. From a sociological viewpoint, the patient is a deviant and the onus implied in his deviance is more forceful in mental than in physical illness.[25] The reason for viewing the sick role as a deviant one is clear: the patient, because of his illness, cannot or is not permitted by community members to perform many of the roles usually expected of him. The mental patient, in particular, in American society is handicapped in fulfilling a set of role expectations that place a great importance upon independent achievement. The passivity and dependence imposed upon the mental patient run counter to the activism of American society. Thus, the mental patient cannot fulfill many everyday tasks and roles and is also unable to meet certain value orientations of the society.[26] As a deviant, the mental patient must be cared for, but the society also believes it must be protected from him. Thus, psychiatric therapists and treatment centers function as agents of social control.

In our society the disengagement process and transition to a new role is much more difficult for deviants than for others, as Kai Erikson points out.[27] In other major role transitions, such as marriage, divorce, graduation from school, and induction into the armed services, formal and often official ceremonies are performed. The individual's change of role is recognized by others who now behave toward him in terms of his new

25 Wilson, *ibid.*, pp. 276–77.
26 Stanley H. King, "Social Psychological Factors in Illness," in Freeman, Levine, and Reader, *op. cit.*, p. 112.
27 Kai Erikson, *Wayward Puritans*, Wiley, New York, 1966, p. 16.

role. This, however, is not generally the case for deviant roles such as that of prisoner, alcoholic, and mental patient. The former mental patient in the community, in many ways, continues his career as a mental patient even though he is no longer under active treatment. Despite professional health efforts to present psychiatric illness as just another sickness, many Americans continue to view the mental patient as a social deviant, even after he has terminated his treatment. The effect of the deviant label remains with the patient even after he is discharged from treatment and is, in one sense, no longer a patient. Others continue to react toward the former patient on the basis of his deviance. He is now an ex-patient, but the term *patient* is still part of his label.

In brief, this study will examine relationships between social class and the outcome of psychiatric treatment. As a continuation of the earlier New Haven studies of social class and mental illness, the current research focuses upon later stages in the career of the mental patient—his follow-up status a decade after the original study, his 10-year treatment experience, and his adjustment in the community if discharged from the hospital

research methods

This chapter describes the research procedures employed to achieve the goals of the study. The details of the principal methodological operations are presented as they were undertaken in the development of the research, beginning with the determination of social-class position, proceeding through case follow-up and data collection, and concluding with data processing and analysis.

SOCIAL-CLASS POSITION

Social class is measured in this study by Hollingshead's *Two Factor Index of Social Position* in which the number of years of school completed and occupation are scored on appropriate educational and occupational scales.[1] The scale value for education is multiplied by a weight of 4 and the scale for occupation by a weight of 7. The resulting score is assumed to be an index of the individual's position in the class structure of the community. The scores on the Index range from 11 to 77, a score of 11

---

[1] We did not use the *Three Factor Index of Social Position* utilized in the 1950 Psychiatric Census because it includes ecological area of residence and many patients and their families lived outside the metropolitan community where ecological ratings were not available. Furthermore, Hollingshead and his associates in recent works have discarded the *Three Factor Index of Social Position* and substituted the *Two Factor Index of Social Position* which can be used more widely. The correlation between the two- and three-factor indices is 0.968. See Appendix 3 for a detailed description of the *Two Factor Index of Social Position*.

representing the highest position an individual can reach by a combination of outstanding educational and occupational achievements; to receive a score of 11 an individual must have a graduate or professional degree and be engaged in a profession or a high executive position, while a score of 77 is assigned to an individual with less than 7 years of schooling who is an unskilled laborer. All degrees of education and types of jobs fall within these extremes.

The scores group themselves into five clusters, and a single score is assigned to each cluster so that in the New Haven community we have five social classes, strata, or levels which represent subcultures. People in these classes live differently and have different attitudes and values toward many of the important things in life. In other words, differential behavior patterns or ways of life are associated with different social levels. The highest prestige stratum is class I and the lowest class V. A description of these classes is given in Chapter 3.[2]

CASES STUDIED

On June 1, 1960, we reexamined the treatment status of those residents of greater New Haven (1563 in number) who between May 31 and December 1, 1950 were in either psychiatric outpatient clinic or psychiatric hospital treatment.[3] *Greater New Haven,* as defined in this study, includes New Haven and the towns of West Haven, East Haven, North Haven, Hamden, and Woodbridge, Connecticut. The residence requirement eliminated students and other patients who were under psychiatric treatment in New Haven at that time but whose homes were elsewhere; it did include residents of greater New Haven who were in psychiatric treatment elsewhere.[4]

The 359 patients (19 per cent of the original Psychiatric Census) treated by private practitioners in 1950 were not included in the present study because of commitments the research group made to those physicians at that time. When the original Psychiatric Census was taken in

---

[2] For a detailed description of the New Haven social-class system, see August B. Hollingshead and Fredrick C. Redlich, *Social Class and Mental Illness,* Wiley, New York, 1958, pp. 66–136.

[3] We define *psychiatric outpatient clinics* and *psychiatric hospitals* as agencies under the supervision of psychiatrists that care for and treat patients with mental and emotional problems through the support of public funds and/or private resources. (In hospitals for the mentally defective, only those persons diagnosed as psychotic were included in the study.) We define a *psychiatrist* as a person who holds the degree *Doctor of Medicine* and has completed or is undergoing training in a psychiatric hospital or clinic in accordance with the criteria of the medical profession.

[4] The original Psychiatric Census is described in detail in Hollingshead and Redlich, *op. cit.,* pp. 19–24.

1950 there had been few studies of patients of private psychiatric practitioners; a major concern of these doctors was that their patients might come to be identified, with a resulting violation of confidence. Since the cooperation of the private practitioners was essential for the success of the original study and their concern for their patients' privacy was so great, we did not request a patient's name or even his exact address if the psychiatrist did not wish to give it to us. At that time we assured the private practitioners that we would never contact their patients without their consent.

In 1960 we explored the possibility of contacting the private practitioners to seek permission to include their patients in the follow-up study, but several serious problems arose: A number of psychiatrists had died, some had moved to far-distant communities, and others could not be contacted for personal reasons. Even if we had been able to trace the patients of these psychiatrists we felt it would be unethical to do so since we did not have their permission. Those psychiatrists who were still in private practice in the community and would have been willing to cooperate in the present study were mostly psychoanalysts or analytically oriented psychiatrists with small case loads. The identifying data for their patients were often poor, so considerable time would have been spent locating them. Also, such patients were disproportionately upper- and middle-class professionals and executives of Protestant and Jewish background and represented less than 25 per cent of the total number of patients treated by private practitioners. In view of the financial resources available for the research, we decided that the small size and biased nature of the sample did not warrant its inclusion in the study. Therefore, because of the commitment made in 1950 and the effort required to trace a small unrepresentative sample, we did not study the patients who had been under the care of private practitioners.

The number of patients studied was determined in the following manner: In the 1950 Psychiatric Census, 1531 patients with a known class position were enumerated; their distribution by psychiatric agency was—state hospitals, 1259; veterans hospitals, 81; private hospitals, 36; and clinics, 155. Owing to major clerical errors in the 1950 hospital and clinic records, five patients, one in clinic treatment and four in a state hospital,[5] were incorrectly listed on institutional records as being in treatment. By 1960 the records had been corrected to show that they had terminated their treatment before May 31, 1950. In 1950, 51 hospital and clinic cases were dropped from analysis because of insufficient informa-

---

[5] Three of the cases were class V and two class IV: two were white females and three white males; their ages ranged from 27 to 66; all were Catholic; three were married, one was single, and one divorced.

TABLE 2.1

	1950 Treatment Agency				
	State Hospital	V.A. Hospital	Private Hospital	Clinic	Total
Included in 1950 Psychiatric Census	1259	81	36	155	1531
Treatment terminated before May 31, 1950	(−)4			(−)1	(−)5
Case records lost				(−)12	(−)12
Included on basis of additional information	(+)47	(+)1	_	(+)1	(+)49
Total	1302	82	36	143	1563

tion. Additional materials secured in the 1960 institutional records enabled us to include 49 of these cases; their social class distribution is—class V, 42; class IV, 6; class III, 1. A final modification resulted from the loss of the records of 12 patients treated in 1950 at two community clinics; in 1960 we were unable to locate their records.

As a result of the above deletions and additions, we restudied 1563 cases in 1960, as tabulated in Table 2.1.

LOCATION OF CASES

In the spring and summer of 1960, Myers and Pepper contacted all of the original treatment agencies either personally or by letter.[6] The co-operation of all agencies was secured with minimal discussion beyond the initial contact. In fact, most clinic and hospital superintendents offered every possible assistance. In the few cases of initial concern, cooperation was secured rapidly after a more detailed explanation of the project's aims. We cannot overemphasize the genuinely enthusiastic reception we received.

There were 29 original treatment agencies contacted: 6 state hospitals,

---

[6] Generally, a letter on the official stationery of the Department of Psychiatry, Yale University was sent to the psychiatrist in charge of the hospital or clinic. Each letter was typed individually and signed by Pepper and Myers, as a personal communication to explain the objectives of the Follow-Up Study and its relationship to the original Psychiatric Census. When either Pepper or Myers knew personally the psychiatrist in charge, permission was requested during a visit instead of by letter, and in a few other cases personal visits were made when it was felt the chances for cooperation would be greater. The Commissioner of Mental Health of the State of Connecticut was contacted to coordinate the efforts of state agencies.

5 Veterans Administration hospitals, 11 private hospitals, and 7 clinics. The state hospitals and clinics were located in Connecticut, while the Veterans Administration hospitals were located in Massachusetts, New York, and Connecticut. Of the private hospitals, five were located in Connecticut and six were out of state.

The search of records at the original treatment facilities indicated that during the 10 years from 1950 to 1960 patients had been treated or cared for at other institutions both in and out of state: 6 Veterans Administration hospitals, 5 state hospitals, 7 other psychiatric institutions, and 40 private convalescent and nursing homes licensed to care for psychotic patients. Consequently, letters were written to 58 agencies in addition to the original 29. Most replied favorably within a short time; a second letter, visit, or telephone call which was used to follow up tardy replies resulted in complete cooperation. As in the case of the original agencies, cooperation was enthusiastic in the vast majority of additional agencies. In sum, in order to review the records of the patients, we contacted and secured permission from 29 original and 58 additional agencies, a total of 87 agencies.

The records at the original and additional agencies were examined to determine (1) those patients who died while in continuous treatment, (2) those patients who died after a period of discharge and readmission, (3) those patients who were alive and had been in continuous treatment, (4) those patients who had had a period of discharge and were again in treatment, and (5) those patients who had been discharged and were no longer in treatment in any of the original or additional agencies on June 1, 1960.

A thorough search of psychiatric agency records was made to help locate discharged patients. We recorded the patient's address at the time of discharge, any address ever listed for him, the names and addresses of all known relatives, friends, employers, or other persons who might have pertinent information, and institutions or organizations with which the patient had ever had contact. We checked the lists of patients discharged from each treatment agency at all other agencies. We attempted to abstract any information which might be utilized to trace the discharged patients; newspaper clippings, correspondence, telephone calls, and other contacts or inquiries by or about the patient after discharge were especially helpful. This information provided the basis for tracing most patients through national libraries of city directories and telephone directories and through the local post office mailing-list service.

The task of tracing patients not yet located by this method was left up to the individual interviewers. When current addresses were un-known, the survey interviewers started their tracing procedure by re-turning to the last known address of the patient, his family, or friends. Generally, family members were cooperative in providing information concerning the location of the patient. Neighbors, as one might expect in an urban environment, could provide little information, although they were extremely valuable in some cases as were local tradesmen. In tracing former patients we did not indicate the nature of our study or that the person had been a mental patient; we stated simply that we were doing an interview study and were interested in contacting the individual.

Following out the linkage of friends, relatives, and others who might know the location of former patients proved to be a time-consuming but very important way of tracing persons. By doggedly pursuing every possible lead, we were able to locate some former patients whose where-abouts were not known even by their families. For example, one inter-viewer following the path of a former patient learned that he lived a solitary life and had not been seen by his family for many years. His father told the interviewer that a friend had reported seeing his son around a junkyard near the city dump. After several visits to the junk-yard, the interviewer finally located the former patient who was living in a shack in the swamps behind the city garbage dump and subsisting on the city's refuse.

In 1960 a total of 387 persons, excluding those who had died in the hospital, were no longer hospitalized. They included those persons un-der outpatient treatment as well as those no longer under any treat-ment. The status of these individuals is tabulated in Table 2.2.

Several factors facilitated our efforts in locating former patients: For part of the 10-year period when they were in hospital or clinic treatment, the patients' freedom of movement was limited. After their discharge, we had access to the records of the agencies in which they had been under care. If death occurred in the community, it was re-corded by the Bureau of Vital Statistics and possibly by the treatment agency or other public agencies.

Factors hindering the tracing of patients included the stigma attached to mental illness. Some families and former patients, wanting to hide their past experiences, moved and tried to start life anew in another community. Other patients, especially the few awol cases interviewed, feared hospitalization if they remained in the immediate community. The length of time between the original Psychiatric Census and our follow-up was another problem in tracing the former patients. In some cases the patient had been discharged from treatment in 1951 and, since

TABLE 2.2

	1950 Treatment Agency		
Former Patients	Hospital	Clinic	Total
Had died in the community	27	5	32
Could not be located	8	10	18
Located but inaccessible for interview	3	3	6
In prison	3	1	4
Refused	10	5	15
Interviewed	204	108	312
Total	255	132	387

we did not complete our data collection until 1963, nearly 12 years had elapsed before we conducted the follow-up interview. A final factor was the patients' geographical mobility which was typical of other Americans; at the time of our contact, former patients were living in Malaya, Sweden, Italy, Germany, Washington, D.C., and 14 different states including Hawaii.

Of the 1563 former patients studied, we were able to locate 1545 or 99 per cent. We traced 1412 of the 1420 patients hospitalized in 1950 and 133 of the 143 patients in clinic treatment.

Of the 355 living former patients no longer hospitalized, we interviewed 312 (88 per cent), received partial information on 10 (3 per cent), could not locate 18 (5 per cent), and had 15 (4 per cent) refusals.[7] Of the 10 persons not interviewed directly, six were living in

---

[7] Selected characteristics of the patients we could not locate and of the refusals are:

	Refusals	Could Not Be Located
Diagnosis		
Neurotic	5	5
Schizophrenic	6	7
Affective	2	1
Alcoholic	1	5
Other psychotic	1	0
Social Class		
I–III	8	7
IV	4	3
V	3	8

foreign countries or were not approached at the request of their psychiatrists, and four were in prisons throughout the United States. We did, however, receive partial information about them through various records, through correspondence with them, or through others. Seventy per cent of the discharged patients resided in greater New Haven, 15 per cent elsewhere in Connecticut, 7 per cent in other parts of the northeastern United States, 7 per cent elsewhere in the United States, and less than one per cent abroad.

In summary, we employed every possible means available for tracing the patient, short of paying the patients and employing the Pinkerton Detective Agency—techniques used in other follow-up projects.

SOURCES OF DATA

The data in this study come from three sources: the original records collected in the 1950 New Haven Psychiatric Census which were reexamined; patient records abstracted from the original 1950 treatment agencies and from subsequent agencies in which the patients were treated between December 1, 1950 and May 31, 1960; and intensive personal interviews completed with (1) patients who were in the community and not hospitalized in 1960, (2) a member of the patient's household, and (3) a control group of persons (never treated for mental illness) individually matched with the patient on the basis of six variables: sex, race, social class, religion, age, and marital status.

	Refusals	Could Not Be Located
Age, 1960		
Less than 39	4	7
40–59	9	10
Over 60	2	1
Sex		
Male	9	15
Female	6	3
Religion		
Catholic	6	6
Protestant	5	9
None	1	1
Unknown	3	2
Marital Status		
Unmarried	5	10
Married	7	5
Separated, divorced, widowed	3	3

1950 Psychiatric Census Schedule

In 1950 psychiatric and social data on all hospitalized and clinic patients were collected by means of a schedule.[8] Social data included name, address, race, sex, age, religion, occupation, education, marital status, number of children, place of birth and rearing, sibling relationship, a synopsis of the patient's family history, the national origin, occupation, and marital status of his parents, and, if married, the education and occupational status of his spouse.

Psychiatric data included the type of referral, payment for treatment (full or partial rates or treatment without expense to the patient or his family), date of first visit to a psychiatrist, date when current treatment began, number of past psychiatric hospitalizations, number of past outpatient courses of treatment, length and intensity of previous psychiatric treatment, type of psychiatric treatment being received, frequency and duration of therapeutic sessions, patient's diagnosis, and a brief synopsis of the patient's psychiatric history.

1950 to 1960 Treatment Agency Schedule

A 43-item schedule was developed to record the data contained in hospital and clinic records about the patient's social, medical, and psychiatric history during the 10-year period from 1950 to 1960, until the time of discharge from treatment or death. The schedule is a compromise between what we desired and what could be obtained from the records.

A number of field trials was made in various clinics and hospitals with preliminary schedules. The pilot schedules contained more questions than could be used in the final schedule. Because of the limitations of clinical records, the preliminary schedules were modified gradually until they contained only questions which could be answered from most of the records available. The final schedule covered the patient's social, psychiatric treatment, health, and remission history during the period covered. The social section included the patient's age in 1960, at death, or at time of discharge; his name; social-class position; occupation; marital status; education; religion; birth of any children; and, if married, spouse's occupation and education. The psychiatric materials covered diagnostic changes during the period of study, psychiatric treatment record in detail, and current psychiatric treatment. The health section covered the history of nonpsychiatric diagnoses since December 1, 1950 and current treatment for such illnesses. If the patient had died, information was collected on

---

[8] These data are described in detail in Hollingshead and Redlich, op. cit., pp. 24–26.

date of death, cause of death, circumstances of death, and, if an autopsy was performed, reasons for and results of the autopsy.

The final items included the discharge and readmission record since December 1, 1950 and the record of other institutional history, such as nonpsychiatric hospital, correctional institution, or nursing home. If the patient was discharged from and readmitted to a psychiatric treatment agency, the following data were gathered: initial type of commitment, final type of commitment, place from which patient was admitted, person accompanying patient, initial source of referral, type of living arrangement at readmission, occupation and employment status at readmission, changes in type of living arrangement, occupation, or employment status between discharge and readmission, mental and physical status at readmission, and precipitating factors (social, behavioral, and psychiatric) in the readmission.

The above schedule represents all materials collected for persons who died in continuous or noncontinuous treatment and who were in hospital treatment on June 1, 1960 (continuous or rehospitalized). The data for each schedule were abstracted from the patient's institutional record by a sociologist or psychiatrist.[9] Collection of data began for this part of the study in June 1960; most materials were gathered by the summer of 1961, but the final abstraction was not completed until April 1962.

Patient and Family Interview Schedules

Persons not under hospital treatment were interviewed in the community. They included persons being treated in outpatient facilities as well as those under no psychiatric care. Information on persons who had died in the community was collected from family members, friends, and other available sources, such as nonpsychiatric hospital records. A patient schedule and a family schedule were constructed to secure information concerning the former patient's current social,

---

[9] These persons included Max P. Pepper and Josef Hes, psychiatrists, Jerome K. Myers, Lee L. Bean, and Robert N. Wilson, sociologists, and nine graduate students in sociology. After the hospital superintendent or clinic supervisor gave permission to use the records at a given institution, Bean, Myers, or Pepper, because of age and professional qualifications and status, set up data-collection procedures. Other sociologists then gathered the information at those agencies with large numbers of cases. However, in many of the institutions with only a few patients the data were collected by Pepper, Myers, Bean, Hes, or Wilson at the time of the initial contact with the hospital or clinic authorities.

behavioral, and mental status functioning or adjustment; his social, psychiatric, and health history since discharge; his attitudes toward psychiatric illness and treatment; and his incorporation into his family, his job, and the community since his discharge from treatment.[10]

Work on these schedules began in August 1960. In April and May 1961 the schedules were pretested on 10 former, psychiatric outpatient clinic patients and 10 former, state hospital patients and their families who were not part of our study group and who had been discharged from treatment during the previous two years. Final revisions were made after the pretest, and by June 15, 1961 we were ready to begin interviewing former patients and their families.

Areas of inquiry covered in the patient schedule are: history of physical illness and its treatment, psychopathological history, psychiatric treatment record, current mental status, family structure, family dynamics, housing, recreation, education, occupation, economics, cost of medical and psychiatric care, friendship patterns, religion, leisure-time activities, ethnic background, attitudes toward psychiatric treatment, personality measurement, social mobility, and social class. Specific questions relating to these areas were developed into a 51-page schedule which includes 215 questions.

Areas covered in the family schedule are: circumstances surrounding patient's treatment and discharge from treatment; occupation; economics; cost of psychiatric and medical care; role-performance expectations for the patient in the family, on the job, and in the community; circumstances surrounding patient's reentry into psychiatric treatment (if applicable); family dynamics; housing; recreation; leisure-time activities; religion; attitudes toward psychiatry; and psychiatric treatment. Specific questions relating to these areas were developed into a 35-page schedule which included 129 questions.

The schedule designed to be given to former patients required between one hour and 45 minutes and eight hours to complete. Most patient interviews, however, lasted about two and one-half hours. The other schedule, for the most significant family member or friend, required about one hour to complete, with actual times ranging from 45 minutes to four and one-

---

[10] Certain questions in the schedules were obtained from interview instruments developed by Srole and his associates, Leighton and his associates, and Simmons and Freeman. See Leo Srole, et al., *Mental Health in the Metropolis: The Midtown Manhattan Study*, Vol. I, McGraw-Hill, New York, 1962; Charles C. Hughes et al., *People of Cove and Woodlot*, Basic Books, New York, 1960; and Howard E. Freeman and Ozzie G. Simmons, *The Mental Patient Comes Home*, Wiley, New York, 1963.

half hours. Our major objective was to interview the person who had had the most intimate contact with the patient since his discharge from treatment. For married patients, the most common respondent was the spouse; for single patients, a parent or sibling was most often interviewed. At times, however, other relatives or even nonrelatives were interviewed.[11]

Control Schedule

At the same time that the patient and family schedules were being developed, we compiled a schedule to be administered to members of the control group. We began constructing it in November 1960 and pretested it on 15 individuals drawn at random from the *New Haven City Directory* in April 1961. It was similar to the patient schedule and was used as a basis for evaluating the former patient's functioning on the job, in the community, and in his family; his mental status; and his social and medical history during the 10-year period 1950–1960.

We would have liked to administer a schedule to a family member in the control sample, but we had neither the time nor financial resources to do so. Therefore, all our comparative data on the former patients and controls were included in those two schedules, while details of the patient's discharge from psychiatric treatment, his incorporation into his family, and his family's treatment and expectations of him as a former patient were concentrated in the family schedule.

The areas of inquiry in the control schedule cover history of illness and its treatment, psychopathological history, current mental status, family structure, family dynamics, housing, recreation, education, leisure-time activity, occupation, economics, cost of medical care, friendship patterns, religion, ethnic background, attitudes toward psychiatry and psychiatric treatment, personality measurement, social mobility, and social class. Specific questions relating to these areas were developed into a 45-page schedule consisting of 198 questions. The first section includes questions to determine whether or not the individual was an appropriate matched control for a patient; if he was not, the interview was terminated after this screening section.[12] Although interviewing ranged from one to four hours, most schedules were completed in about one hour and 15 minutes.

---

[11] The respondents were: husbands, 45; wives, 41; mothers, 49; fathers, 17; brothers, 14; sisters, 35; other relatives, 25; nonrelatives, 21. The number of household interviews is less than the number of patient interviews because in some cases there was no household informant, in others the patient requested that we not interview a family member, and in a few cases the household member refused or could not be located.

[12] See page 31 of this chapter for further discussion of the screening technique.

INTERVIEWING

Interviewing of former patients, family members, and controls began on June 15, 1961 and concluded on March 10, 1963. In the summer of 1961, 16 interviewers worked full time.[13] All interviewed all three types of respondents, i.e., former patients, family members, and controls. During the academic year 1961 to 1962, most of these interviewers were unavailable because of their studies. Consequently, interviewing slowed down and was carried out on a part-time basis.[14] Most of the remaining interviews were completed in the summer of 1962 with a research team of 10 members.[15] The final interviews were completed on a part-time basis by March 1963.[16]

Bean, Myers, and Pepper conducted a number of patient and family interviews with individuals living in other states, with patients who requested that a senior member of the study staff interview them, or with cases in which special circumstances indicated that the chances of success were greater if the interview was conducted by an older, more fully qualified, and higher-status professional person. Generally, regular staff members interviewed persons within a radius of several hundred miles of New Haven. In addition, staff members made several trips throughout parts of the United States. However, when there was only one case at a great distance from others, we hired associates at other universities to conduct interviews with patients and their families located in their areas, and sociologists on trips abroad for other purposes conducted a few interviews.

Interviewers were thoroughly trained before being sent out to the field. Group sessions were held to discuss each item on the schedule. The interviewers then interviewed each other and also had a private training session with one of the professional staff. Finally, before the interviewer was sent out on his first study case, several practice interviews were held with persons not included in the study.

---

[13] These interviewers included three graduate students in psychology, three nurses, two advanced undergraduate sociology students, one medical student, and seven graduate students in sociology.

[14] These interviewers included three social workers, two school teachers, two graduate anthropology students, three graduate sociology students, and two medical students.

[15] These interviewers included nine graduate sociology students and one school teacher.

[16] These interviewers included three graduate sociology students and a research assistant.

Permission to Interview

Permission to contact those patients living in the community was secured from the appropriate agency. Pepper and Myers, either singly or together, contacted all of the clinics and hospitals in which the discharged patients had been treated. The procedure used to contact the former patients varied, depending upon the wishes of the agency personnel. Some agencies wrote or telephoned the former patients; others requested us to do so. If the agency had no preference for the procedure to be used, we contacted the patient directly by visiting him for an interview without any previous notification. Over the years, our field experience in interviewing has indicated that this direct approach results in the lowest refusal rate.

Regardless of the specific approach to the patient, we contacted him directly to seek his permission for the interview; we did not work through a family member. With the household informant, we identified ourselves and our interest in the former patient only after we had received the patient's permission to do so.

We approached the control population directly, calling upon them at their homes without previous communication. The interviewers were instructed to call back at least four times before they returned the card containing the name and address of the individual to the study office. Each interviewer carried a letter of identification, describing the study, written on official stationery of the Department of Sociology, Yale University and signed by Myers as Director of the Community Health Survey.

We felt it was essential to locate and interview as many cases as possible. We appealed to all groups for cooperation on the basis of the research value of the study and we guaranteed the complete confidentiality of the materials gathered. In most cases the agencies not only cooperated but went out of their way to assist us in every way possible. We offered no services to the patients and their families, although we did emphasize that research is essential if we are to learn more about psychiatric illness and its treatment. Most patients and their families not only cooperated but also seemed pleased that we were taking so much interest in them and were willing to visit them in their homes. The high rate of cooperation was due to the interest of the former patients as well as to our persistence in locating them and calling back an unlimited number of times until the interview was completed. If a former patient refused one interviewer we sent out at least two others before we gave up on the case. We were gratified with the cooperation of the treatment agencies, the former patients, their families and friends, and members of the control population.

CONTROL SAMPLE

One of the purposes of the Follow-Up Study is to determine the adaptation of former patients to community and family living outside of the hospital and the level at which they are presently functioning. Such questions cannot be answered meaningfully when based upon data furnished through a study of only the discharged patient population. Such a study would result in a descriptive analysis of a given aggregate of individuals without providing any information about the effects of psychiatric treatment or hospitalization upon the life patterns of the population. Without a control population it is impossible to determine if adjustment variations are unique or simply reflections of differences to be found among any population.

It might be argued that the former patient population is, in some sense, a nonnormal population and that, therefore, the control sample should consist of a group of normal individuals. However, at our present state of knowledge it is exceedingly difficult to define operationally the concept of normality in a control group.[17] Consequently, we used an alternative criterion for defining the control group. Since in the original study a patient was defined as an individual under psychiatric care, psychiatric treatment was selected as the crucial variable for distinguishing the two groups. Therefore, we included in the control sample only those individuals who had never been under treatment for psychiatric disorders.

The two groups were matched on six social and demographic characteristics which are related to the patterns of human behavior we study in measuring adjustment, such as occupational performance and social participation. These factors are: (1) *social-class distribution* (I–II, III, IV, V); (2) *age distribution* (0–19, 20–39, 40–59, 60 and over); (3) *sex* (male, female); (4) *marital status* (single, married or remarried, widowed, separated, or divorced); (5) *religion* (Protestant, Catholic, Jewish); and (6) *race* (white, Negro).

---

[17] For an excellent discussion of the concept of normality and the difficulties in operationalizing it, see F. C. Redlich, "The Concept of Health in Psychiatry," in A. H. Leighton, J. A. Clausen, and R. N. Wilson (eds.), *Explorations in Social Psychiatry*, Basic Books, New York, 1957.

Method of Selecting Sample

There are a number of problems to be considered in the selection of a control sample best handled by setting up a theoretical procedure which provides the best sample possible. We then attempt to come as close as possible to the ideal. We begin with a specified patient population stratified in terms of six variables, each in turn categorized for a total of 19 categories, so that theoretically there could be 768 possible types of patients in the stratified sample. If we wish to match the control with the patient we then need an accurate listing of all persons who fall into each of the 768 cells, that is 768 mutually exclusive lists. Obviously, such lists are not available or even necessary. Instead, the sample may be drawn from a random list of individuals in the community, matching for the six control factors until the control sample includes a population of randomly selected individuals who, as a group, correspond to the patient population. This was done in the following stages:

First, the sampling frame was selected; a list was compiled of individuals in the community. The alphabetical listing of individuals in the 1961 *New Haven City Directory* served as a basis since these listings were obtained in 1960, the year of our follow-up. Using systematic sampling we then selected a sample of names from this listing. Individuals were assigned randomly to interviewers until the control population was completed. Individuals who obviously failed to correspond with the characteristics of the patient sample were discarded at two stages—before assignment to an interviewer and after ascertainment in the first part of the interview that the individual did not correspond to the stratification requirements of the sample. In addition, whenever any individual was found to have been under psychiatric treatment for mental illness that individual was dropped from the sample; in such an instance the interview was terminated at the earliest possible time, although in some cases the respondent's psychiatric treatment was not discovered until the entire interview was completed.

By use of the above method, bias in the selection was reduced to a minimum. Even though the control characteristics may not be distributed randomly throughout the population, the original selection of the list ensures equal probability of selection or nonselection of individuals with the required characteristics. As long as the individual is randomly selected from the prepared list before he or she is excluded from the control sample, then every individual meeting the requirements of the control sample has equal probability of being included.

We compiled a master control sheet based on the known characteristics of the patients at the time of their discharge from treatment, although our final matching was on 1960 characteristics. We knew the age, sex, and race of the patients and felt there was little likelihood of changes in their religion. However changes were possible in marital status, class position, and treatment status. For example, until we located a former patient *thought* to be living in the community we could not know if he was actually living in the community, if he was hospitalized in another part of the country which had not been covered in our search of the records, or if he had died before June 1, 1960. Consequently, the number of patients in any cell in our control matrix could change. This caused problems in selecting control cases because of the possibility of shifting.

We could have avoided this problem by waiting to interview the control sample until we had completed patient interviewing, but this would have caused a delay of about two years; the advantages gained did not seem worth the time lost. As it was, the length of time involved in data collection covered nearly three years, and we could not see any point in adding several more years to the project. Therefore, we decided to base our original control matrix on the information available and to interview the patient and control samples at the same time. We simply kept modifying the matrices as necessary, adding more controls if we needed them and dropping the most recently interviewed cases if we found we had too many controls in a given cell. This resulted in our interviewing more controls than we needed, but the only alternative was to delay our interviewing process.

Our initial interviewing procedure was to contact each prospective control case directly without any previous contact. This was done to ensure the lowest possible refusal rate. However, as the interviewing proceeded an increasing number of persons contacted and partially interviewed did not fit into the cells we needed. This became a greater problem as the easy-to-be-filled cells of the control matrix were completed. We finally reached a point at which about one half of the cases did not fit into the needed cells. With about 80 hard-to-locate control cases still to be interviewed (for example, class V, Jewish, widowed, female 28 years old), we decided to make preliminary telephone calls to get the information necessary to determine if a given person could be used. We called those with listed telephone numbers, identified ourselves as a community health survey, and secured information about age, sex, religion, marital status, occupation, and education. We then followed up with a home interview in those cases which would fit.

Persons without listed telephones, of course, still had to be contacted directly.

The control sample is based upon 1960 data as listed in the 1961 city directories. The ideal procedure would have been to draw our matched control sample from the 5 per cent sample of residents of New Haven used in the original study, but the practical problems of tracing and interviewing large numbers of people who had moved out of the community made this impossible; we simply did not have the financial resources to follow this group. If we had interviewed only those remaining in the community we would have had an extremely biased sample in terms of geographic mobility. By basing our sample on the population of greater New Haven in 1960 we were able to overcome this bias because we had a 10-year mobility history on all people in our interviews. Of course many of this group lived elsewhere in 1950. Since our primary emphasis is upon the current adjustment of the patients (most of whom do reside in greater New Haven), it seems reasonable to use as a control group persons also residing in the community in 1960 regardless of where they lived in 1950.

The sample drawn from the city directories consisted of 3366 names which can be broken down into five different groups: (1) 608 cases contacted and interviewed—some fully, some only through the screening section: 310 used as matched controls; [18] 22 rejected because they had been treated for mental illness; and finally 276 not included because they failed to match the patients. (2) 1234 persons contacted by telephone who did not match the patient group. (3) 47 individuals not interviewed for a variety of reasons: 9 could not speak English; 17 were so ill that they could not be interviewed; and 21 very old people were senile and could not communicate. (4) 187 refusals which included individuals contacted by telephone as well as in person; some of these would have matched a patient, while for some we could not ascertain the detailed characteristics. (5) And finally, 1290 cases not contacted directly; of this group, 272 were not contacted because they were in atypical positions such as nuns or priests attached to schools or hospitals, could not be found at home, or knew of this study; an additional 224 had moved from the New Haven area; 76 had died by the time we attempted to contact them; 46 were in convalescent homes; and 672 cases were not interviewed because the study had been completed by the time these persons were assigned to be contacted.

---

[18] We did not secure control cases for two young adolescents who were originally treated in a clinic specializing in the treatment of children, because most of the questions with which we deal are not relevant to these two cases.

In brief, for the control sample we contacted 2076 individuals and had 187 refusals (9 per cent).[19] The attrition rate in securing the proper number of cases was extremely high: of the 3366 potential case matches originally drawn, we were able to use only 310 (9 per cent). The difficulties we faced in matching cases are similar to those of other researchers who have conducted comparable field work.[20]

Our completion rate for the controls is extremely high for a survey, although the refusal rate is higher than that among former patients. At least two factors were responsible for this: First, for controls, we gave up on a case after a minimum of four recalls, whereas for the patients we continued to call back until we actually found them at home. Second, the patients represent a special-interest group who shared a common problem. Most of them were surprised that anyone was interested in them after such a long period of time, and most were pleased and highly motivated to participate in the study.

DATA PROCESSING AND ANALYSIS

To test the hypotheses of this study, the analysis required determination of the relationship, if any, between the independent variable, social class, and the range of indices used to measure treatment outcome, relapse, and community adjustment. Next, tests were required to eliminate spurious relationships or to determine if a finding of no relationship could be accounted for by some confounding influence. This "sifting

---

[19] The persons who refused represent a cross section of the social-class structure. The occupational characteristics classified by occupational scale of Hollingshead's *Two Factor Index of Social Position* of this group, obtained from the city directories, are:

Occupation	Refusals Number	Refusals Per Cent
1	1	—
2	13	8
3	10	6
4	36	21
5	38	22
6	20	12
7	52	31
	170	
Unknown	17	
Total	187	100

[20] See, for example, P. K. Whelpton, A. A. Campbell, and J. E. Patterson, *Fertility and Family Planning in the United States*, Princeton University Press, Princeton, 1966.

process" required thousands of cross-tabulations and statistical tests. This type of repetitive and time-consuming task is easily adaptable to computer technology, and to facilitate such an analysis the Yale Computer Center provided a programmer who was able to complete a program which allowed us to speed up the analyses through the use of the IBM 704 and 7090–7094 systems.

The availability of the computer added nothing new to the data-processing procedure. It simply allowed us to do an accurate and thorough job in a much shorter period of time. Moreover, the cost of analyzing the data was probably lower than it would have been under older systems, but this is difficult to determine since we were able to analyze materials which time and cost considerations might have forced us to ignore in the past. In general, the processing of the data involved standard techniques completed by a computer in a shorter period of time.

The statistical procedures used in this study are not confined by a rigid adherence to a given statistical test or level of statistical significance. Statistical tests, at best, are analytical devices of which appropriateness is determined by a number of factors such as sampling and measurement; moreover, their usefulness ultimately depends upon the logical problem of interpretation. This does not mean, as some have argued, that statistical tests should not be used unless the researcher has followed rigidly all requirements specified for a range of tests. Rather, appropriate statistical tests provide standards of judgment which aid the researcher in his interpretation of the data.

In the analyses presented here, the following procedures are used: Wherever possible, statistical tests are made and the level of confidence, whatever it happens to be, is given. The statistical test used is normally the chi-square test.[21]

SUMMARY

In this chapter we have examined the methods of research employed in this follow-up study. We have described the method used to measure social class, the cases studied, the location of cases, sources of data employed, interview procedures and schedules, selection of the control sample, and methods of data analysis. In the next chapter we describe the setting in which the study is undertaken—New Haven, Connecticut—and the psychiatric facilities available to the patients.

---

[21] Actual numbers are used in all statistical calculations.

the social
setting

chapter
three

In this chapter we examine the social structure of the New Haven community from which the patient population was drawn in 1950 and to which the discharged patient returns. First, the community social structure is examined and particular attention is paid to possible alterations which occurred in the social fabric of the city between 1950 and 1960. Second, the various social classes of the New Haven community are described. Third, the availability of and changes in the psychiatric facilities of the New Haven community are discussed.

COMMUNITY STRUCTURE

In 1950 the social structure of the New Haven community was found to be highly compartmentalized, marked by both vertical and horizontal cleavages.[1] Vertical cleavages follow racial, ethnic, and religious lines. Along racial lines two distinct, parallel social structures have evolved, one for whites and one for Negroes. Within the white structure, however, further vertical cleavages exist—along religious lines and along ethnic lines.

---

[1] For an analysis of the social structure of New Haven in historical perspective, see A. B. Hollingshead and F. C. Redlich, *Social Class and Mental Illness*, Wiley, New York, 1958, pp. 47–65. A detailed and comprehensive history of the community is provided in Rollin G. Osterweis, *Three Centuries of New Haven*, Yale University Press, New Haven, 1953.

36

Cross-cutting each vertical division is a series of horizontal cleavages, further separating the community into distinct social strata or social classes. The horizontal cleavages are based upon commonly shared values attached to such factors as occupation, residence, education, and associations. Individuals of a particular occupation and education are similarly ranked within each of the vertical dimensions. For example, an unskilled factory worker with little education residing in one of the slum sections of the city is ranked low within each of the vertical dimensions of the community, whether Negro or white, Catholic, Jewish, or Protestant, Polish, Italian, Irish, or Old Yankee. The social framework both differentiates and integrates social life in the community; the differentiation arises from the combination of vertical and horizontal cleavages in the community, and the integrating mechanisms stem from the same factors.

Two integrating factors are found in the community. First, each stratum of each vertical division is similar in its cultural characteristics to the corresponding stratum in the other divisions. Second, the cultural pattern of each stratum or class was set by the Old Yankee group. This core group initially established and has maintained the cultural mold which shaped the status system of each racial, religious, and ethnic group.

Since 1950 the physical structure of the community has been altered through massive redevelopment programs and the population has grown and been redistributed through the process of suburbanization, but the basic social structure in the community remains much the same. Although New Haven has become increasingly well known throughout the United States for its redevelopment program, the impact of the program by 1960 was essentially in terms of the physical aspects of community living and was restricted to the central city.[2] The patient, returning to the community by 1960, found the city skyline changed and certain improvements made: Where rats once scurried past children playing in refuse heaps behind tenements, fashionable young girls from a new office building now rush along the street during lunch hour, but there are still slums in the city. What was once the deteriorating section of the city is now the dilapidated section; the residents await the bulldozer to hurry them into another deteriorating section or into a public housing project in which the same social world will be re-created. This exodus of slum dwellers is followed by the construction of public housing units,

---

[2] For a brief description of the redevelopment program in New Haven, see Howard W. Hallman, "New Haven, Connecticut: What One City Can Do," in Robert E. Will and Harold G. Vatter (eds.) *Poverty in Affluence*, Harcourt, Brace, and World, New York, 1965.

in which an increasingly large number of low-income families live, or by an influx of middle- and upper-class persons who move into newly constructed high-rise apartment houses. Each group, in turn, re-creates its own separate social world.

The population changes occurring over the 10-year period are common to other areas of the United States. The community, as a whole, increased from 250,000 [3] to 273,429, but the central city, New Haven, declined from 164,443 to 152,048, a population decrease of 7.5 per cent. The growth of the community reflects the general pattern of decentralization found in other American metropolitan areas. As the central city lost population, the surrounding towns which encapsulate New Haven grew rapidly. None increased by less than 34 per cent (West Haven), and the smaller towns of 1950 increased by as much as 75 per cent (East Haven).

While the spatial distribution and size of the population of the New Haven community changed somewhat during the period 1950 to 1960 as described, the basic ecological structure was modified only slightly by the shuffling of various ethnic, racial, or religious groups. Foreign immigration was minimal, continuing the trend which began in 1915. By 1960, only 11 per cent of the population of the New Haven community was foreign born, although persons of foreign stock, first- and second-generation immigrants, made up a large proportion of the population, 41 per cent. The relative distribution of ethnic groups remained the same between 1950 and 1960; those of Italian extraction are the largest group of foreign stock, followed by the Irish, and Russian-Polish, Austrian, and German Jews.[4]

---

[3] The figures reported here are for the community which includes New Haven, West Haven, East Haven, North Haven, Hamden, and Woodbridge. The population in 1950, reported here as 250,000, is slightly higher than the figures reported by Hollingshead in 1950 when the census reporting was less complete than for 1960 and some items were not available for small communities. Because of the absence of available figures for such towns as Woodbridge, East Haven, and North Haven, the figures utilized in the original study were for the urbanized area for 1950 which excluded parts of West Haven, North Haven, and all of Woodbridge. The urbanized area of 1960 is more inclusive than the original definition (1950) and includes areas other than those in the original description; the figures reported here for the town include New Haven, East Haven, West Haven, Hamden, North Haven, and Woodbridge. The data were taken from *Census of Population, 1960, Volume 1, Characteristics of the Population, Part 1, Connecticut,* United States Department of Commerce, Bureau of the Census, Washington, D.C.

[4] Exact distribution figures for the various ethnic groups are unavailable at the present time for the New Haven community. Census figures report only first- and second-generation foreign stock, and such figures do not represent the extent of

Consistent with the pattern of redistribution of the Negro population in the United States, New Haven experienced some growth in the number of Negroes between 1950 and 1960. In that decade the proportion of Negroes in the community increased from 4 to 9 per cent, with most settling in the central city. In addition some Puerto Ricans had settled in New Haven by 1960, but they comprised less than 1 per cent of the population.

Thus, by 1960, there had been no radical change in the social structure of New Haven. New Haven remains a city with a status structure differentiated both by vertical and horizontal lines of cleavage. No essentially new vertical cleavages have appeared, and nothing has occurred to erase the existing vertical or horizontal cleavages.

THE SOCIAL CLASSES

We now turn to a description of the various social classes in the New Haven community which provides evidence of the differentiation of the social structure. In large part, this section derives from the 1950 study; however, the follow-up study interviews with patients and controls in the community strongly indicate that the general outline is valid for 1960.

Class I

Class I is the smallest stratum in the New Haven community, comprising about 3 per cent of the population. In this class nearly every individual recognizes the existence of social classes in the community, and more than 9 out of 10 persons identify themselves as upper class or upper-middle class.

The men of class I families work as executives or professionals. In business, these men are trustees, presidents, vice-presidents, secretaries, or treasurers of large industries, construction and transportation companies, banks, stores, brokerage firms, or utilities. Two thirds of the men in the professions are in independent practice as lawyers, physicians, architects, or engineers, while one third are salaried clergymen, professors,

---

ethnic identification. Despite the acculturation which has taken place, third- and fourth-generation individuals still identify and are closely linked to the specific ethnic lineage groups. Nevertheless, the census figures which, in part, reflect the difference in timing by arrival of the various ethnic groups indicate that the rank order of ethnic groups in the foreign stock remains the same as that of the detailed census carried out by the staff of the 1950 study of social class and mental illness which identified the population of various ethnic origins irrespective of generational differences.

or engineers. Women in class I do not work; they occupy themselves in family, social, and charitable activities.

Old Yankees, who trace their lineage directly from the colonial period and then from British, Scottish, Dutch, or French Huguenot refugee ancestors, comprise nearly 60 per cent of class I. Religion and ethnic background are closely related: 61 per cent of class I families are Protestant, 24 per cent, Catholic, 13 per cent Jewish, and 2 per cent have no religious affiliation.

Persons in class I are the most educated in the population, and, with the number of male heads of household in the professions, the educational difference between husbands and wives is greater in this class than in any other. The median years of school completed is 17.6 years for husbands and 14.4 years for wives.

The nuclear family of husband, wife, and dependent children constitutes the primary family and common household unit. Family stability is valued highly, and divorce is avoided if possible. Marriage within the same class, religious, and ethnic group is considered desirable.

Family homes are large, spacious, and located only in the best sections of the community, protected from encroachment by rigid zoning laws limiting the size of lot and home. The home contains between 8 and 30 rooms, with the modal home consisting of 12 to 15 rooms.

A distinguishing feature of the class I family is its membership in exclusive clubs. The club memberships are generally multiple, consisting of a gentlemen's or ladies' club, a family club, or a special-interest club. Clubs are rigidly divided by ethnic and religious lines. Separate yachting, fishing, hunting, and beach clubs, for example, are maintained by the Gentiles and the Jews.

Class II

Nine per cent of the New Haven community is placed in class II by the Index of Social Position. The members of this class are the most status sensitive of the community: 96 per cent of the respondents know there are classes in the community and can identify their own positions in the class structure. Status sensitivity stems in part from the pivotal position occupied by the class II individuals in the social structure; 74 per cent of the class II adults have been upwardly mobile in the course of their lives. They are close enough to the established families and community leaders to know how they think and act, and at the same time they understand, frequently from firsthand experience, the problems of the small business owners, white-collar workers, and blue-collar workers.

In addition to social mobility, many have also been geographically mobile. The majority of the socially mobile men in this class work for national organizations with offices in major cities throughout the United States. To achieve their aspirations for promotion and advancement, they have moved from office to office, from community to community, as they advance within the company.

Occupationally, the adult men are usually employed as business executives or salaried professionals, engineers, teachers, social workers, pharmacists, opticians, accountants, and proprietors of businesses valued between $35,000 and $100,000. The business executives are never at the top of the organization; they implement rather than make policy decisions. These men and their families are marked by their quest for success and security, the younger executives looking forward to advancement and the older ones concerned with "holding on" to their positions. To supplement family income, especially for the younger executive and minor professionals, approximately one sixth of the wives are employed as teachers, social workers, office managers, secretaries, or clerical workers.

The family home for class II is more closely tied to the family life cycle than in class I. Residence early in the marriage is frequently a small apartment in New Haven or some other city. Family saving at this stage in life is primarily for the purpose of purchasing a home, one which must be in the "right" area and in the "right" school district. Older homes in established districts are considered more desirable by many families than the ranch-type or split-level houses common in newly developed areas. In the New Haven community, the majority of the class II families view two of the older areas with well-established school districts as the "better" areas. Movement into these areas for the young couples frequently means that they are "overhoused," and the mortgage payments are a continuous strain.

The modal residential unit for the class II family is located on the slopes of the hills and ridges where class I homes are located. The class II home, however, is situated on a considerably smaller lot and the house is smaller, usually 6, 7, or 8 rooms.

Most of class II adults were educated in public schools, colleges, and universities. The majority of the men and somewhat less than half of the women are college graduates; the balance, for the most part, completed one to three years of college. Few completed only high school. Similar to the class I males, the class II males are better educated than the females although the educational difference between husbands and wives is somewhat smaller than for the class I couples.

Religiously and ethnically, class II families differ from those in class I. Since the majority of the class has been upwardly mobile, Yankee or "American" households are in the minority—approximately one fifth;

Russian and Polish Jews make up the largest single group, one quarter, with the remainder of the population being English-Scottish or Welsh, northern European (Germany, Scandinavia, the Netherlands, France, Austria), Irish, and Italian. Protestants are the largest single religious group, 45 per cent, followed by Roman Catholics, 29 per cent, and Jews 26 per cent.

The modal family unit is made up of the married adults and their minor children. Family disruptions more frequently occur as the result of death than of divorce or separation; the ratio of widows and widowers to separated or divorced individuals is 9 to 1.

In their leisure time the men and women of class II participate actively in a number of formal and informal associations. Memberships include neighborhood cliques, local church organizations, political clubs, fraternal societies, social clubs, business organizations, and charity organizations. Most adults belong to two or more organizations. Weekday evening recreation includes active participation in clubs and community associations. Recreation also frequently involves participation in a family club. In the home, recreation centers around the television set and reading.

Class III

The 21 per cent of the community's population comprising class III are well aware of the social-status system and of where they fit into it. About one half of the employed class III males are engaged in clerical, sales, and administrative pursuits; one fourth own small businesses; 16 per cent are plant supervisors or skilled workers; and 9 per cent are semi-professionals or technicians. Administrative personnel include section heads in governmental, industrial, and large business offices and shop, service, and chain-store managers. Many class III women are in the labor force, concentrated primarily in clerical and sales jobs. Usually a class III woman is working at the time of marriage and continues until her first child is born. Many of these women then leave their jobs permanently, although some seek employment again when their children are in school and making demands that the fathers' income cannot meet.

Although three out of four class III persons are employees, they do not identify with labor. They resist unionization and remain unorganized, preferring to identify with management. However, they are not treated as equals by their superiors; they are a relatively powerless group caught between higher management and organized labor. They have job security, but they are not well paid and do not have much opportunity for advancement.

In contrast to employees, the small businessmen in this class are well organized through neighborhood trade associations and the Chamber of Commerce. In greater New Haven there are approximately 80 district and neighborhood trade associations composed of small businessmen. These groups exert considerable political pressure to preserve their business interests which they justify in terms of "community interest" and "service to the public." The small businessman has a higher income than the salaried worker, but he fears the competition of the large, national chain concern.

The typical class III individual is a high school graduate. The average number of years of school completed is 12.4 for husbands and 12.1 for wives. In nearly half of the families both husband and wife have the same amount of education. In those families in which there is a difference, twice as many husbands as wives have more education than their spouses, although it is usually only one more year. Most children attend public schools, and 89 per cent graduate from high school. Of this group, nearly 70 per cent begin a postsecondary education, most at publicly supported colleges such as teachers colleges, community junior colleges, and state universities. However, about one third leave college after the first year and another quarter drop out after two years.

The modal class III residence is a five- or six-room single-family house in a "good" residential area. Many such homes are over 30 years old, located on narrow streets with lots 30 to 50 feet wide. The houses are close to the street and not as well landscaped as the homes of higher-class families. Newer homes are built on larger lots, mainly in developments, but they are smaller in size and cost more than the older houses. Most persons living in single-family homes own them; renters live in apartments and two-family dwellings.

Class III is heterogeneous in ethnic composition: six out of seven adults trace their ancestry directly to European countries rather than to old American stock of the pre-Revolutionary War era, the largest proportion to the period of the Old Immigration of 1830 to 1860. Roman Catholics comprise the largest religious group, 47 per cent, followed by Protestants, 39 per cent, and Jews, 14 per cent.

People in all denominations in this class take religion seriously; they belong to a church, attend it regularly, support it financially, and participate in its organizational life. The church is a center of social activity, for religion performs as important a social function as a spiritual one for class III persons. Being a "good" Catholic, Protestant, or Jew gives one prestige and status in the community. Religious participation, like community participation, is considered necessary for good citizenship.

In class III, approximately 93 per cent of adults have been married at some time in their lives, and 79 per cent are currently married. Of

8

the remainder who are widowed, divorced, or separated, the ratio of widows and widowers to separated and divorced persons is 6 to 1. The modal family, including 48 per cent of all households, consists of parents and minor children with no other relatives or nonrelatives present; 84 per cent of all children in this class live with both parents.

Class III persons belong to community organizations of all types: fraternal orders, church couples' clubs, church auxiliaries and guilds, veterans' organizations, athletic clubs, Boy Scouts, Girl Scouts, the Parent-Teacher Association, etc. Membership is most widespread, however, in church-related lodges or veterans' groups for men and in church-related associations for women; 82 per cent of the men and 87 per cent of the women belong to at least one formal organization, and about 70 per cent of each sex belong to two or more. Both men and women are active in their groups, believing that some participation is necessary for the "good of the community." The most popular leisure-time activities are visiting and entertaining friends and relatives, viewing television, and reading local newspapers and popular magazines such as *Life, Reader's Digest,* and *The Saturday Evening Post.*

Class IV

Class IV, as identified by the Index of Social Position, is the largest, single class group. Members of this social class make up 49 per cent of the population of the New Haven community. While these individuals are less sensitive to the class structure and their relative position in it than individuals in other classes, nearly nine out of ten individuals believe there are social classes.

Nearly three quarters of the adults in class IV have been intergenerationally stable and most are not committed to a life of striving to better their position. They are generally satisfied with their way of life. Stable class IV individuals have a sense of personal dignity and self-esteem which sustains them in their life position; they identify themselves with the working class in a significantly large number.

One third of the class IV adult males are employed as skilled manual workers, slightly more than one half as semiskilled employees, and the balance are clerical and sales workers or petty proprietors. The skilled manual workers, such as auto body repairers, electric welders, linotype operators, masons, or yard superintendents for the railroad, feel secure in their jobs and in their homes; they have few worries about the future and are less concerned than the semiskilled workers about the possibility of a future major depression. Many are enthusiastic about their work, and few feel that it is just a job.

The semiskilled workers are usually employed on the assembly lines of larger manufacturing companies in the community. The skilled and semiskilled workers jointly look to the union and economic conditions in the country for their security. Two thirds are employed in organized industries and believe that their greatest safeguards against economic insecurity are "the union" and state and federal legislation.

Many women in this stratum are in the labor force. The largest proportion of females employed in manufacturing industries is drawn from this stratum. After leaving school, the young women work in the factories or in clerical positions and continue to work after marriage at least until the first pregnancy. Normally, after the children have left home, the women again return to work.

Nearly one half of the families in class IV have title to a home, but four out of five of the homeowners are still making mortgage payments. The type of home purchased by the family is dependent upon ethnic background. Many first- and second-generation families feel that a single-family home is a luxury. They believe that a two- or three-family home will pay for itself, even in "hard times." Such families normally live on the first floor of the house, using the rent from the upper floors to meet housing payments. Younger families, however, and in particular the third- and fourth-generation families, have moved into the single-family, mass-produced, ranch-type home in the suburbs.

The educational pattern of the class IV adult is distinctly different from that of his counterpart in class III. Few have completed high school and, on the average, the adult females have more education than their husbands. However, their is little difference in the educational level of husbands and wives. While the children tend to remain in school longer than their parents, a significant proportion of the older children leave to take a job in a factory before completing high school. Education for class IV is generally in the public elementary and secondary schools, although a considerable percentage attend Roman Catholic schools. For those few who do complete high school, further education is limited to a year or two at the community, state teachers, technical, or business colleges.

Ongoing acculturation is the hallmark of the class IV individual. Partially assimilated European ethnic stocks make up the majority of the heads of the household. Less than 10 per cent trace their lineage to Old Yankee stock; the largest ethnic groups are the Italians (30 per cent), Irish, and Scandinavians, and the balance are distributed in small proportions among the Poles, Polish and Russian Jews, Greeks, Hungarians, Lithuanians, and Bulgarians. Nearly two thirds are Catholic, 30 per cent Protestant, and 7 per cent Jewish.

The typical family constellation in class IV differs from the family patterns of class III in the following ways: more broken homes, more households with boarders and roomers, larger families, and more three-generation families residing in the same household. The amount of disorganization in the class IV family is indicated by the fact that the ratio of widowed to separated and divorced individuals is 2 to 1, in contrast to the ratio of 9 to 1 in class II, and 6 to 1 in class III.

Leisure-time activities, as usually pursued by the upper- and middle-class families, are normally absent in the class IV household. Time away from the job is frequently spent in performing household chores around the house. Reading occupies little of the spare time of the class IV adult, with the type of reading usually restricted to a local newspaper, a weekly sensational newspaper, *Life*, or one of the home-improvement magazines. Contact with the mass media normally comes through the television set or the radio enjoyed by the housewife during the day and by the whole family during evening and weekend hours. Outside of the household, family leisure-time activities are normally taken up with visiting relatives or taking short outings as a family to a local amusement park or public beach.

Formal associations are utilized infrequently. The one formal organization to which nearly two thirds of the adult males belong is generally a union. Involvement in formal organizations is minimal; the majority of those individuals who do belong to a formal association rarely attend the meetings.

Class V

Class V individuals, who comprise 18 per cent of the community's population, are less aware of a distinct class system than persons in any other social stratum, although they recognize their low position in the community structure.

Approximately one half of the males are semiskilled workers; nearly one half are unskilled laborers; a few have never had a regular job. Jobs at this level are poorly paid, require long hours of work, and are generally in nonunionized industries. People in this class start working as soon as the law permits. Although men are expected to work and support their wives and children, wages are so low that a large number of wives and mothers work. Nearly 50 per cent of all married women are gainfully employed outside the home as semiskilled or unskilled workers.

The educational level in class V is the lowest of any stratum. The median education for men is the sixth grade and slightly less than eighth grade for women; 54 per cent of the adult men and 30 per cent of the women have less than a seventh-grade education. Children today leave school in the middle teens—usually at 16, the minimum legal age for leaving school in Connecticut.

Class V housing is concentrated in the worst slum areas of the city and in low-rent public housing. Many families live in multifamily tenements built 60 to 80 years ago in which the small apartments are almost all the same and consist of a few small rooms. This housing is overcrowded, dirty, unsanitary, and overpriced. Increasingly larger numbers of these families, however, are finding their homes in public housing which offers the advantages of newness, more space, and better equipment in terms of heating, cooking, and sanitary facilities; three types of units are available—variable-rent units in which cost depends upon family income, fixed-rent units, and housing units for the elderly.

In class V, most persons, with the exception of Negroes, are new immigrants and their descendants—Italians, Poles, Slavs, and Russian and Polish Jews. Although the majority of class V persons are Catholic, few are practicing Catholics in any sense of the term; they affiliate themselves with the Roman Catholic Church, but they are often in difficulty with the parish priest. Antagonism to the Church is widespread. To many class V persons the Catholic Church represents a money-grasping organization, and priests are viewed as more interested in money than in religion. This attitude prevails also among class V Protestants, both white and Negro, who are inactive in their church and distrustful of ministers. Only Russian and Polish Jews, who comprise 4 per cent of the class V population, are practicing members of their faith; these Orthodox, first-generation immigrants have remained loyal to their religion and do not feel hostile or skeptical toward it.

The nuclear family of father, mother, and children is the dominant form of the households in class V, but the three- or four-generation family and broken nuclear families of one parent and minor children are common. Two of every five children under 17 years of age live in homes broken by death, desertion, divorce, or separation. In most of these families the mother lives with the children; however, desertion by the mother is not uncommon, and when this occurs the father and children usually move in with a relative.

The isolation of class V families, first in the slums and then in ethnic and racial groupings, tends to keep them beyond the mainstream of community life. Outside the hours spent on the job and in school, most of the family's social activity takes place within the narrowly confined slum areas and ethnic enclaves of their particular group. Three quarters of class V families are completely isolated from formal community associations except for their nominal church affiliation. The lack of clubs and organizations with regular meeting places, combined with the overcrowding in their homes, leads to the use of commercial and public facilities for recreation or simply to spilling out into the streets. Favorite out-of-home recreation includes movies, athletic events, local amusement parks, public beaches, or nearby public parks. Children play games in the streets, alleys, open areas around factories, and parking lots. Older children move in gangs to the downtown areas, taverns, parks, and beaches, and on exploring expeditions to other communities. Viewing television and listening to the radio are the most common home pastimes in class V. The television or radio is set at high volume in the morning and is not turned off until the last member of the household goes to bed at night. Little reading is done except for local newspapers, nonlocal tabloids, and an occasional picture magazine. Visiting is a common pastime, but many persons in this class have few friends. Many middle-aged and older persons, in particular, have few social contacts outside their immediate families.

PSYCHIATRIC FACILITIES

In this section the organization of psychiatric care and treatment facilities are described for the period 1950 to 1960. The history of these facilities prior to 1950 is described in detail in the original study.[5] During the period of the follow-up study, some changes occurred in the organization of psychiatric care and facilities, but many of them came too late to affect the patients.

State Hospitals

In 1950 there were in operation three state mental hospitals, approximately of equal size, dating individually from 1866, 1903, and 1931. This had not changed by 1960. Of the total patient population in the follow-up study (1563 in number), 83 per cent were in treatment in one of the three state hospitals in 1950. By 1960 the total patient population in the three state hospitals had increased slightly (0.4 per cent), but the numerical distribution had assumed a better balance. Since patient assignment is on a geographical basis, the majority of state hospital patients from the New Haven community were in treatment in one facility, the oldest state hospital. In this hospital the patient population decreased by 5.7 per cent between 1950 and 1960, while in the newest and smallest hospital it increased by 8.9 per cent.

The overall slight increase in the number of resident patients hides two important facts: First, the increase occurred during the first part of the

---

[5] Hollingshead and Redlich, op. cit., pp. 137–161.

decade, and since 1955 the number of patients in state hospitals on any given day has declined. Second, despite this half-decade (1955 to 1960) decline in the number of occupied beds, the total number of patient contacts and different patients seen in state hospitals has increased. For example, in 1950, the three hospitals admitted 2943 patients and in 1960, 5311 patients. In other words, while the number of inhospital patients at any given time was declining, both the admission and discharge rates were increasing.

In 1958 an administrative decision was made to hold the line on the number of general-patient beds in the existing state hospitals, while increasing facilities elsewhere. The building programs in the state hospitals were then designed to modernize and to alleviate the overcrowded conditions present in 1950. Thus, the number of patient beds in the three hospitals has increased by only 6 per cent (1950 to 1960), and the overcrowding has been reduced so that mental hospitals in the state which were operating at 103.9 per cent of capacity in 1950 operated at 89.7 of capacity in 1960.

Other direct attempts to alleviate certain problems existing in 1950 involved staffing and money changes. In 1950 the staff-patient ratio in state psychiatric facilities was 35 to 100; in 1960 it had increased to 47 to 100. Financially, the greater investment in psychiatric patient care is reflected in two ways: First, staff salaries were improved so that between 1950 and 1960 this item in the budget of the oldest state hospital increased from 1.9 million dollars to 4.7 million dollars. Second, expenditures per patient nearly doubled, increasing from $3.85 per diem to $7.30 per diem. However, despite the drop in total patient load, the modernization programs, and greater financial investment, the patient pressure on facilities is still relatively great. The physical and staff facilities of the three state hospitals are overtaxed by the large number of patient admissions and discharges generated by the more rapid turnover of the patient population which first began to appear at mid-decade.

Beyond the modernization program affecting the physical plant of the state hospitals, several other specific changes took place during the ten years: Dynamic milieu therapy brought a change in attitudes toward treatment. As one facet of the program, the "open-door" policy was activated simultaneously in the three state hospitals, following a joint visit by the three hospital superintendents to England where the program had been initiated.

A second set of changes involved specific forms of therapy. Of particular importance during the decade was the introduction of psychotropic drugs—tranquilizers as well as psychic energizers—which appeared around 1955. Their major effect on the large body of chronic hospitalized patients included in the Follow-Up Study resulted in the termination of the traditional physical forms of restraint; the pill was substituted for the camisole. Not only the use of the camisole but also of the various forms of hydrotherapy, which calmed agitated or aggressive patients, was discontinued in the state mental hospitals. The use of psychotropic drugs, of course, became common in the community and opened a new modality of treatment, one no longer administered solely by psychiatric medical personnel. The impact of these drugs in the community has not been widely studied so that we know little about their influence.

In contrast to the initiation of new therapies, two traditional forms of treatment in some vogue in 1950 were utilized less frequently by the end of the decade or had disappeared altogether. By 1960 insulin shock therapy was rarely used, and psychosurgery had fallen into disrepute. Specifically, of the 150 patients in the Follow-Up Study who had been treated by psychosurgery, only 21 were so treated after 1950 and the majority of these lobotomies were carried out in 1951 and 1952; the last lobotomy performed on a patient in the Follow-Up Study took place in 1958—five years after the next most recent lobotomy. While insulin therapy and hydrotherapy were utilized with decreasing frequency and psychosurgery was terminated, electroshock therapy was utilized about as often in 1960 as in 1950. In general, the use of electroshock therapy has remained relatively constant.

The remainder of the changes in the state hospitals are more diffuse than the changes in form of therapy. They stem, in part, from certain organizational reforms. In 1955 the Connecticut Legislature passed a law authorizing the creation of the Office of the State Commissioner of Mental Health. The first commissioner assumed office in 1956 and was replaced by the current commissioner in 1958. The Office of the Commissioner of Mental Health not only centralizes authority for the state psychiatric facilities but also controls the licensing of private psychiatric facilities, controls and maintains standards, supports and coordinates inservice training programs, and secures and distributes federal funds received through the National Institute of Mental Health, the Department of Health, Education and Welfare (which now contributes approximately 5 per cent of the total budget for the care and treatment of the mentally ill by state-supported agencies).

The creation of the State Department of Mental Health has served to coordinate the various state psychiatric facilities and stimulate integration of these facilities with other health-oriented agencies and programs such as that of the Yale University School of Medicine. Many new programs now in operation were in embryonic form in 1960 and more are only now in the planning stage.

Some changes result from the reorientation of psychiatric treatment, much of which is not restricted to the confines of the state hospitals. Indeed, the overwhelming significance of these changes is the reduction of the isolation of treatment facilities and of the independence of psychiatric agents and agencies. Prior to 1950, the state hospital was an independent, isolated facility whose concern for the patient, by and large, began at admission and terminated at discharge. The role of the psychiatrist was circumscribed by the traditional treatment role of the physician. The functions of other staff members were limited to minor services, frequently to maintaining the patient until a psychiatrist became available. However, the introduction of dynamic milieu therapy involved the awareness that services traditionally provided by the psychiatrist might be provided by a nurse, psychologist, or other members of the staff. Thus, the psychiatrist's functions were extended beyond the traditional treatment role to providing inservice training, coordination, and consultation with hospital and nonhospital agents involved in the care and rehabilitation of the mentally ill. Thus, dynamic milieu therapy has modified the traditional structure. The state hospital is increasingly viewed as only one element in the treatment process in which effective therapy involves linking hospital care to outpatient psychiatric facilities and community agencies. Moreover, the role of the psychiatrist has been expanded to include consultation services with community agents, nonpsychiatrically trained physicians, and paramedical personnel.

These changes mirror a common trend in medical practice toward team functions—pooling of the resources and talents of teams of specialists to provide comprehensive care at the highest technical level. In order to maintain a high level of competency in the face of rapid technological advances, the medical specialist (in this case the psychiatrist) turns part of his less technical responsibilities over to others. Similarly, the state hospital relies on other agents and agencies to complement the types of services it offers. This pattern of increasing functional integration of specialized services reflects the changes associated with any division of labor arising in response to rapid technological developments.

Several objective conditions reflect these changes in the role of the state hospital in the psychiatric treatment process: First, increasing attention is devoted to the patient at discharge. Patients are channeled into outpatient agencies funded, staffed, and maintained by the state hospital and other community agencies which are, in turn, supported by state, local, hospital, and university funds. Second, the staffs of the state hospitals have established closer ties with such institutions as the Yale University School of Medicine. Third, hospital staff members increasingly provide consultation services to nonmedical community agencies, such as the Family Service Agency.[6]

The changes described above took place late in the decade. The impact on the mentally ill patient will most likely be seen in the current and following decades. The patients in this study are, in general, not directly concerned with the changes to the degree that the current patient population will be. For many of the patients entering treatment for the first time shortly before the 1950 study, to say nothing of those who were already deteriorated by then, the pattern of chronicity and deterioration had been established. For these patients, changes in therapy and organization had little impact on the course of their illness. It is the 1960 and after, first-admission patient who will most likely benefit. While it should be indicated that, in the latter part of the decade, interest in rehabilitation programs extended and renewed interest in even the chronic, deteriorated patient, nevertheless it would be premature to suggest that these programs have been particularly effective with the hard-core chronic patient. At present, such programs are best viewed as demonstration projects.

Veterans Hospitals

In 1950, 5 per cent of the patients included in the Follow-Up Study were in treatment in Veterans Administration hospitals. The majority of the patients were treated in neuropsychiatric hospitals populated largely by psychotics. Assignment to the various Veterans Administration hospitals in 1950 depended upon a number of factors: Generally, veterans from World War I were in a single hospital in one adjoining state, and veterans from World War II were in a single hospital in another adjoining state. Since 1950 a few of the patients in our study have received treatment in a new psychiatric hospital in an adjacent state. Also, a veterans hospital, which includes psychiatric wards, has opened in the New Haven community, thus making treatment facilities for veterans available locally. A few male patients in our study were readmitted to psychiatric treatment in this institution, avoiding separation from the community which previously was the result of treatment outside the state.

Several of the veterans hospital patients who had received treatment in a psychiatric hospital in a neighboring state have returned to the New Haven community, going periodically for treatment in Veterans Ad-

---

[6] One additional change which hopefully symbolizes the fact that the state hospital is no longer a separate dead-end institution with prime responsibility for the custodial care of the mentally ill is the fact that all three state hospitals changed their names removing the word *state* in each case.

ministration clinics or the Veterans Administration general hospital. New forms of treatment, such as psychotropic drugs and milieu and group therapies, have been utilized widely in Veterans Administration hospitals as well as in other types of hospitals.

Private Hospitals

Few of the patients studied (2 per cent) were treated in private hospitals. These private hospitals are widely scattered; only one is located in the New Haven community. Their accommodations range from luxurious cottages on carefully landscaped, country estates to dismal, decaying, old mansions that are poorly maintained. The private hospitals are generally small institutions except for one which has over 300 beds.

Discharge from the private hospital comes about in two distinct ways: the patient is discharged as "cured," or treatment is terminated with the exhaustion of the patient's financial resources, and the patient is subsequently transferred to public facilities. There are some interesting reversals of this process. Patients hospitalized for long periods in state institutions occasionally are transferred to private institutions at the insistence of family members who make a final heroic effort to provide "better care." Mrs. L., for example, after years in the state hospital, was transferred to a private hospital when her family unexpectedly fell heir to several thousand dollars; when the money ran out, she was again returned to the state hospital.

Therapeutic orientations vary among the different private hospitals. The range of treatment runs from psychoanalysis and psychoanalytic therapy to primarily organic methods including drugs and electroshock.

In contrast to state hospitals, the private institutions are better staffed: the ratio of employees to patients is much higher and, particularly, the number of psychiatrists available per capita patient population is higher. Moreover, the psychiatrists receive a greater financial reward for their work in these hospitals.

Despite the advantages offered by the private hospitals in terms of physical facilities, staff, and selectivity, most of these agencies were less able in 1960 to provide the integrated services of other psychiatric institutions. Basically, these hospitals are not community-oriented agencies since they draw their patient population on a regional and, in some cases, a national basis. The nature of the private hospital makes follow-up programs nearly impossible, as it is difficult to provide treatment continuity in the disengagement process during which the patient moves from hospital treatment back into the community. Thus, while the institutions maintain some outpatient services, their scope is restricted to the relatively few local patients. This problem is found similarly among Veterans Administration hospitals which also draw their patient population regionally. However, the national network of Veterans Administration hospitals and clinics partially mitigates this problem.

Because of the improvements in state facilities, expansion of veterans hospitals, other alternative treatment facilities, and rising costs, the private hospitals are finding it increasingly difficult to survive. This is particularly true of those hospitals catering to the middle-class patient.

Outpatient Clinics

In 1950, 9 per cent of the patients were in treatment in psychiatric outpatient clinics. At the time of the original study it was clear that emphasis upon the clinic as a psychiatric treatment agency was growing, and this growth has continued during the period of the Follow-Up Study. Ten years ago the patients in the study were utilizing seven clinics, of which five were located in the New Haven community. These clinics have continued to operate and their operations have expanded as their case loads have increased.

The two Veterans Administration clinics continue to be used by the patients in our study. These clinics are located in two separate Connecticut metropolitan areas and are used by patients for diagnostic consultation and ongoing treatment.

The largest community clinic accounts for half of the patients from greater New Haven who use clinics each year: it is the clinic most frequently utilized by discharged patients from various inpatient agencies. This clinic is located in the community hospital and is supported by a variety of sources: state, general hospital, university, and federal government. It provides diagnostic and treatment services to adults through the hospital and the school of medicine's psychiatric-residency training program. The therapeutic orientation in the clinic in 1950 was analytic-psychological, but today it tends to be more eclectic.

A separate psychiatric clinic is maintained in a sectarian hospital in the community. Between 1950 and 1960 few changes were made in this clinic, although since 1960 expansion of facilities and deemphasis of directive-organic therapy has been initiated. Its patient case load was small in 1950 and did not expand greatly over the 10-year period. With its past therapy orientation, few patients remained in treatment for any extended period.

Other clinics in operation since 1950 include one maintained for alcoholics by the State Commission for Alcoholism. Several patients originally treated in this clinic have continued on a sporadic basis over the 10-year period. Two additional clinics specializing in the treatment of children have operated under the support of, first, the community and state, and, second, the university.

New Psychiatric Facilities and Utilization Patterns

By 1960 several entirely new psychiatric facilities had been made available to the mentally ill of New Haven: (1) A local outpatient clinic operated by one of the state mental hospitals is maintained to provide ongoing treatment for former hospitalized patients. A number of the patients we studied were seen in this clinic. (2) A residence facility (halfway house) for chronic-drunkenness offenders was started as a pilot program to establish a milieu climate for treatment and care. At the time of the Follow-Up Study several patients had been or were located in this agency. (3) Two children's facilities, both residential, one privately sponsored and one state sponsored, were opened. No patients from the original study were involved with these institutions. (4) Privately owned and operated convalescent homes have been increasingly converted for the care and treatment of psychiatric patients. These institutions may be considered new in the sense that following a mid-decade change in the social security laws it became possible for individuals to collect benefits while living in nonpsychiatric institutions. To reduce the chronic-patient load in state hospitals, many older patients were discharged and transferred directly to these convalescent homes where the same type of "treatment"—custodial care only—is continued.

The care provided in most of the convalescent homes is variable. Although such institutions are licensed by the state, requirements are minimal and conditions are extremely poor in some. Few institutions provide any medical care other than the necessary physical treatment available from a nurse or a general practitioner who has the token connection with the home required for the state license.

To many of the smaller, more poorly managed convalescent homes, the body of state hospital patients is attractive. First, transfers from the state hospital eliminate the cost incurred by operating with empty beds. Second, the older chronic cases are placid and easy to manage. (The convalescent homes are selective and accept only those cases in which management problems are minimal.) Third, the body of state hospital patients often provides service staff for the convalescent home; patients who are capable of cleaning, cooking, and building maintenance, but who lack a family or job in the community to which they may return, find sheltered employment in such institutions.

Many of the former state hospital patients in our study were transferred to these convalescent homes during the 10-year period. In 1960 these patients were located in 40 homes. For the most part, such patients are older, chronic, deteriorated cases whose transfer has served to reduce the load of chronic patients in the state hospitals, freeing facilities for the treatment of new, acute cases for whom chance of recovery is higher. In general, these institutions provide a safety valve to the pressure of chronic patients in the state hospital, but they do not provide comprehensive treatment facilities. However, patients transferred to these hospitals are often considered past the point at which psychiatric intervention might be effective. The patients' demands are generally physical, and many of these demands can be and are provided by the convalescent home which often serves as a way station to the cemetery.

Private Practice

As indicated in Chapter 2, patients originally in private psychiatric treatment in 1950 were not followed up in this study. It is, however, important to describe briefly the availability of such services in the community as a number of patients have been treated at various times since 1950 by private practitioners.

In 1950, 22 psychiatrists were practising full time and eight others part time in the New Haven community. The psychiatrists at that time represented two distinctive therapeutic orientations: one group with a psychological and analytical orientation was described in the original study as the A-P group; a second group had a directive and organic orientation, the D-O group. Two criteria were utilized to distinguish these groups—the principal method of therapy and training for such therapy. The analytic approach consists essentially of analyzing behavior, relationships, and unconscious and conscious motivations according to psychoanalytic theories; an almost purely psychological approach is stressed. The directive approach consists of changing attitudes, opinions, and behavior by directive and supportive methods; these procedures are combined with organic medical techniques.

In training, the A-P psychiatrists went through full or partial psycho-analytic and/or psychodynamic training and orientation; little training took place in the basic biological and clinical sciences during their years of specialization. D-O psychiatric training was more closely oriented to the organic medical approach, and considerable training was undertaken in neurology and basic biological sciences.[7]

While this A-P—D-O dichotomy emphasized the extremes of a very real polarity in 1950, the same general model, with two important modifications, applies in the community today. First, a number of psychiatrists

---

[7] For a more complete discussion of this distinction, see Hollingshead and Redlich, *op. cit.*, pp. 155–161.

who represented the extremes of this polarity have died since 1950, and their absence is reflected in a convergence of extreme points of view. Second, new men entering practice in the community have been trained in programs reflecting this convergence. Exposed to more eclectic training programs, they tend to cluster closer to the midpoint of the D-O—A-P continuum but still on one or the other side of the same dividing line. Although there is evidence of some agreement among the various practitioners, certainly the formation of a single monolithic orientation, for which some hoped, has not taken place.

In 1960, one and a half as many psychiatrists are in private practice in the New Haven community, and 48 patients in the follow-up population have been, or are, in private treatment. The cost of such treatment is so high, however, that the patients are drawn, in general, from the middle and upper classes. Some private psychiatrists maintain an affiliation with a public clinic, but the patients they see in the clinic also tend to be of higher social status.

The general characteristics of the community structure, the five social classes, and psychiatric facilities should be kept in mind as the patients' 10-year treatment experience is examined. We shall turn to this topic in the following chapter.

treatment experience and its outcome: 1950 to 1960

part two

This part examines the 10-year experience of the patient population. First, we analyze the relationship between social class and follow-up status in 1960 of patients from New Haven, Conn., who were in psychiatric treatment in 1950. Next, the treatment experience of these patients is studied for the decade 1950 to 1960. Finally, the relationship between psychiatric treatment and outcome is described.

social class and treatment status at follow-up

Data are presented in this and following chapters to test the proposition that social class is related to treatment outcome. In this chapter we test our first hypothesis: *social class is related to treatment status in 1960 at follow-up* of patients from greater New Haven who were in psychiatric treatment in 1950. Since 1950 is the base line for the 10-year follow-up, the 1950 social-class position of patients was used to determine the effect of class position on treatment outcome. The treatment status of all hospital and clinic patients was examined on June 1, 1960, and follow-up status was divided into three major categories: [1]

1. Hospitalized. Patients in any psychiatric inpatient facility are included in this category. In addition to state hospitals, Veterans Administration hospitals, and private psychiatric hospitals, this category includes psychiatric wards or units in general hospitals. Psychiatric patients who were transferred from mental hospitals to convalescent homes and nursing homes licensed to care for psychotic patients are also classified as hospitalized; patients with nonpsychiatric diagnoses in these homes are not considered to be under psychiatric care.

Patients hospitalized in 1960 are subdivided into two groups: those hospitalized continuously from 1950 to 1960, and those hospitalized inter-

---

[1] The 18 persons who could not be located in 1960 are excluded from all analyses. Therefore, in this chapter, 1545 patients are studied instead of 1563.

mittently during the period and in hospital treatment at the time of the Follow-Up Study.

Patients on parole or on an extended visit of more than 30 days are considered as discharged although possibly still classified administratively as patients. In many state hospitals it is customary to place patients on extended visit or parole for one year before granting them a final discharge. Patients are "kept on the hospital books" for such an extended period in order to facilitate the readmission process if it should be necessary; if the patient returns during this period, less administrative work is required than if he has to be handled as a new admission. Usually, there is little or no supervision or care during this period, and final discharge at the end of the period is automatic. On the other hand, visits under hospital supervision are mostly for short periods of less than 30 days. From a review of cases, it is apparent that patients on an extended visit or parole of over 30 days generally consider themselves discharged, and hospital authorities treat them as such except for administrative purposes.

2. *Dead.* Persons who died any time between December 1, 1950 and June 1, 1960 are included in this category, regardless of their treatment status at the time of death. Later in the chapter this category is subdivided in terms of the patients' treatment status at death.

3. *Not hospitalized.* This category is subdivided into two groupings: not under psychiatric care (former patients not under psychiatric care on June 1, 1960), and under outpatient care (patients receiving any type of outpatient psychiatric care—private practitioner, private and public outpatient clinics).

Treatment status in 1960, 10 years after the patients were studied originally, is shown in Table 4.1.[2] The social-class distribution of patients by follow-up status differs significantly from the totals; many more persons in the lower classes were still under hospital care 10 years after the original 1950 study; the percentage increases steadily from the higher to the lower classes. Most hospitalized patients in 1960 had been under continuous hospital care during the 10-year period, with the percentage increasing from classes I–II to class V. However, the proportion of persons under intermittent care does not differ greatly nor in any consistent manner among the classes. In fact, if only the hospitalized patients are considered, the proportion under intermittent care is lowest in class V. In other words, among the 1960 hospitalized patients,

---

[2] Percentages are rounded to the *nearest whole number* in all presentations. Classes I and II are always combined because of the small number of cases in class I.

TABLE 4.1

1960 Treatment Status and Social Class (Per Cent)

Treatment Status	Social Class				
	I–II	III	IV	V	Total
Hospitalized	34	41	47	54	49
Continuously	28	34	38	48	43
Intermittently	6	7	9	6	6
Dead	26	20	28	31	29
Not hospitalized	40	39	25	15	22
Not under treatment	27	34	22	13	19
In outpatient treatment	13	5	3	2	3
$n = 53$		149	616	727	1,545

$\chi^2 = 62.8, \ df = 6, \ p < .05$ [a]

[a] Categories used in the statistical test were (1) hospitalized, (2) dead, and (3) not hospitalized.

relatively fewer in class V than in any other class had ever been discharged during the 10-year study period.

Class differences in hospital discharge and readmission are reflected even more dramatically in the proportion of persons living in the community and not hospitalized at follow-up in 1960: the percentage declines from 40 in classes I–II to 15 in class V so that the proportion of persons not hospitalized in the community in the two highest classes is more than two and one half times as great as in the lowest. Although most persons in the community were no longer under any type of psychiatric care, those receiving outpatient therapy were concentrated in the middle and upper classes. Only 2 per cent of class V former patients were being treated in a clinic or by a private practitioner, whereas in classes I–II the percentage rose to 13. These percentages are based upon the total cohort of 1950 cases, and thus they include persons who had died by 1960 and those who were hospitalized, as well as those no longer under inpatient care. A more realistic way of revealing the extent of outpatient treatment is to base percentages only upon those living in 1960 who were no longer hospitalized. On this basis the percentage declines from 33 in classes I–II to 13 in class V.

Class differences in the proportion of persons who died are not great although the smallest percentage of dead in 1960 is found in class III. This difference is due primarily to a smaller proportion of older people in class III than in the other classes. Several factors may explain the

TABLE 4.2

**Age-Specific Mortality Rates: Comparison of Patients
with Connecticut Population**

	Mortality Rate [a]	
Age at Death	Patients	Connecticut [b] Population
15–24	1.9	0.8
25–34	4.2	1.2
35–44	7.5	2.5
45–54	16.2	6.6
55–64	29.3	17.4
65–74	55.1	39.7
75–84	119.3	91.5
85 and over	179.3	191.8

[a] Per 1000 population. See Mortimer Spiegelman, *Introduction to Demography*, the Society of Actuaries, Chicago, 1955, p. 55, for computation of mortality by 10-year periods.
[b] Based upon 1950 State of Connecticut Registration Report.

younger age of class III. First, this group in the community has fewer aged persons. In a community sample taken in 1950,[3] the lowest proportion of persons 55 years of age and over was found in class III (15 per cent) and the highest in class V (23 per cent). Next, this class has been expanding in size because of changes in the occupational and educational structure of the society, and it is younger rather than older persons who have the training and skills to move upward into it. Finally, older persons in class III may be less likely to be hospitalized for psychiatric problems than those in other classes since most of these families do not have the financial resources available to class I and II families for private hospitalization and there is a greater stigma attached to hospitalization in a state institution at this level than in classes IV and V.

Since age is a crucial factor in determining mortality rates, we computed age-specific rates by 10-year categories (see Table 4.2). It is clear that at all ages, except 85 and over, the mortality rates for the patients are higher than for the general population. Other studies also have found

[3] For a discussion of the 5 per cent community sample, see A. B. Hollingshead and F. C. Redlich, *Social Class and Mental Illness*, Wiley, New York, 1958, pp. 30–37.

much higher death rates for mental patients than for the general population.[4] Many factors are responsible for these higher mortality rates among patients. For example, persons hospitalized for psychiatric disorders often have serious physical illnesses or disabilities as well, which shorten their life span. Also, emotional problems leading to hospitalization are sometimes associated with cardiac decompensation and arteriosclerotic diseases. Among the elderly, in particular, physical and mental symptoms are difficult to distinguish in such cases, and the mental symptoms frequently lead to psychiatric hospitalization before the physical ones become acute enough to require general hospitalization. Even in cases of acute illness, such as pneumonia or cardiac decompensation with edema, the mental concomitants may lead to admission to a mental rather than to a general hospital. In fact, the death rate for patients in our study is twice as high during the first year after admission to the hospital as during any subsequent year. Finally, factors such as malnutrition, resulting from the refusal to eat properly, not uncommon among psychiatric patients especially those with depressive symptoms, probably help account for the higher mortality rate of mental patients.

Although we do not have data to allow us to determine social-class differences in mortality for the general Connecticut population, age-specific death rates for the patients differ markedly by class. As shown in Table 4.3, mortality and class are related: generally, age-specific mortality rates are lowest in classes I–III. This finding is not unusual since studies of the general population indicate the same pattern.[5] Since many of the hospitalized patients are lower class, the higher death rates in class V may be one of the factors accounting for the higher mortality among the patients in general in our study.

Also as demonstrated in other studies, age at death is directly related to class: the higher the class, the older the individual at death.[6] Thus, we find the percentage of patients 75 years of age and older at death increases from 39 in class V, to 45 in class IV, to 53 in class III, and to 57 in classes

[4] For example, see Leta M. Adler, James W. Coddington, and Donald D. Stewart, *Mental Illness in Washington County, Arkansas: Incidence, Recovery, and Posthospital Adjustment*, University of Arkansas Research Series, No. 23, Fayetteville, Ark., 1952; and B. A. Lengyel, "Remission and Mortality Rates in Schizophrenia," *American Journal of Hygiene*, 33, 16 (1941).

[5] For example, see Jacob Tuckman, William F. Youngman, and Garry B. Kreizman, "Occupational Level and Mortality," *Social Forces*, 43, 575 (1965); I. M. Moriyama and L. Guralnick, "Occupational and Social Class Differences in Mortality," *Trends and Differentials in Mortality*, Milbank Memorial Fund, New York, 1956.

[6] *Ibid.;* C. Sheps and J. H. Watkins, "Mortality in the Socioeconomic Districts of New Haven," *Yale Journal of Biology and Medicine*, 20, 51 (1947).

TABLE 4.3

Age-Specific Mortality Rates for Patients by Social Class

Age at Death	Mortality Rate [a]		
	Classes I–III [b]	Class IV	Class V
25–34	0.0	5.2	5.2
35–44	6.7	3.8	11.0
45–54	10.2	16.4	17.4
55–64	30.3	25.1	31.9
65–74	22.2	63.9	54.5
75–84	103.4	132.5	113.8
85 and over	200.0	183.3	168.0

[a] Per 1000 patients per class. See Spiegelman, *loc. cit.*
[b] Classes I, II, and III are combined because of the small number of cases in classes I–II.

I–II.[7] The primary cause of death for about two thirds of these patients is arteriosclerosis or another cardiovascular ailment. In an additional 1 out of 7 cases the primary cause of death is infectious disease. There are no class differences in the cause of death.

Although most patients died while in hospital treatment, there are social-class differences in the place of death. Specifically, the higher the class the more likely the person to have been already discharged from the mental hospital by the time of his death: classes I–II, 14 per cent; class III, 10 per cent; class IV, 9 per cent; and class V, 6 per cent.[8] As would be expected, fewer patients in classes I–II died in state hospitals and more in private hospitals than in the other classes.

The materials just presented demonstrate a strong relationship between social class and 1960 follow-up treatment status; they support Hypothesis One. Since factors other than social class may be related also to treatment outcome, however, it was necessary to analyze our data further to determine if class is the crucial factor in follow-up status or if other factors confound the assumed linkage between class position in 1950 and treatment status in 1960. The first control introduced was the 1950 treatment agency.

---

[7] Chi-square test indicates $p < .20$.
[8] Chi-square test indicates $p < .05$.

CONTROL FOR TREATMENT AGENCY

Data for patients hospitalized and for those in clinic treatment in 1950 were analyzed separately for a number of reasons. First, the diagnoses of clinic and hospital patients differ: 72 per cent of patients in clinic treatment in 1950 were diagnosed as neurotic, 20 per cent as alcoholic, and only 8 per cent as some other type of psychotic; the corresponding percentages for hospitalized cases were 4 per cent neurotic, 4 per cent alcoholic, and 92 per cent other psychotic. Next, the experience of being hospitalized and isolated from normal community and family living is markedly different from that of being treated in an outpatient clinic. Undoubtedly, there are also differences between the two groups in pathways to the treatment process itself, in precipitating events related to entering treatment, and in attitudes toward treatment. Finally, hospitalized patients so greatly outnumber clinic cases that any analysis of total cases would reflect to a large extent the obviously distinctive experience of the former.

1950 HOSPITAL PATIENTS

Of the 1420 patients who were in state, private, and veterans hospitals at the time of the original study, 1412 were located in 1960. Of this number in 1960, 54 per cent were still hospitalized,[9] 31 per cent had died, 13 per cent were no longer hospitalized or under any psychiatric treatment, and 2 per cent were discharged from the hospital but under outpatient care.

The data in Table 4.4 demonstrate a significant relationship between social class and 1960 treatment status. The percentage of patients still

---

[9] At follow-up in 1960, 94 of the 756 hospitalized patients, or 12 per cent, were persons over 65 years of age in private nursing or convalescent homes licensed to care for psychotic persons. These persons were listed on state hospital records as discharged, which gives a false picture if recovery rates are based on hospital discharge as they are in many studies. If these 94 persons were added to those discharged from hospitals, they would increase the percentage discharged considerably. In fact, these older persons would represent 31 per cent of all discharged persons. The patients were shifted to private nursing homes because of changes in the social-security legislation in the late 1950's not because of any changes in the patients' mental condition. Under the new legislation, the federal government provided more financial support for patients with organic diagnoses cared for in private nursing homes than in state mental hospitals. This is an excellent example of how social and economic factors influence mental-hospital discharge statistics.

TABLE 4.4

1960 Treatment Status and Social Class of Hospital Patients (Per Cent)

	Social Class				
Treatment Status	I–II	III	IV	V	Total
Hospitalized	39	49	52	57	54
Continuously	*32*	*42*	*43*	*51*	*46*
Intermittently	*7*	*7*	*9*	*6*	*8*
Dead	30	24	30	33	31
Discharged from hospital	31	27	18	10	15
Not under treatment	*22*	*23*	*16*	*9*	*13*
In outpatient treatment	*9*	*4*	*2*	*1*	*2*
$n =$ 46	121	559	686	1,412	
$\chi^2 = 39.80,\ df = 6,\ p < .05$ [a]					

[a] Categories used in the statistical test were (1) hospitalized, (2) dead, and (3) discharged from hospital.

hospitalized 10 years after the original study increases steadily from classes I–II to class V. The proportion of patients who had died in the 10-year period does not differ significantly among the classes.[10]

While there are no great differences in the percentage dead, the percentage no longer hospitalized and living in the community declines steadily from 31 in classes I–II to 10 in class V. Thus, the proportion of persons discharged from hospital treatment in the two highest classes is three times as great as in the lowest class. Most persons discharged from the hospital were no longer under any type of psychiatric therapy. However, those receiving outpatient care were concentrated in the middle and upper classes. Only 1 per cent of class V former patients were being treated in a clinic or by a private practitioner, whereas in classes I–II the corresponding figure was 9 per cent. These percentages are based upon the total cohort of 1950 cases and include persons who had died by 1960, those who were still hospitalized, and those no longer under inpatient care. If percentages are based upon only those persons who were living in 1960 and were no longer hospitalized, a more realistic picture of the extent of outpatient treatment is obtained. Although class differences decline on

---

[10] The 9-point difference in the percentages in class III and class V is not significant. A chi-square test between the dead and the living produces a probability of greater than .20 that the class differences are due to chance. Furthermore, in class III the average age of patients is lower.

this basis, they remain striking, the percentages being 33 in classes I–II, 12 in class III, 10 in class IV, and 10 in class V.

Two further tests of the first hypothesis may be made by (1) examining the treatment status at follow-up in 1960 of only those patients still living, and (2) determining the treatment status of dead patients at time of death as well as the treatment status of those still living in 1960. If the follow-up status of the 976 persons living today is examined, the same class differential is found as for all patients; the percentage of persons no longer in hospitals declines from 44 in classes I–II to 15 in class V, so that the proportion of discharged patients remains three times as great in the highest as in the lowest class.[11]

An examination of the treatment status of patients at time of death or in 1960 reveals the same pattern of class differences in treatment outcome already found: the higher the class, the greater the proportion of patients discharged from the hospital. Specifically, the percentage of persons living in the community either in 1960 or at the time of death increases by class as follows: V—12, IV—20, III—29, and I–II—35.[12] Thus, the ratio of patients discharged from the hospital continues to be three times as great at the highest class level as at the lowest.

CONTROL FOR TWO FACTORS: HOSPITAL PATIENTS AND ONE OTHER FACTOR

The materials presented so far demonstrate a significant relationship between social class and follow-up treatment status for patients who were hospitalized in 1950. Other factors which may be related to social class and treatment outcome should be examined also to determine if they may account for the relationships we have found. Therefore, in addition to 1950 treatment agency, we have controlled as well for the following 10 biological, social, and psychiatric factors: sex, race, age, religion, marital status, length of hospitalization at time of original study, previous psychiatric treatment history, major type of 1950 psychiatric treatment, type of hospital by sponsorship, and psychiatric diagnosis.[13]

---

[11] The total number of living patients in each class and the percentage discharged from the hospital are as follows: I–II—32 (44 per cent), III—92 (36 per cent), IV—392 (26 per cent), and V—460 (15 per cent). $\chi^2 = 34.96$, $df = 3$, $p < .05$.

[12] The total number of patients in each class is as follows: I–II—46, III—121, IV—559, V—686. $\chi^2 = 38.40$, $df = 3$, $p < .05$.

[13] Patients are classified according to their 1950 status on each of these variables. See A. B. Hollingshead and F. C. Redlich, *op. cit.*, pp. 28–29 and 253–57, for a description of the diagnostic scheme employed and for the classification of types of psychiatric treatment facilities.

Each of the above factors was divided into the categories shown in Table 4.5, and two analyses were made. First, a chi-square test was made for each category to determine if there was a significant relationship be-

TABLE 4.5

Treatment Agency, One Other Factor, and Social Class of Hospital Patients Discharged from Hospital by 1960 (Per Cent) [a]

	Social Class			
	I–II	III	IV	V
A. Sex				
Male	32	22	16	10
Female	29	29	20	10
B. Race				
White	30	26	19	11
Negro	—	50	9	7
C. Age				
Under 35	60	59	40	30
35–44 [b]	60	25	20	14
45–54 [c]	38	19	18	9
55 and over	13	(spanning I–II, III)	8	4
D. Religion				
Catholic	28	(spanning I–II, III)	20	12
Protestant	31	29	15	17
Jewish [b]	33	9	27	9
E. Marital Status				
Unmarried	30	22	16	10
Married	46	45	27	12
Separated, widowed, divorced [c]	22	(spanning I–II, III)	22	8
F. Year of Hospitalization				
1949–50	52	53	42	31
1948 or earlier	10	(spanning I–II, III)	8	4
G. Previous Psychiatric Hospitalization				
Hospitalized previously	29	25	22	13
Never hospitalized previously	33	32	14	8
H. Major 1950 Psychiatric Treatment				
Psychotherapy [c]	53	50	34	27
Organic	35	(spanning I–II, III)	27	17
Custodial [d]	2	(spanning I–II, III)	5	4
I. Type Hospital				
State	24	25	17	10
Private or veterans	38	(spanning I–II, III)	33	15

TABLE 4.5 (Continued)

	Social Class			
	I–II	III	IV	V
J. Psychiatric Diagnosis				
Schizophrenic, paranoid	32	24	18	8
Neurotic [e]	71	63	50	
Affective [d]	42		38	30
Intoxication, organic [e]	50	14	7	9
Senile [d]	—	6	—	1

[a] Unless otherwise indicated, $p < .05$ for the two chi-square tests made for each of the individual control categories.
[b] $p < .10$ for total cases and for living only.
[c] $p < .10$ for total case.
[d] $p > .20$ for total cases and for living only.
[e] $p < .20$ for total cases and for living only.

tween social class and treatment outcome. Three categories of follow-up status were used: hospitalized, dead, and discharged from hospital. Next, a chi-square test was made for only patients living in 1960 in terms of two categories of treatment: hospitalized and discharged from hospital. Data on follow-up status of 1950 hospital patients are presented in Table 4.5. To simplify the presentation, patients who were dead or hospitalized in 1960 are omitted from Table 4.5, and only the percentage of patients discharged from the hospital is shown. The results of these analyses are described below. They are summarized on pages 73–74 for the reader who is not interested in the details.

Sex

In Table 4.5, Section A, the data are presented for answering the question: *If the sex variable is controlled, will social class continue to be a significant factor in treatment outcome?* As can be seen, the percentages of both male and female patients discharged from the hospital in 1960 at each class level are very similar to those of the total hospitalized population summarized in Table 4.4. For both males and females there are approximately three times as many class I–II individuals as class V persons living in the community and no longer under hospital care. The proportion of patients discharged from the hospital by class is similar for both sexes.

Race

Definite relationships exist between class and follow-up status for both Negroes and whites. Although there were no class I–II and few class III Negroes in the study group, the patterns for Negroes and whites are quite similar: the lower the class, the smaller the proportion of patients discharged from the hospital.

Age

The same relationship between social class and treatment outcome is found for all four age categories: the higher the social class, the greater the proportion of former patients living in the community. Although the chances of discharge declined with age, approximately two to four times as many class I–II persons as class V individuals in each age group were discharged from hospital treatment by 1960.

Religion

Within each religious group, the same class differential is found: the percentage of patients discharged from the hospital increases as class position increases.

Marital Status

Significantly more married persons than unmarried, separated, widowed, or divorced were no longer hospitalized in 1960. However, within each marital status group, three to four times as many class I–II as class V persons had been discharged from the hospital by 1960.

Length of Hospitalization

Although persons hospitalized in 1948 or earlier are less likely to be discharged by 1960 than those more recently hospitalized, the proportion discharged decreases steadily from the highest to the lowest social class regardless of length of hospitalization.

Previous Psychiatric Treatment

The same general relationship between class and follow-up treatment status is found regardless of whether or not the patient had a previous record of psychiatric hospitalization: the higher the class, the higher the proportion of discharged individuals.

Major 1950 Psychiatric Treatment

Social class is related significantly to hospital discharge for persons receiving psychotherapy or organic treatment. Although a higher percentage of patients receiving psychotherapy than those receiving organic therapy had been discharged at all class levels, we found that for each type of treatment about twice as many higher-class as lower-class individuals were out of hospital. There are no class differences, however, for persons receiving custodial care, of whom 96 per cent were never discharged from the hospital.

Type of Hospital

In all types of hospitals the chances of discharge increase steadily and significantly from the lower to the higher social classes.

Diagnosis

With the exception of the category senile psychoses, in which only two of 180 persons were discharged, the same class pattern of discharge is found: the higher the class, the greater the proportion of persons no longer under hospital treatment. This pattern is least pronounced among the affectives as are the class differences in prevalence for this diagnostic group in the original study.

In 1950 the prevalence rates for the affective disorders were two and one half times greater in class V than in classes I–II, whereas the rates were from 8 to 28 times greater for all other types of psychosis.[14] The fact that the diagnosis of affective disorder is the most clear-cut of the diagnoses of functional disorders may help account for the smaller class differentials in treated prevalence and hospital discharge. Since affective psychosis is the most discrete, nonorganic illness episode and its symptoms, like depression, are circumscribed, social factors may play a less important role in determining the original diagnosis. Not only is there general agreement about the clinical picture but also about the treatment for it. Therefore, social factors are not as likely to enter into the decision on the treatment to be administered; electroshock therapy or drugs are more likely to be standard treatment than in the case of other psychotic diagnoses. Finally, since there were small class differentials in treated prevalence to start with, the chances of large class differences in hospital discharge are not as great.

We summarize the control for two factors by stating that the introduction of 10 biological, social, and psychiatric controls for patients hospitalized in 1950 generally does not negate the class differences found for 1950 treatment status. In nearly all cases, the same relationship is found

---

[14] *Ibid.*, pp. 232–33. Other studies have found similar class patterns; see, for example, Robert E. L. Faris and H. Warren Dunham, *Mental Disorders in Urban Areas*, University of Chicago Press, Chicago, 1939.

within each grouping: the higher the social class, the greater the percentage of patients discharged from hospital care. Two separate analyses were made for each of the control categories shown in Table 4.5: one for all cases and one for the living only. Then a chi-square test of significance was applied to each of these. In 50 of these 56 tests, social-class differences are clear-cut; the distribution of significant levels found is: 39 tests, $p < .05$; 7 tests, $p < .10$; 4 tests, $p < .20$; in only 6 tests is $p > .20$, and 4 of these 6 tests were for custodial care and senile psychoses in 1950. These exceptions represent a select portion of the study group—older patients and those with little chance of hospital discharge. Only five of 180 seniles and only 26 of 675 persons receiving custodial care were ever discharged. The remaining two tests were for the affective psychoses where the trend is the same as for all patients but where $p > .20$.

SIMULTANEOUS CONTROL OF THREE FACTORS:
HOSPITAL PATIENTS AND TWO OTHER FACTORS

We have already held constant 1950 treatment agency (hospitalized patients only) and each of 10 other factors to determine if social class is related significantly to follow-up status under these conditions. We now go one step further; in addition to 1950 treatment agency, we hold constant at one time two of the above factors. The results of the analyses are summarized on page 76 for the reader who is not interested in the detailed account.

Because the number of cases in any cell is reduced greatly as we introduce each additional control, some modifications were made in the procedure used in the two-factor control analyses to provide enough cases in all cells to make statistical tests. First, follow-up status was dichotomized into those hospitalized in 1960 or at time of death and those not hospitalized in 1960 or at time of death. Next, classes I, II, and III were combined at times. Finally, some of the categories into which the control factors were divided were also collapsed. These modifications were as follows: (1) Negroes were eliminated from all analyses because of the paucity of cases; (2) age was dichotomized into those under 45 and those 45–64; age 65 and over was dropped because only 29 of 359 patients in this category had ever been discharged from hospital care; (3) Jews were dropped because there were only 117 cases of which 20 were discharged; (4) all persons not married were included in one category; i.e., the unmarried were combined with the separated, widowed, and divorced; (5) custodial care was eliminated because only 26 of 675 patients receiving this treatment were ever discharged from the hospital; (6) seniles were dropped because only five were ever discharged from hospital care; and (7) affective, intoxication, and organic psychoses were combined. The control categories finally employed are as follows: (1) *Sex*—male, female; (2) *Race*—white; (3) *Age*—under 45, 45–64; (4) *Religion*—Catholic, Protestant; (5) *Marital Status*—married, not married; (6) *Length of Hospitalization in 1950*—hospitalized in 1949 or 1950, hospitalized in 1948 or earlier; (7) *Previous Psychiatric Treatment*—previous hospitalization, no previous hospitalization; (8) *Type 1950 Psychiatric Treatment*—psychotherapy, organic therapy; (9) *Type Hospital*—state, private/veterans administration; and (10) *Psychiatric Diagnosis*—neuroses, schizophrenia, other psychoses (excluding seniles).

In our method of analysis, we may ask, for example, the question: *Is class related to treatment outcome when treatment agency, age, and 1950 major psychiatric treatment are held constant simultaneously?* An examination of Table 4.6 indicates that the same relationship between class and treatment outcome is found for all four control categories: the higher the class, the greater the percentage of patients discharged in 1960 or at death.

To make similar tests for the three-factor control of the 10 variables we examined 179 matrices. In this analysis we included hospital cases plus two other factors in all combinations. This is a complicated analysis, but if we continue to find the same class patterning of treatment outcome, we increase the likelihood that the relationship is a true or a real one rather than an artifact of the combination of other factors.

The analyses we made with three factors under control demonstrate

TABLE 4.6

	Discharged in 1960 or at Death (Per Cent)		
	Classes I–III	Class IV	Class V
Hospitalized patients under 45 years of age receiving psychotherapy in 1950	75	49	41
Hospitalized patients 45–64 years of age receiving psychotherapy in 1950	54	45	21
Hospitalized patients under 45 years of age receiving organic therapy in 1950	46	34	22
Hospitalized patients 45–64 years of age receiving organic therapy in 1950	31	23	19

that there is, indeed, a significant linkage between social class and treatment outcome. In all cases but six, the chances of discharge from the hospital increased as social-class position increased. The level of significance in the chi-square test is: 112 cases—$p < .05$; 19 cases—$p < .10$; 27 cases—$p < .20$; 6 cases—$p > .20$;[15] 15 cases—too few to run a test but the class differences were in the predicted direction.

Briefly, extensive analyses demonstrate that social class is strongly related to treatment outcome for hospital patients when 2 of the 10 factors are held constant in all possible combinations. These factors did not account for the characteristic pattern we kept finding of a direct relationship between class and hospital discharge, i.e., the higher the class, the greater the proportion of individuals living in the community.

1950 CLINIC PATIENTS

The experience since 1950 of persons treated in clinics at the time of the original study was markedly different from that of hospitalized patients. At the time of the follow-up research, 80 per cent of the 133 former clinic patients studied were living in the community and no longer under psychiatric care, whereas for hospitalized cases the corresponding percentage was 13.[16] Only 6 per cent of clinic patients had died contrasted to 31 per cent of hospital patients. Another 6 per cent of former clinic patients were hospitalized, but 54 per cent of the 1950 hospital patients were still under such care. Finally, 8 per cent of former clinic patients were under outpatient care in 1960 compared to 2 per cent of hospital patients.

Many of the above contrasts are related to differences in the social and psychiatric characteristics of the two groups. The low proportion of dead and hospitalized reflects the younger average age of clinic patients and the large number of neurotics among them (see Appendix 1, Table A1.1, Sections A and B). Hospital and clinic patients differ in terms of other social and psychiatric variables (see Appendix 1, Table A1.1, Sections C,

---

[15] The 6 instances in which the usual class pattern did not hold are as follows: (1) 37 cases—other psychotics who received psychotherapy; (2) 41 cases—neurotics under 45 years of age; (3) 385 cases—not married persons 45–64 years old (but only 38 had been discharged from the hospital); (4) 259 cases—not married, other psychotics (but only 45 were discharged from the hospital); (5) 211 cases—females hospitalized in 1949 or 1950 (104 hospitalized, 107 discharged); (6) 226 cases—Catholics hospitalized in 1949 or 1950 (124 hospitalized, 102 discharged).

[16] Ten of the 143 clinic cases could not be located so they are not included in the analyses.

D, and E). Clinic patients included higher proportions of upper- and middle-class persons, males, and married individuals.[17] The two groups differ also in their psychiatric treatment experience. Fewer clinic than hospital patients (19 per cent compared to 48 per cent) have a history of previous psychiatric hospitalization. The opposite relationship is found for previous outpatient treatment: 22 per cent of clinic patients had received such care, but only 6 per cent of hospital patients. As would be expected, differences in major 1950 treatment are striking: most clinic patients (81 per cent) were in psychotherapy; most hospital patients received custodial care (48 per cent) or organic treatment (41 per cent).

Despite these differences in the characteristics and experiences of the two groups of patients, the same pattern of social-class variations in treatment outcome is found among the clinic as among the hospitalized patients. Examining the social status of former clinic patients in 1960 or at the time of their death, we find the higher the class the smaller the percentage hospitalized, while the opposite relationship is found between social class and outpatient care—the higher the class the greater the percentage in outpatient treatment [18] (see Table 4.7).

The former clinic patients who were hospitalized at follow-up in 1960 or at death are atypical of general clinic patients in a number of ways: [19] proportionately more of them were alcoholics, older, Catholic, and separated, divorced, or widowed; although only 20 per cent of clinic patients were diagnosed as alcoholic in 1950, 45 per cent of those hospitalized at follow-up were in this diagnostic group; 10 per cent of clinic patients were over 44 years of age in 1950, but 64 per cent of those hospitalized in 1960 were in this age grouping; half of the total clinic population, but 91 per cent of those hospitalized, were Catholic; although only 14 per cent of the clinic population were separated, divorced, or widowed, 45 per cent of those hospitalized were of this marital status.

As would be expected, hospitalized patients were more severely disturbed psychologically and had records of long and intensive psy-

---

[17] There are no significant differences in the two groups by race or religion; 94 per cent of hospital and 96 per cent of clinic patients were white; the percentage of hospital patients by religion is Catholic—58, Protestant—31, Jewish—9, and other—2; the corresponding percentages for clinic cases are 50, 31, 16, and 4.

[18] Because of the small number of former clinic patients who were dead or in treatment in 1960, it was not possible to control extensively for other variables possibly related to treatment outcome as was done for patients hospitalized in 1950.

[19] There are no differences between total and hospitalized clinic patients by sex or race.

TABLE 4.7

Treatment Status of Clinic Patients in 1960 or at Death (Per Cent)

	Social Class			
Treatment Status	I–III [a]	IV [a]	V	Total
Hospitalized	6	5	15	8
In outpatient treatment	14	5	7	8
Not under treatment	80	90	78	84
$n = $	35	57	41	133
$\chi^2 = 3.14$, $df = 1$, $p < .10$ [b]				

[a] Classes I, II, III, and IV were combined in the chi-square test because of the small number of hospitalized cases.
[b] Categories used in the statistical test were (1) hospitalized, (2) not hospitalized.

chiatric care from 1950 to 1960. For example, the diagnosis of several of the alcoholic patients had been changed to borderline schizophrenia, and the diagnosis of one neurotic was changed to schizophrenia over the 10-year period.

SUMMARY

The findings reported in this chapter support the hypothesis that there is a significant relationship between social class and patients' treatment status in 1960 at follow-up: the lower the social class of the patients the higher the proportion under hospital care.

The follow-up status of those patients who were hospitalized and those in outpatient-clinic treatment in 1950 differs significantly: whereas most of the former were still hospitalized 10 years later, most of the latter were no longer under any type of psychiatric therapy. This difference is not unexpected owing to variations between the two groups in the types and severity of psychiatric illnesses, age distribution, and other factors at the time of the original study. However, in both groups the same pattern of class differences is found: the lower the social-class position of patients, the greater proportion under hospital care in 1960 or at the time of their death.

Among patients living in the community the opposite relationship is found between social class and psychiatric treatment: the lower the social class, the smaller the proportion of patients in outpatient care, either in clinics or private practice.

These striking class variations in treatment outcome indicate the influence of social, as well as medical and psychiatric, factors upon the history of mental patients. In the following chapter we shall examine the influence of these three factors upon treatment status at follow-up by analyzing data concerning the treatment process over the 10 years 1950 to 1960.

social class and the treatment process

In the previous chapter data were presented supporting our first hypothesis that social class is related to treatment status at follow-up. In this chapter we shall examine data to test the second hypothesis that *social class is related to the patients' treatment and readmission experience during the period from 1950 to 1960*. Three major analyses are made to test this hypothesis: (1) the 1950 to 1960 hospital discharge and readmission history of 1950 hospital patients; (2) the 1950 to 1960 treatment experience of 1950 hospital patients and its relationship to follow-up status, and (3) the psychiatric treatment experience of 1950 clinic patients.[1]

HOSPITAL DISCHARGE AND READMISSION—1950 TO 1960

In the preceding chapter we examined the treatment status of patients 10 years after the original study; in this chapter we analyzed the details of the treatment experience for the entire 10-year period (1950 to 1960). Of the 1412 persons hospitalized at the time of the original study in 1950, 27 per cent were discharged some time during the 10-year period. However, this percentage varies significantly by social class, declining

---

[1] In testing the second hypothesis we continue to use the 1950 social-class position of patients.

80

steadily from the top to the bottom of the social-class hierarchy as follows: I–II–43, III–36, IV–33, and V–20.[2] (see Appendix 1, Table A1.2).

To determine if other factors might account for these striking social-class differences, we controlled for the same 10 biological, social, and psychiatric variables as used previously (see Chapter 4, p. 69). When this is done, class continues to be related significantly to hospital discharge.[3]

Once discharged, about three out of five patients were readmitted to a psychiatric hospital. The proportion readmitted increases steadily from classes I–II to class V, although the class differences for readmission are not nearly so great as for discharge rates. Of the 382 patients discharged, the percentage readmitted to a hospital by social class is I–II–50, III–56, IV–58, and V–63.[4] (see Appendix 1, Table A1.3).

---

[2] The total number of patients in each class is as follows: I–II–46, III–121, IV–559, and V–686. $\chi^2 = 38.77$, $df = 3$, $p < .05$.

[3] Each of these factors is divided into the same categories utilized in Chapter 4, and a chi-square test is made for each category to determine if there is a significant relationship between social class and the proportion of persons discharged from hospital care. In 25 of the 28 tests made, there are clear-cut social-class differences: the higher the social class, the greater the percentage of patients discharged from the hospital between 1950 and 1960. The distribution of significance levels found is: 20 tests, $p < .05$; 1 test, $p < .10$; and 4 tests, $p < .20$. Of the three cases in which class is unrelated to discharge rates ($p > .20$), two are groups in which few patients were discharged from hospital treatment at any time: senile psychotics and patients in custodial care in 1950. The third group are affective psychotics of whom sizeable numbers of patients (87) were discharged and sizeable numbers (63) remained in hospital treatment during the 10-year period. A discussion of possible reasons for this exception is given in Chapter 4, pp. 73–74. In summary, when the 10 factors are controlled, class continues to be related significantly to hospital discharge.

[4] The total number of patients in each class is as follows: I–II–20, III–43, IV–184, V–135. $\chi^2 = 1.78$, $df = 3$, $p > .20$. When we examine the relationship between social class and readmission for the 10 control factors the same pattern generally holds: the higher the class, the lower the proportion of persons readmitted to the hospital. Because of the small number of cases some categories had to be dropped and only 21 analyses were made.

The following analyses were made. Control Category: *Sex*—male, female; *Race*—white; *Age*—44 years and under, 45 years and older; *Religion*—Catholic, Protestant; *Marital Status*—unmarried, married, separated–widowed–divorced; *Year of Hospitalization*—1949 to 1950, 1948 or earlier; *Previous Psychiatric Hospitalization*—previous hospitalization, no previous hospitalization; *Major 1950 Psychiatric Treatment*—psychotherapy, organic therapy, custodial care; *Type Hospital*—state; *Psychiatric Diagnosis*—schizophrenic, affective, other psychotic. The level of significance is $p < .05$, 2 analyses; $p < .10$, 6 analyses; $p < .20$, 7 analyses; and $p > .20$, 6 analyses. Thus in 15 of the analyses the class differences are in the expected direction. In the others there are essentially no differences by class in the percentage readmitted to the hos-

Once rehospitalized, subsequent discharges and readmissions follow the same class patterns already described (see Appendix 1, Tables A1.2 and A1.3). For example, all readmitted patients in classes I–II were discharged again, 79 per cent in class III, 66 per cent in class IV, and 67 per cent in class V.[5] After living in the community for some time, 68 per cent of these persons in class V were readmitted to the hospital but only 59 per cent in classes I–III.[6] Class differences are less for the third discharge, and they finally disappear for the third readmission.

In summary, social class is a crucial factor not only in initial hospital discharge but also in subsequent discharge: the higher the class, the greater the percentage of patients discharged. Although more lower-class individuals, generally, were readmitted to the hospital, the relationship between class and readmission is not nearly so strong as that between class and discharge. However, even though the class differences in re-admission are not great, there is a "piling up" of more lower-class cases after the first two readmissions because of these differences.

The class differentials in hospital discharge and readmission just described result in marked social-class differences in follow-up treatment status among discharged patients. As seen in Table 5.1, the lower the class, the higher the percentage of discharged patients who were again hospitalized in 1960 or at the time of their death and the smaller the percentage under outpatient care. Approximately two out of five class IV and V discharged patients were again hospitalized by 1960 or at death but only about one out of five patients in classes I, II, and III.

---

pital, but in no case was there a reversal of the pattern. These six cases where no class differences were found are: persons under age 45; unmarried; separated, widowed, or divorced; no previous hospitalization; custodial care; and other psychotics.

[5] The total number of patients in each class is as follows: I–II–10, III–24, IV–106, V–85. $\chi^2 = 4.79$, $df = 2$, $p < .10$. When we test for the 10 control variables, we continue to find the same relationship between class and discharge rate. Because of the small number of cases some categories had to be combined or eliminated. The following categories were used: Sex–male, female; Race–white; Age–44 years or under, 45 years or over; Religion–Catholic, Protestant; Marital Status–unmarried, married, separated–divorced–widowed; Year of Hospitalization–1949 to 1950, 1948 or earlier; Previous Psychiatric Hospitalization–previous hospitalization, no previous hospitalizaton; Major 1950 to 1960 Treatment–psychotherapy, organic therapy; Type Hospital–state; Psychiatric Diagnosis–neurotic, schizophrenic, affective, senile. In 18 of the 21 tests, class differences are clear-cut. The levels of significance are: 11 cases $p < .05$; 2 cases $p < .10$; and 5 cases $p < .20$. In 3 cases $p > .20$–males, Catholics, and senile psychotics.

[6] The total number of patients in each class is as follows: I–III–29, IV–70, V–57. $\chi^2 = 3.39$, $df = 2$, $p < .20$. Classes I, II, and III are combined at times because of the small number of cases in classes I and II.

TABLE 5.1

Treatment Status of Discharged Hospital Patients at Follow-Up or Death, by Social Class (Per Cent)

Social Class	N	Treatment Status (Per Cent)		
		In Hospital	Outpatient Care [a]	No Treatment
I–II	20	20	20	60
III	43	19	12	69
IV	184	38	7	55
V	135	39	6	55
	382			

$$\chi^2 = 8.40, \, df = 3, \, p < .05$$

[a] Combined in computation of chi square with "no treatment" category as "in community."

In contrast, the percentage under outpatient care jumps from only 6 in class V to 20 in classes I–II.

A number of factors appear to be related to class differences in discharge rates. As the social class of patients becomes lower, the hospital staff, the patient, and his family are more likely to "give up" on the patient, especially after a hospital readmission. The hospital staff generally considers patients low in the class hierarchy as "poorer risks" for discharge than persons higher in the social structure. Professionals also have more negative attitudes toward lower-status persons, and they are more frustrated and irritated when such persons reappear in the hospital after having been discharged.[7] Their negative values are reinforced when the patients fail to adjust successfully to community life after their initial discharge.

Staff members know that fewer community resources are available to lower-status individuals. The staff is willing to take greater risks in discharging class I, II, and III patients. Even after the failure of the first discharge, professionals continue to believe that more community

---

[7] See, for example, Robert H. Hardt and Sherwin J. Feinhandler, "Social Class and Mental Hospitalization Prognosis," *American Sociological Review*, 24, 815 (1959); J. K. Myers and L. Schaffer, "Social Stratification and Psychiatric Practice: A Study of an Outpatient Clinic," *American Sociological Review*, 19, 307 (1954); L. Schaffer and J. K. Myers, "Psychotherapy and Social Stratification," *Psychiatry*, 17, 83 (1954).

resources are available to upper- and middle-class persons (see Chapters 8 and 9 for a discussion of these resources). The staff may be concerned about what will happen to lower-class patients in the community, and their reluctance to grant an initial discharge becomes even greater after the patient has been readmitted. Even if the patient's mental condition improves, the staff is likely to consider the social conditions outside as unchanged and undesirable. Since they feel helpless to change the social conditions to which the patient must return, they are less willing to discharge class IV and V patients.

Hospital staff also may be influenced by other community authorities such as social workers and police who regard lower-class patients as problems and question the wisdom of discharging them. The spoken, or unspoken, question that recurs is: "Why bother us with these crocks? Why don't you keep them locked up where they belong?" Such attitudes may have an effect on the staff members who become increasingly reluctant to discharge lower-class patients a second or third time.

The "piling up" of lower-class patients in the hospital also may distort the views of the psychiatrist and other staff members. Over the years there is movement in and out of the hospital of middle- and upper-class persons, while a larger proportion of the same class V patients remains. The staff sees middle- and upper-class faces moving in and out of treatment, but they grow accustomed to the lower-status patients who remain. Numerically, of course, class IV and V patients are by far the largest group in the hospital, and the staff can easily get the impression that it is hopeless to try to deal with these persons through discharge.

In addition, the lower-class patient's family is less likely to accept the patient back home. These families sometimes do not have adequate facilities at home to care for the patient and because of different values they are less willing than upper-class families to accept back into their midst a member who has been hospitalized for mental illness. Lower-class families are less satisfied with the patient's treatment than higher-status persons. They are hostile toward doctors and other hospital personnel and they have little comprehension of psychiatric illness and therapy. Once a patient is hospitalized, however, he is no longer a burden on the rest of the family. As time goes on, the family displays less and less interest in him.[8] For example, 83 per cent of class I, II, and III families visited hospitalized patients, now discharged and interviewed in the second phase of the study, while only 53 per cent of class V families

---

[8] J. K. Myers and B. H. Roberts, *Family and Class Dynamics in Mental Illness*, Wiley, New York, 1959, p. 217.

did so. Similarly, the proportion who sent packages or money declines from 75 per cent in the highest three classes to 43 per cent in class V and the proportion who wrote to the patients from 42 per cent to 26 per cent.

The case of Ralph M., a class V male, illustrates these points. Ralph's parents had moved out of the state during his hospitalization. The four siblings remaining in Connecticut lost all contact with him. When his condition improved markedly in the hospital, the authorities initiated action to find him a home with one of his family, as he was still single at the age of 38. A brother, Bill, finally agreed to accept the patient. When Bill was contacted later by the study interviewer, he indicated that Ralph had lived with him less than a month and he did not know his whereabouts. He suggested we see his sister Grace. Although Grace was not certain of Ralph's address, she thought he still lived in New Haven, because she had seen him within the past year. She said, "Once I seen him walking down Maytown Avenue but he didn't see me and we didn't talk none."

This sister told us that during the patient's hospitalization a hospital orderly, who accompanied him on a visit to her home, requested her signature on a paper to release the patient from the hospital. She felt Ralph had not recovered so she did not sign the paper. "Anyway," she went on, "what do you expect me to do? How can I look after Ralph? My God, I got eight of my own kids to look after." Much of Grace's uncertainty about Ralph's condition stems from his violent behavior. She was the one who had him arrested originally, after which the prosecuting attorney recommended the state hospital instead of jail. She said, "I had him put away for his own good and for the safety of the rest of us. Once I had to keep him from stabbing himself. I wasn't proud to put him away; I don't think anyone would be. Still, we were all scared stiff of him and I don't want him around no more. Besides, he don't look cured to me."

During her brother's hospitalization, Grace never visited, wrote, or had any contact with him. Currently, Ralph lives alone in a rented room and seldom sees any of his relatives. His sister and brother believe that he should still be in the hospital because he is not cured.

If the patient fails once, the lower-class family is even less interested in having him return home a second or third time. The patient himself becomes more isolated and alienated and is more likely to live alone (see Chapter 9). Thus, according to the present system of managing former mental patients, the lower-class patient is a poor risk. In many cases commitment was made because the family was unwilling or unable to give the patient care, and persons who live alone often are not discharged because they have no place to go.

The case of Mrs. K. is an illustration of this problem. She was a class V woman, 48 years old, separated from her husband at the time of her hospitalization in 1950 and diagnosed as schizophrenic. She was discharged 15 months later. Previously, at age 28, she had been hospitalized for three months for a postpartum psychosis. At the time of the 1950 hospitalization she had a 20-year-old daughter, also separated from her husband, living at home and a married son living away from home. Her son and daughter both believe that their mother should not have been hospitalized and would not have been except for the family situation. Her husband would not look after her, her son's wife did not want her living with them, and the daughter claims she could not handle her mother without the help of a man.

Mrs. K., the son, and the daughter all blame Mr. K. for the unnecessary hospitalization. However, when the patient was ready to be discharged, the daughter's second husband did not want Mrs. K. to live with them. She went to live with her son, but this did not work out. In the meantime, the daughter became separated from her husband, and Mrs. K. then lived with her daughter.

Patients in the lower classes may, themselves, give up more easily, thereby becoming permanent institutional cases. Hospital existence may be relatively attractive to them in contrast to living conditions in the lower-class community, especially after a series of readjustment failures. In addition to possible class differences in motivation to be discharged, there are class differences in the patients' attempts to be released from the hospital. Higher-status persons are far more active and persistent in their efforts than lower-class individuals. Furthermore, class V patients more often feel neglected by their families and believe that their families do not want them to return home. There is some basis, in fact, for their belief, since 20 per cent of the families in class V felt it would have been better for the patient to have remained longer in the hospital. In classes I and II no families were of this opinion.

Ralph M., whose story is told on page 85, was not interested in leaving the hospital. He said: "They made me leave before my treatment was finished. They only finished the needle treatment on me and then didn't do no more. I didn't want to leave. My folks moved away, and none of my brothers or sisters wanted me. I had no place to go."

Ida J., gives us an extreme example of the class differences in family attitudes. In 1960 she was a single, 36-year-old, class III schizophrenic, living with her parents in the community for a period of five years after discharge from psychiatric hospitalization. She had been in six private hospitals and the state mental hospital for a total of eight years from age 21 to 31. For four of those years she was in private hospitals, until the family could no longer afford such treatment. Since her discharge from a state hospital in 1955, she has functioned on a regressed but stabilized basis. She seldom goes out alone, keeps to herself, is uncommunicative, and is extremely dependent upon her parents, especially her mother. However, through the care of her family and attendance regularly at an outpatient clinic connected with the hospital, she is able to get along at home.

During the entire period of hospitalization the parents visited their daughter faithfully each week. Whenever possible, they consulted with hospital authorities about her possible release and pressured them to allow her to come home. Although the authorities were reluctant, they finally consented. Her mother said, "We wanted Ida home with us. Whenever I had the opportunity when I was up there visiting, I saw the hospital authorities about it. Finally, they allowed us to bring her home. We've shown them that Ida can get along fine at home and does not have to be hospitalized."

Another illustration is Mrs. W., a class III, married, schizophrenic who was hospitalized in 1942 at the age of 23, after the birth of her first child. For the next eight years she was in a state mental hospital, but since her discharge in 1951 she has never required any further treatment. Her husband, parents, and siblings visited her regularly during her hospitalization. The husband, who rose from the position of salesman to branch manager for an appliance company in this time period, had her home on visits whenever possible so that she could maintain her family and community relationships, at least to some extent. Living in the community since 1951, she is well adjusted and attributes much of her success to her family.

Her first year home from the hospital was especially difficult because her long absence made it necessary to become reacquainted with her son. During this period, her husband gave up all his regular leisure-time activities to be home with her and help her readjust. Gradually she resumed her activities. Neighborhood friends were of considerable help; they were not only understanding, but they also made great efforts to help her readjust.

In contrast to the negative attitudes expressed in the lower classes, class I, II, and III families are mostly satisfied with the patients' hospital treatment. They visit the patients frequently, are interested in their welfare, and want them to return home. In classes I, II, and III, 60 per cent of the patients' families consulted with hospital authorities about the patients' discharge; in classes IV and V the corresponding figures are 44 per cent and 41 per cent, respectively.

Turning from discharge to readmission, we have examined some of the circumstances associated with readmission for a better understanding of the process. Although our data are far from definitive, they do offer some clues to the slightly higher readmission rates for lower-class persons.

The circumstances surrounding readmission were examined in terms of the readmission process, social and economic conditions at the time of readmission, and psychiatric signs and symptoms. It is clear that in most cases, the patient's disturbed, bizarre, or dangerous behavior, coupled with his inability to adjust socially and economically, led to his rehospitalization. In most cases the readmission process was involuntary and was initiated by someone other than the patient. Most patients were readmitted from their homes and were accompanied by a friend or relative.[9]

Imposed upon these common patterns, however, are significant variations by social class. Lower-class persons were more likely to be referred to the hospital by the police or courts and less likely to refer themselves or be referred by their families than higher-class individuals.[10] Although the majority of initial commitments were involuntary, the percentage of such commitments increases steadily from 58 in classes I–III through 73 in class IV to 84 in class V.[11] Similarly, the percentage of probate commitments rose from 52 in classes I–III through 80 in class IV to 85 in class V. The greater importance of the legal system in the readmission process in the lower classes is seen further in the distribution by class of the persons accompanying the patient to the hospital. Lower-class persons are more likely to be accompanied by the police and less likely by relatives than higher-class individuals.

The class differences in the frequency of legal and police intervention in the rehospitalization process support the findings of the original Psy-

---

[9] During the 10-year period, 225 persons were readmitted at least once to a psychiatric hospital as indicated in footnote 5. The circumstances surrounding readmission were analyzed for the first readmission if there was more than one. Thus, the number of cases is always 225.

[10] Problems of reliability and validity are especially difficult in studying the referral process. For example, how can we determine the "true" source of referral? Was the source of referral the wife who called the police when her husband became violent or the police who took him to the state hospital instead of to jail? Our policy has been to determine the source of immediate referral to a psychiatric facility, since the further back in the process we go, the less reliable and less valid the data become.

[11] Voluntary admissions started to become fashionable during the decade 1950 to 1960, although this practice did not reach its peak until after 1960.

TABLE 5.2

Employment Status	Social Class (Per Cent)		
	I–III	IV	V
Self-supporting	50	33	37
Partially self-supporting	11	11	14
Unemployed	39	56	49

chiatric Census.[12] Such class differences are less at readmission than at the time of the original hospitalization, but they remain important. In the higher classes, the patient, his relatives, or friends are more likely to recognize that hospitalization is necessary and to initiate action. In the lower classes, such action is frequently not taken until the patient's behavior becomes so bizarre or violent that community authorities must be called upon. Despite, or perhaps because of, first-hand experience with psychiatric treatment, class V patients and their families are less likely than higher-status persons to be involved in the readmission process.

At the time of rehospitalization most patients were living in their own homes or with their parents. However, about twice as many class V patients as persons in other classes lived alone, 21 per cent compared to 10 per cent, and a smaller proportion lived with their parents.

Although most patients were not fully self-supporting at the time of rehospitalization, there were interesting class differences. More patients in classes I, II, and III were self-supporting and fewer unemployed than in the two lower classes, as can be seen in Table 5.2.

These class differentials in employment at time of readmission may be related to class differences in rehospitalization rates, according to a study by Maisel of a selected group of patients drawn from the Follow-Up Study.[13] In a study of the decision to rehospitalize, he interviewed the families of 60 white males, 17 to 60 years of age, who had been diagnosed as psychotic without organic impairment, hospitalized in state or veterans hospitals in 1950 but discharged some time between 1950 and 1960. Nearly all the cases were in classes IV and V. This study found rehospitalization related to the family's perception of the patient's mental condition but related much more strongly to his ability to work.

---

[12] A. B. Hollingshead and F. C. Redlich, *Social Class and Mental Illness*, Wiley, New York, 1958, pp. 183–191.

[13] Robert Maisel, *The Mental Patient and His Family: A Study of the Success of Ex-Mental Patients in the Community*, unpublished Ph.D. dissertation, Yale University, 1964.

On the basis of family ratings on a symptom list, Maisel classified discharged patients as either normal or abnormal; 62 per cent of patients rated normal by their families, but only 47 per cent of those judged abnormal, remained out of the hospital during the entire 10-year period. Much more important, however, were work records. At the end of one year, 37 patients had worked regularly and 23 patients had not; of those working regularly, 89 per cent were still out of the hospital, but of those not working only 48 per cent were in the community. By the end of two years, 97 per cent of those working regularly were still out of the hospital, but of those not working only 45 per cent. The relationship between long-term success in living in the community and working is remarkably high; of the 60 men, 27 succeeded in remaining out of the hospital for the entire 10-year period and 26 of these worked consistently; the one exception was an elderly patient living with two retired brothers. Moreover, Maisel found this high correlation between working and success whether or not the patient's behavior was noticeably odd in other respects.

Maisel hypothesized that perception of mental illness is strongly influenced by the patient's work performance. If the patient does not work, something is considered wrong with him. The tolerance of parents for nonworking sons, for example, grows thin as pressing financial and physical difficulties strike the aging family members. Wives are even less tolerant of husbands who do not work. Thus, class differences in readmission rates may be related to employment patterns.

In the Follow-Up Study, most patients exhibited severe psychiatric signs and symptoms at rehospitalization. The rate of occurrence, however, of all the symptoms is high and supports the findings of other studies.[14] The most common signs and symptoms were delusions and hallucinations, antisocial verbal aggressiveness, paranoia, antisocial physical aggressiveness, depression, physical disorders, failure in self-care functions, and disorganized thought process, as shown in Table 5.3.

Although most patients exhibited several of the symptoms shown in the tabulations, there are interesting class differences (see Table 5.4). Anxiety, depression, obsessions, compulsions, and phobias are directly related to class: the higher the class, the larger the proportion of patients exhibiting such symptoms. The opposite relationship holds for memory

---

[14] See, for example, H. E. Freeman and O. G. Simmons, *The Mental Patient Comes Home*, Wiley, New York, 1963, pp. 61–67; S. Angrist, S. Dinitz, M. Lefton, and B. Pasamanick, "Social and Psychological Factors in the Rehospitalization of Female Mental Patients," *Archives of General Psychiatry*, 4, 363 (1961).

TABLE 5.3

Readmission Symptoms	Per Cent
Delusions and hallucinations	35
Aggressive, antisocial verbally	32
Paranoia	31
Aggressive, antisocial-physical (other than sexual)	25
Depressive syndrome	23
Physical disorders or illnesses	23
Failure in self-care functions	21
Disorganized thought process	20
Orientation and/or memory disturbance	17
Manic syndrome	17
Anxiety	16
Suicidal or self-mutilating threat or attempt	14
Alcoholism, drug addiction	10
Obsessions, compulsions, phobias	8
Aggressive, antisocial-sexual	4
Hysteria	3
Vagrancy	2
$n =$	225

or orientation disturbances, disorganized thought processes, delusions and hallucinations, aggressive verbal behavior, and aggressive physical behavior: these symptoms are less common as we move from the lower to the higher classes.[15] The presence of these more severe symptoms in the lower classes does not necessarily mean milder ones are not present; the more severe symptoms may mask other less severe ones which are reported more commonly among higher-status patients. Psychiatrists, for their part, may not probe as deeply for milder symptoms among lower-class persons because of the overwhelming nature of the more serious ones, or they may not bother to note these milder symptoms.

Nevertheless, certain symptoms such as delusions, hallucinations, and disturbances of orientation and thought process are common in the lower classes; they are more likely to be considered as signs of serious emotional difficulty and lead to hospitalization. Maisel found, for example, that antisocial behavior is related to rehospitalization rates. Thus, the fact

---

[15] Other studies have found similar class differences. For example, see T. S. Langner and S. T. Michael, *Life Stress and Mental Health: The Midtown Manhattan Study*, Vol. II, The Free Press of Glencoe, New York, 1963, pp. 406–408; and J. K. Myers and B. H. Roberts, *op. cit.*, pp. 222–240.

TABLE 5.4

Symptoms of Hospital Patients at Readmission, by Social Class (Per Cent) [a]

	Social Class		
Symptoms	I–III	IV	V
Anxiety	30	15	11
Depression	30	33	7
Obsessions, compulsions, phobias	18	7	4
Orientation and/or memory disturbance	6	19	20
Disorganized thought process [b]	9	21	24
Delusions and hallucinations [b]	24	33	42
Aggressive behavior (physical) [b]	17	24	29
Aggressive behavior (verbal) [b]	21	31	39
$n =$	34	106	85

[a] $p < .05$ for chi-square test unless indicated otherwise.
[b] $p < .10$.

that aggressive behavior (both verbal and physical) is more common in the lower than upper classes at readmission may help account for class differences in rehospitalization rates. Even if family members do not rehospitalize the patient, his symptoms are more likely than those characteristic of higher-status persons to come to the attention of community authorities who will rehospitalize him.

The results of the analysis presented in this section support the first major analysis made to test the second hypothesis that social class is related to the patients' 10-year treatment experience. Examination of the 1950 to 1960 hospital discharge and readmission history of 1950 hospital patients indicates significant social-class differences. For the initial and subsequent discharges from psychiatric hospitals during the 10-year period, a strong direct relationship is found between social class and discharge rates: the higher the class the greater the proportion discharged. The chances of being readmitted increase slightly from the highest to the lowest class for the initial readmission, but the class differences diminish with each subsequent readmission sequence. Factors associated with readmission are also related to social class. These factors, in combination with the class differences in discharge, appear to account in part for the apparent piling up of lower-class patients in the hospital. To test this notion further as well as to extend the test of our second hypothesis, we now examine the complex relationship between social class, 1950 to 1960 treatment experience, and treatment status at follow-up or at time of death.

SOCIAL CLASS AND 1950 TO 1960 TREATMENT EXPERIENCE OF HOSPITAL PATIENTS

Hospital treatment between 1950 and 1960 has been classified into four major types: psychotherapies, somatotherapies, drug therapies, and custodial care. This system of treatment classification is a modified form of that employed in the original study.[16] Psychotherapy and custodial care are defined in the same manner in both studies. Organic therapy in the present study is divided into two groupings: somatotherapies and drug therapies; the reason for this division is that psychotropic drugs have been introduced as a major new form of treatment since the original study. The four types of therapy are described below.

Psychotherapies

This category encompasses all the various types of individual and group psychotherapies. Psychotherapy includes all behavioral methods, largely verbal in nature, by which attempts are made to help patients suffering from behavioral disturbances. Types of treatment range from orthodox Freudian methods of psychoanalysis to nondirective group therapy. All are based on the assumption that a patient's difficulties may be eliminated or ameliorated through discussion and reeducation.

Somatotherapies

These therapies are directed principally toward an organ or organ system (the central nervous system) and are based on the assumption that the patient's symptoms may be eliminated or controlled by some form of physical or chemical intervention. They include many types of medical and surgical therapy, neurosurgical procedures (such as lobotomies and topectomies), and various shock treatments (such as electroconvulsive therapy and insulin coma therapy). The most common type of treatment in this category is electroconvulsive shock.

Drug Therapies

Any major form of treatment in which patients receive drugs of any type (sedatives, tranquilizers, alkaloids, or antidepressants) as their major form of therapy is included in this category.

---

[16] A. B. Hollingshead and F. C. Redlich, *op. cit.*, p. 257.

TABLE 5.5

**1960 Follow-Up Status and Principal Type of 1950 to 1960
Therapy of Hospital Patients**

1950 to 1960 Therapy	N	1960 Status (Per Cent)		
		Hospitalized	Dead	In Community
Psychotherapy	119	47	11	42
Somatotherapy	416	58	14	28
Drug therapy	426	65	31	4
Custodial care	444	41	53	6

$$\chi^2 = 315.06, \ df = 6, \ p < .05$$

Custodial Care

This treatment is based on the assumption that little can be done for the patient beyond providing for his physical needs and physical health until he either recovers spontaneously or dies. It refers exclusively to patients who receive no psychotherapy, somatotherapy, or drug therapy but who do receive essential medical, surgical, and nursing care. Patients who help maintain the hospital by working on the wards or in the kitchen, dairy, farm, or shops are included here if they receive none of the specific therapies described above.

Our first step in analyzing the relationships between class, treatment, and follow-up status was to determine the relationship between 1960 follow-up status and the principal type of therapy received after December 1, 1950 and prior to initial hospital discharge. As shown in Table 5.5, the principal type of therapy is strongly associated with follow-up status.[17] The proportion of patients who had died by 1960 is very much greater among those receiving custodial care and drug therapy than among those receiving psychotherapy or somatotherapy. Conversely, the proportion no longer hospitalized is greater for those patients receiving psychotherapy or somatotherapy. If treatment status is examined at time of death as well as in 1960, the same relationship is found between principal type of therapy and outcome; the treatment of those persons no longer hospitalized was: psychotherapy, 47 per cent; somatotherapy, 31 per cent, drug therapy, 5 per cent, and custodial care, 8 per cent.

---

[17] In the analyses which follow, 7 cases are not included because of incomplete information in the hospital records. Thus 1405 cases are analyzed instead of 1412.

TABLE 5.6

1960 Follow-Up Status of Hospital Patients by Type of Therapy (1950 to 1960)

Therapy (1950–1960)	N [a]	1960 Status (Per Cent)		
		Hospitalized	Dead	In Community
Psychotherapy				
Individual psychotherapy	98	31	7	62
Group psychotherapy	77	64	6	30
Somatotherapy				
Electroshock	382	65	13	22
Insulin coma	38	61	3	36
Drug therapy				
Tranquilizers	650	79	12	9
Antidepressants	61	90	5	5
Sedatives	485	63	27	10
Custodial care	444	41	53	6

[a] An individual may receive several types of therapy so the numbers total more than 1405 as in Table 5.5.

Since some patients received multiple therapies, we examined each specific therapy, as well as the major type, to determine whether or not treatment outcome was similar to that for principal type of therapy. As seen in Table 5.6, the results for each specific type of therapy are, in general, similar to those for major type.[18] A much higher proportion of patients who received individual psychotherapy than any other type of treatment were in the community in 1960. The chances of being discharged from the hospital are also relatively high for persons receiving group psychotherapy, electroshock, and insulin coma therapy. In contrast, few individuals receiving any type of drug therapy or custodial care were residing in the community in 1960.

Frequently, a secondary type of therapy may consist of only an occasional tranquilizer or sedative when necessary while the patient is receiving, for example, a series of 20 electroshock treatments or undergoing regular psychotherapy. We shall deal, therefore, only with the major type of therapy since the results of the specific therapies are generally similar to major type and since the intensity and extent of the

---

[18] If an individual is listed as receiving custodial care in Table 5.6, by definition it is also his major type of treatment. Treatment by surgery is not listed in Table 5.6 because of the small number.

secondary types of therapy vary so greatly that they are not so meaningful as the major type in indicating the treatment the patient received.

In order to determine how this relationship between treatment and outcome occurred, initial hospital discharge rates must be examined. The percentage of patients discharged from the hospital at any time drops sharply from 61 in psychotherapy and 50 in somatotherapy to 13 in custodial care and 8 in drug therapy.[19]

Since the major type of psychiatric treatment received from 1950 to 1960 is related so strongly to treatment outcome, it was necessary to determine the class pattern of treatment. The percentage of patients receiving either psychotherapy or somatotherapy, for whom chances of discharge were high, declines from 55 in classes I–II, through 47 in class III and 42 in class IV, to 32 in class V.[20] Conversely, the percentage receiving drug therapy or custodial care increases from classes I–II to class V.

From the materials presented so far, it can be seen that chance of discharge is related to type of therapy received, and type of therapy, in turn, is related to social class. To summarize, proportionately about five times as many persons receiving psychotherapy or somatotherapy (53 per cent) as those receiving drug therapy or custodial care (11 per cent) were discharged. In terms of social class, the higher the class, the greater the percentage of patients receiving psychotherapy or somatotherapy.

The relationships between social class, type of therapy, and chances of discharge just described are found also among rehospitalized patients. The percentage of those receiving drug therapy or custodial care during their rehospitalization increases from classes I–II to class V. In turn, the major type of therapy received during rehospitalization is related to the chances of being discharged again. The figures for redischarge after rehospitalization are: psychotherapy, 50 per cent; somatotherapy, 45 per cent; custodial care, 39 per cent; and drug therapy, 22 per cent. It is interesting that the discharge rate for drug therapy is lower than that for custodial care. It may be that after rehospitalization those patients who were most disturbed and had the poorest prognosis were put on drug therapy so that they could be managed more easily. Since the advent of drug therapy, drugs are frequently substituted for physical

---

[19] The percentage for psychotherapy and somatotherapy combined is 53 and for drug therapy and custodial care combined, 11. The total number of patients by type therapy is as follows: psychotherapy–119, somatotherapy–416, drug therapy–426, and custodial care–444. $\chi^2 = 306.3$, $df = 3$, $p < .05$.

[20] The total number of patients in each class is as follows: I–II–44, III–119, IV–556, and V–686. $\chi^2 = 23.2$, $df = 3$, $p < .05$.

restraints and indeed have come to be thought of as "chemical restraints," among their other functions.

The relationships between social class, type of treatment, and discharge for subsequent rehospitalizations follow the same general pattern as described. Consequently, the percentage of readmitted hospital patients living in the community in 1960 or at time of death declines from 66 in classes I–II to 40 in class V.

The complicated relationship between class, 1950 to 1960 hospital treatment, and outcome can be summarized as follows: (1) Type of treatment is strongly related to initial discharge rates; 53 per cent of persons receiving psychotherapy or somatotherapy but only 11 per cent of those receiving drug therapy or custodial care were released initially from the hospital. (2) Social class is related to discharge but not so strongly as type of therapy; the percentage discharged decreases from 44 in classes I–II, to 36 in class III, 33 in class IV, and 20 in class V. (3) Finally, social class is related to principal type of therapy: the higher the class, the greater the percentage receiving psychotherapy or somatotherapy.

To determine if class differences in discharge rates are due primarily to the uneven distribution of types of therapy by class, principal type of therapy was held constant and outcome by class was determined. Table 5.7 shows this operation.

It is clear that there is a strong relationship between class and outcome for patients receiving therapies which are related to high rates of discharge: the higher the class, the greater the proportion of patients discharged from the hospital. On the other hand, social class is not related systematically to discharge among patients receiving drug therapy or

TABLE 5.7

Social Class	Psychotherapy and Somatotherapy		Drugs and Custodial Care	
	Number of Patients	Per Cent Discharged	Number of Patients	Per Cent Discharged
I–II	24	71	20	5
III	56	59	63	11
IV	235	58	321	14
V	220	43	466	9
Total	535	53	870	11
	$\chi^2 = 15.98$, $df = 3$, $p < .05$		$\chi^2 = 6.1$, $df = 3$, $p < .20$	

custodial care, but only 11 per cent of such patients were discharged from the hospital at any time.

Since we have been dealing with *all* hospitalized cases, there were many chronic, long-term patients for whom there was little hope of discharge. To determine if chronicity might be accounting for the class differences in the follow-up status described above, we controlled for date of hospitalization and record of previous psychiatric treatment as well as for type of 1950 to 1960 treatment. First, we controlled for length of hospitalization at the time of the original study in 1950 by dividing the patients into two groups: (1) those hospitalized in 1949 or 1950, and (2) those hospitalized before 1949. Each of these two groups was then subdivided into two further groups: patients with previous psychiatric hospitalization and patients with no previous psychiatric hospitalization. Each of the resulting four groups was then divided into two therapy groupings: (1) psychotherapy and somatotherapy, and (2) drug therapy and custodial care. In the four analyses involving psychotherapy and somatotherapy, the same class patterns are found: the higher the class, the larger proportion of patients in the community in 1960 or at time of death. On the other hand, there are no significant class differences in follow-up status for patients receiving drug therapy or custodial care. It is clear that deteriorated patients, given custodial care or managed by drug therapy alone, are seldom discharged, and social class is unrelated to their slim chance of discharge. Many of these persons are the aged and senile who ultimately die in the hospital.

To summarize briefly, social class is related to differential rates of hospital discharge in several ways. The higher the class, the more likely the patient is to receive a type of therapy associated with favorable treatment outcome. In addition, among those persons receiving such therapies other factors are involved, for the higher the class, the more likely the chances of hospital discharge.

Having established relationships between social class, hospital treatment, and discharge, we turn now to the patients' treatment experiences once they have been discharged from the hospital. Only 54 of the 373 patients (14 per cent) discharged and studied received outpatient care after their initial hospital discharge.[21] Whether or not a patient received such outpatient care is related to his chances of remaining out of the hospital. While 52 per cent of patients receiving outpatient care after initial discharge were never again readmitted to the hospital, only 39 per cent of those not receiving outpatient care remained out of hospital

---

[21] Nine discharged cases were dropped from the analysis because of incomplete information. Thus, 373 cases are analyzed instead of 382.

treatment.[22] Since some patients were readmitted to the hospital, data for all discharged patients were examined in terms of outpatient care after the last hospital discharge. When this was done the differences in outcome were more pronounced. Of the 68 persons receiving outpatient care after their last hospital discharge, 87 per cent were no longer hospitalized in 1960 or at their death, whereas the corresponding figure for those who did not receive such care was 59 per cent.[23] Since few discharged patients received any outpatient care, it must be emphasized that most persons who remained in the community received no outpatient therapy; 81 per cent of those who remained out of hospital after initial discharge and 75 per cent of those who remained out after last discharge were never under outpatient care. Nevertheless, since outpatient care significantly increases the patient's chances of remaining discharged from hospital treatment, we shall analyze it further.

First, the relationship between social class and outpatient care is striking: the higher the class, the greater the proportion of individuals receiving such treatment: I–II–67, III–32, IV–15, V–15.[24] Since outpatient care itself is related to hospital readmission we must differentiate between its influence and that of class.

Therefore, we examined relationships between hospital treatment outcome and outpatient care at each class level and found very important differences (see Tables 5.8 and 5.9). In classes I–III there are no differences in readmission rates between those patients receiving and those patients not receiving outpatient therapy. In classes IV and V, however, the percentage of patients readmitted to the hospital is substantially less among those receiving outpatient care than among those receiving no such therapy. Approximately the same percentage of persons receiving no outpatient care after initial discharge were readmitted to the hospital in each class: I–III–58, IV–59, and V–66. Among persons receiving outpatient therapy, however, the percentage readmitted drops noticeably from 56 in classes I–III to 45 in class IV and 43 in class V. The class differences are even more striking when outpatient care was received after the last hospital discharge: At each class level somewhere between 84 and 90 per cent of patients receiving outpatient care remained in the community. In classes I–III, 75 per cent remained in the community even

---

[22] The total number of patients receiving outpatient care after initial discharge is 54; the number receiving no outpatient care is 319. $\chi^2 = 3.35$, $df = 1$, $p < .10$.

[23] The total number of patients receiving outpatient care after last discharge is 68; the number receiving no outpatient care is 305. $\chi^2 = 18.95$, $df = 1$, $p < .05$.

[24] The total number of discharged patients in each class is as follows: I–II–18, III–40, IV–181, and V–134. $\chi^2 = 20.13$, $df = 2$, $p < .05$.

TABLE 5.8

Outpatient Care and Hospital Treatment Outcome for Hospital Patients, Controlled for Social Class

	N	Hospital Treatment Outcome (Per Cent)	
		Readmitted to Hospital	Not Readmitted to Hospital
Classes I–III			
Outpatient care [a]	18	56	44
No outpatient care	40	58	42
		$\chi^2 = .02$, $df = 1$, $p > .20$	
Class IV			
Outpatient care [a]	22	45	55
No outpatient care	159	59	41
		$\chi^2 = 1.92$, $p < .20$	
Class V			
Outpatient care [a]	14	43	57
No outpatient care	120	66	34
		$\chi^2 = 3.12$, $p < .10$	

[a] After initial discharge.

with no outpatient care. In classes IV and V, however, this figure drops to 58 and 55 per cent, respectively.

Thus, social class operates in two ways: (1) for class IV and V individuals, outpatient care increases the chances of remaining out of the hospital, but at these social levels proportionately fewer persons than in the higher classes receive such care (classes I–II, 67 per cent; class III, 32 per cent; class IV, 15 per cent; and class V, 15 per cent); (2) among persons receiving no outpatient care, the chances of remaining out of the hospital are better in classes I, II, and III than in classes IV and V.

In discussing the relationships we have found between social class, outpatient care, and treatment outcome, two questions may be raised. First, why are there social-class differences in the use of outpatient facilities? Second, why are outpatient facilities more important in keeping patients out of the hospital in the lower classes than in the higher classes?

In answer to the first question, among the many factors related to differential class use of outpatient facilities are attitudes toward psychiatry, the perceived stigma attached to mental illness, attitudes toward outpatient clinics, and economic resources. Many studies have shown that

TABLE 5.9

**Outpatient Care and Treatment Status for Hospital Patients in 1960
or at Death, Controlled by Social Class**

	N	Treatment Status (Per Cent)	
		In Hospital	In Community
Classes I–III			
Outpatient care [a]	22	14	86
No outpatient care	36	25	75
		$\chi^2 = 1.14,\ df = 1,\ p > .20$	
Class IV			
Outpatient care [a]	25	16	84
No outpatient care	156	42	58
		$\chi^2 = 6.98,\ df = 1,\ p < .05$	
Class V			
Outpatient care [a]	21	10	90
No outpatient care	113	45	55
		$\chi^2 = 8.60,\ df = 1,\ p < .05$	

[a] After last hospital discharge.

negative attitudes toward psychiatry increase as social status decreases.[25] The proportion of former patients who were dissatisfied with their hospital treatment increases from classes I–II to class V. As a result, fewer lower-class persons after their hospital discharge were interested in the continuation of any type of psychiatric therapy.

Dissatisfaction with their hospital experiences was expressed by patients in class V. Mrs. K. stated, "The attendants up there [state hospital] on the ward treated all the patients the same, just like cattle. They didn't treat you like no human being. They swore all the time and pushed you around."

Mrs. G. told us: "That [state hospital] was a terrible place. I wouldn't put my dog up there. It was filthy and dirty, and the stink was terrible. You never got to see a doctor to speak to up there. They always gave you the brushoff. Besides, they shocked you or put you in a strait jacket if you didn't agree with them about something."

[25] See, for example, E. G. Jaco, "Attitudes Toward and Incidence of Mental Disorder: A Research Note," *The Southwestern Social Science Quarterly*, June, 27 (1957); J. K. Myers and B. H. Roberts, *op. cit.*, pp. 202–205; and W. S. Williams, "Class Differences in the Attitudes of Psychiatric Patients," *Social Problems*, 4, 240 (1957).

Mr. E. said, "I got no help up at the hospital. Christ, you never saw a doctor except once in a while they came around looking at the ward. They always gave you the run-around if you tried to see them."

Mrs. F. commented, "Lunatics were all over the place. Who wants to be cooped up with a bunch of nuts? The food was terrible. Why, for a couple of months I thought I was in a concentration camp."

The use of outpatient facilities is related to the stigma attached to mental illness and the patient's fear of further identification as a mental patient after discharge from the hospital. Patients hope that discharge will be viewed by their family and friends as evidence that their mental illness has been cured. To continue in psychiatric therapy in a clinic is defined by lower- and working-class persons as evidence that the cure is not complete. Moreover, it may be more difficult to conceal treatment in a public psychiatric clinic than therapy by a private practitioner which is more common in the middle and upper classes.

Mrs. L. is a 43-year-old, class V widow whose late husband's relatives live nearby. They never let her forget that she was a patient in a state mental hospital. She said, "They rub it in about my having been to the state mental hospital. They call me 'that crazy woman.' " A number of people in the neighborhood have asked the relatives in the presence of the former patient, "Is this the one who was up at the state mental hospital?" It is quite clear that Mrs. L. believes that if she goes to a clinic this will type her even further as a mental patient.

When outpatient treatment was undertaken, patients in classes IV and V were less satisfied and more likely to quit than those higher up in the social-class system. Although we do not have evidence in our study, other research has shown the preferential treatment accorded middle- and upper-class persons in clinics and the more favorable attitudes the staff have toward them.[26] We cannot determine or delineate the reasons for the dissatisfaction of lower-class persons with clinic treatment, i.e., whether it is because of actions on the part of the staff, the patients' own actions, or other factors. However, we do know that lower-class patients recognize they receive differential treatment and are less satisfied with it.

A class V man, Mr. D., described his outpatient treatment, which he discontinued after a few sessions, as follows: "I thought the treatment was nutty; the guy talked to me and watched me all the time. That certainly didn't do me no good." His wife told us, "He hated to go to the clinic. He thought he was different than other people because he went there. Those people at the clinic didn't tell me much about it, and they

---

[26] J. K. Myers and B. H. Roberts, *op. cit.*, Chapter 8; J. K. Myers and L. Schaffer, *loc. cit.*

didn't help him none because he didn't want to be helped. He's better now but not because of the treatment he got from them. They could have gave him some needles to calm him down, but they didn't. Going to the clinic doesn't do you no good. It just makes people think you're still sick. At least, it made my old man think he was different than other people."

Economic factors also play a part in the differential use of outpatient clinics by social class. Since outpatient clinics operate generally only during the daytime, class differences in occupational demands provide the upper classes with an advantage in utilizing the clinics. When a lower- or working-class man or woman takes time off from work he is not paid, whereas middle- and upper-class people more frequently have jobs with paid sick leave.

The availability of community resources and the amount of family support are probably answers to the second question of why outpatient facilities are more important in keeping patients out of the hospital in the lower classes than in the higher strata. Upper- and middle-class patients are less likely to live alone, more likely to have jobs, and more likely to receive emotional and financial support from their families and friends. Consequently, outpatient facilities themselves are not as important for the patients' support in the upper and middle classes as in the lower and working classes where they frequently are the only resource available to former patients.

Family interest and support decrease markedly as social-class position decreases. Mrs. L., discussed earlier in the chapter, was hospitalized at the state hospital for two years as a schizophrenic. During this time she had no visitors. According to Mrs. L., when her husband became ill he then remembered her: "He signed me out after he got sick because he needed me to look after him." After her discharge, Mrs. L. did indeed take care of her husband whose illness was terminal. Since his death, she has lived alone. She seldom visits any relatives. Although some of her husband's family live nearby, she has stopped seeing them because they have informed her neighbors of her hospitalization. At present Mrs. L.'s social contacts are limited to a few aged women in the rooming house where she lives. At times she helps these women prepare their meals and takes care of them when they become ill. She was so lonely that she pleaded desperately with the study interviewer to return and talk with her.

Because of the lack of family support and of other community resources, the outpatient clinic becomes very important in maintaining class IV and V former patients in the community. Miss H., a single, class V woman, 36 years of age, had been hospitalized as a schizophrenic. The youngest of eight children, she had many relatives in the community and was discharged to live with an older sister who was also single. One week after discharge, she and her sister had a disagreement, and the patient moved into a small apartment where she still lives alone. She has no friends or acquaintances in the neighborhood and is dissatisfied with her housing, but she is unable to afford an apartment with a private bath which she desires. She has worked on three different occasions as a clerk in a 5-and-10-cent store, once for a year, another time for nine months, and the third time for three and one half months. For the past year and one half, however, she has not worked and lives on state aid.

This woman belongs to no clubs or organizations, seldom sees people socially, and is very lonely. She has no close friends, and although she has several related families nearby she does not see any of them more than once a month. In the past month, no friends have visited her, and she has visited only once at the home of a friend. She stopped going to church about six months ago because she was embarrassed at having no money for the collection. Apparently her weekly visit to an outpatient clinic and her confidence in one of the doctors is the stabilizing force in her life.

The sister with whom Miss H. lived after discharge explained, "I didn't want her sent home to me. She should have stayed up there [at the state hospital] for the rest of her life. I know she'd be happier up there. I'm disgusted with social workers and psychiatrists. They treat everyone like a mental patient, always prying into your affairs. Besides, I don't want to worry about my sister and her problems. I don't feel nobody can help her. As far as I can see, she is beyond cure. They should send her back to the state hospital where she belongs. If you ask me, they let her out too soon. I don't think so many doctors and other people should have been seeing my sister at the hospital. All they did was keep giving her different advice and couldn't agree with each other on what to do. Hospitals are too ready to get rid of patients. They should keep her up there because up there she's better. Now she can't be helped no more. Nothing can help her."

Since the lower-class patients frequently lack access to resources in the community and are without family support, access to and use of psychiatric outpatient facilities become important factors in keeping them in the community. In contrast, while upper-class patients may utilize outpatient facilities more frequently, the support received from their families also plays a critical role in their adjustment after hospital discharge.

A typical illustration is Mrs. R., a class I, married woman with two teenage children. Mrs. R. was hospitalized with schizophrenia four times in private hospitals for a total of 17 months between the age of 31 and 37. Since her last discharge in 1951, she has seen a private psychiatrist regularly about six or eight times a year. During her hospitalization her husband visited regularly and conferred with the doctors every few weeks about her condition. He is very satisfied with the treatment she received; he feels that she improved tremendously and since her discharge has been "as normal" as anyone he knows.

Since her discharge, Mrs. R. has pursued an active social life. She was readily accepted by the membership of a church-related charity organization and is now a member of the board of directors. In addition, she is president of another social club. With the financial support of her husband, a professional man himself, she has opened up a small novelty and art shop which she enjoys. The shop, as well as her occasional "shopping sprees" during which she charges large amounts, has been an added burden to her husband but he tolerates this behavior as being therapeutic. With the financial support of her husband, the acceptance by friends and relatives, and her periodic use of the private psychiatrist, she has been able to adjust quite well and has remained out of the hospital continuously since 1951.

The materials presented in this section indicate a strong relationship between the 1950 to 1960 treatment process and 1960 follow-up status. Patients receiving psychotherapy or somatotherapy are more likely to be discharged and living in the community in 1960 in contrast to those who received drug therapy or custodial care. Upper- and middle-class patients, however, more frequently receive psychotherapy or somatotherapy than working and lower-class patients who are more likely to receive drug therapy or custodial care only. If discharged, class IV and V patients are less likely than higher-status persons to utilize outpatient psychiatric facilities, despite the fact that use of these facilities reduces their chances of rehospitalization.

1950 TO 1960 TREATMENT EXPERIENCE OF CLINIC PATIENTS

An analysis of the treatment history of clinic patients supports further the study's second hypothesis that social class is related to the patients' 10-year treatment experience from 1950 to 1960. Although there were differences between clinic and hospital patients, as described in the previous chapter, the same type of class pattern we demonstrated in hospital treatment characterizes both groups: the lower the class, the higher the percentage of patients hospitalized. For example, the percentage of 1950 clinic patients who were hospitalized sometime during the decade increases from 17 in classes I–III to 23 in class IV and 33 in class V.[27]

Of the 32 clinic patients who were hospitalized at one time or another during the 10-year period, 11 were still hospitalized at follow-up or death, while the remainder had been discharged; 17 of these 21 discharged patients had been hospitalized less than three months, 3 for three months to one year, and only one for over a year. Since most had multiple hospitalizations, the average length of each hospitalization was extremely short compared to that of discharged hospital patients.[28]

When hospitalized, higher-status individuals are more likely to be confined to private hospitals and lower-status persons to public institutions. For example, the percentage of all 1950 clinic patients treated in public hospitals increases from 21 in classes I–III to 22 in class IV and 34 in class V.

The pattern of outpatient care from 1950 to 1960 for former clinic patients differs from that of former hospital patients. Whereas 20 per cent of discharged hospital patients received some type of outpatient therapy, 53 per cent of former clinic patients reentered outpatient treatment after their initial discharge from such care. Moreover, the use of outpatient facilities among former clinic patients is widespread at all class levels in contrast to the greater use of such facilities by middle- and upper-class former hospital patients (see Table 5.1). The percentage of former clinic patients at each class level who received further outpatient

---

[27] Classes I, II, and III are combined in the analysis of clinic cases because of the small number of cases in classes I and II. Although there are 143 clinic cases, some cases are dropped at times because of incomplete information on certain items. Therefore, the number of cases in each class is presented for each analysis. In this instance seven cases are excluded so the total number of patients in each class is as follows: I–III–36, IV–57, and V–43; $\chi^2 = 3.52$, $df = 2$, $p < .20$.

[28] The 10-year hospital experience for clinic patients not hospitalized at follow-up or at time of death is as follows:

Length of Hospitalization Months	Cases N	Hospitalizations N	Average Hospitalization Days
0–3	9	1	24
	6	2	19
	1	3	9
	1	4	14
4–12	1	2	45
	1	6	45
	1	7	30
12–23	1	8	83

care sometime between 1950 and 1960 varies from 51 to 56.[29] Apparently lower-class persons will use psychiatric outpatient facilities once they have had experience with them. If treatment can be initiated in such facilities then the outpatient clinic can be an important community resource for persons with emotional problems at all class levels. However, the reentry of former patients from all class backgrounds into outpatient care does not result in similar therapeutic experiences. In fact, there are sizeable discrepancies in the nature of psychiatric care by class which follow the same pattern found for hospital patients: the higher the class, the greater the amount and intensity of therapy.

For example, treatment on the average is longer in the middle and upper classes, with the percentage of persons treated for three or more months rising from 61 in class V through 66 in class IV to 82 in classes I–III.[30] As would be expected, higher-status persons are also more likely to be treated by a private practitioner than in the clinic. Thus, those persons under private psychiatric care are: classes I–III, 25 per cent; class IV, 9 per cent, and class V, 10 per cent.[31]

If the various types of outpatient therapy are examined, further evidence of social-class differences in the treatment process is found. More higher- than lower-status individuals received individual psychotherapy, for example, and for longer periods of time, as shown in Table 5.10. Thus, there are class differences in the nature of outpatient therapy, although approximately the same proportion of persons from each class utilized such facilities at sometime during the 10-year period.

As time passes, however, class differences again appear even in the proportion of persons receiving outpatient care. Although there are no class differences in the proportion of persons receiving such therapy during the entire 10-year period, 14 per cent in classes I–III were still under outpatient care in 1960 but only 5 per cent in class IV and 7 per cent in class V.[32]

To illustrate the differences in the treatment experiences of the outpatient clinic cases at different social-class levels, we contrast the cases of Mrs. G. and Mrs. U.

Mrs. G., a married, class V housewife, was 35 years old when she

---

[29] The figures for those reentering outpatient care are: classes I–III, 54 per cent; class IV, 51 per cent; and class V, 56 per cent.

[30] The total number of patients in each class is as follows: I–III–40, IV–59, and V–44. $\chi^2 = 4.98$, $df = 2$, $p < .10$.

[31] The total number of patients in each class is as follows: I–III–32, IV–55, and V–40. $\chi^2 = 5.20$, $df = 2$, $p < .10$.

[32] See Chapter 4, Table 4.7, p. 78.

TABLE 5.10

Length of 1950 to 1960 Individual Psychotherapy for Clinic Patients by Social Class

Social Class	N	Treatment (Per Cent)			
		None	1 to 6 Months	7 to 12 Months	Over 12 Months
I–III	36	8	31	22	39
IV	58	22	47	14	17
V	42	24	36	21	19
	136 [a]				

$$\chi^2 = 8.30,^{\text{b}} \; df = 2, \; p < .05$$

[a] Seven cases are excluded because of insufficient information. Thus there are 136 cases instead of 143.
[b] Categories used in chi-square test were (1) 6 months or less, and (2) over 6 months.

was treated in a local outpatient clinic in 1950 for her neurosis. As part of her treatment during the 10-year follow-up period, she visited a social worker at the clinic twice each month, from December 1950 to December 1952. After that she was seen only a few times at the clinic and the last visit was in June 1953. She became dissatisfied with the clinic for a number of reasons: the doctors seemed young and inexperienced; she rarely saw the same doctor; it was time-consuming waiting to see a doctor; and she did not feel any better after her discussions with the doctors.

In 1950, the diagnosis of Mrs. G. was phobic reaction but it was changed to obsessive-compulsive reaction a few years later. For the past 10 years she has had periods of depression and acute anxiety. Although the patient now appears more relaxed and easy to be with, according to her relatives, she still has many fears associated with her mental health and is concerned that she may become mentally ill again. Currently, Mrs. G. appears to be active, energetic, and capable of carrying out the responsibilities of a housewife. However, she seems to be a pessimistic personality and easily gets upset. She believes that her close relatives do not accept or understand her need for psychiatric care, and for this reason she was reluctant to have any of her relatives interviewed.

Since terminating her contact with the psychiatric outpatient clinic, she has been under the supervision of a family physician, but he does not help her with her emotional problems. Her doctor has suggested that she return to the clinic, but she refuses. She feels that the doctors at the clinic were experimenting with her. She feels also that she is not as nervous as formerly nor does she get as easily upset by events. She feels more secure and able to make independent decisions. However, she admits that she is still pessimistic and nervous, and her relatives think that these problems are greater than she realizes. In 1960 Mrs. G. finally consulted a private psychiatrist on the advice of her family doctor. She was much more satisfied with him. She felt he was mature and understanding and that she could make an appointment any time. However, she saw him only a few times and was unable to continue because of the cost of treatment.

Mrs. U. was a 33-year-old, married, class I woman, at the time of the original study in 1950. She also was a patient in the same outpatient clinic as Mrs. G. Her diagnosis was psychoneurotic disorder—psychoneurosis, mixed type. She had a depressive reaction, chronic and severe, related to a postpartum period. She was emotionally unstable and characterized by marked passive dependency, suicidal trends, and barbiturate addiction. Later the suggestion was made that her diagnosis might be a manic-depressive disorder.

Mrs. U. attended the clinic from December 1950 to February 1951. At the suggestion of the psychiatrist there, she was admitted to a private hospital from which she was discharged after a stay of 30 days. In 1951, after her discharge from the private hospital, she received outpatient treatment by its staff for several months.

After her return home from the private psychiatric hospital, Mrs. U. functioned rather well, although she was dissatisfied with her role as a housewife. For some years she had had a strong interest in painting and wanted to do this professionally. With no opportunity to work in this area, she decided any job would be better than remaining at home taking care of the house and children. She first secured a job in New Haven as a semiprofessional clerical worker, supervising the assignment of day laborers to various jobs in the community. After a year she found the work unchallenging; she gave up the job but did not return to the housework or the care of the children which had now become an additional burden on her husband. Free from job demands, she immediately became involved in a variety of community and church activities, pursuing doggedly the clubwoman role.

In the middle 1950's her husband was transferred to Massachusetts. This move created a number of problems for Mrs. U. She had to cope with moving into and arranging a new home and developing new friends, associations, and community activities. She rapidly joined a number of charitable and church groups, accepting duties in each. Her interest in religion, however, bordered on the social. Her family had never been affiliated with any religious group, but as an adolescent she had joined a church in which she had become the church organist. In her new home, she again joined a church and took over the role of organist.

Despite her attempts to integrate herself into the activities of the community, the problems of adjustment were collectively insurmountable. In 1957 Mrs. U. became severely depressed and anxious, threatening suicide again. She sought the help of a psychiatric counselor retained by her church. Upon his advice, she was again rehospitalized—this time for a period of five weeks in a private clinic. She was then discharged with the understanding she would enter treatment with a private psychiatrist. She has been in treatment since, and her recovery has been quite amazing. She has made rapid progress and feels that she is back to normal. She has resumed her duties in the household at their previous level, and she is taking part again in church activities and social organizations.

While both Mrs. G. and Mrs. U. have continued to have psychiatric problems their experiences are quite different. Whereas Mrs. G. feels that her husband and siblings fail to understand her problems, Mrs. U.'s husband is not only understanding but has also been willing and able to provide care in private hospitals and with private psychiatrists. Mrs. G. has been financially unable to continue with a private psychiatrist. Mrs. U. not only is financially able to utilize the services of a private psychiatrist, but, in addition, her position as an organist in an upper-class suburban church provides her with immediate access to a psychiatric counselor retained by her church.

SUMMARY

In this chapter we have made three major analyses to test our second hypothesis that social class is related to the patient's treatment and readmission experience during the period from 1950 to 1960. First, we examined the 10-year discharge and readmission history of the former hospital patients. For the initial and each subsequent discharge, we found class to be directly related to the chances of hospital release. Specifically, the higher the class, the greater the proportion of patients discharged. While the relationship between social class and chances of readmission is less striking, for the initial and second readmission the relationship is in the expected direction: lower-status patients are more likely to be readmitted. By the third readmission, class differences have virtually disappeared, but the class difference in rates of discharge remains.

We then examined the treatment process during the 10-year period. While specific types of treatment are related to the chances of discharge, a significant relationship is found for the various types of treatment: Upper- and middle-class patients more frequently receive psychotherapy or somatotherapy, the dominant form of treatment for those patients who are likely to be discharged and living in the community in 1960. Further, we found that for the discharged patients, the lower the class the less likely the patient was to be in outpatient treatment during the 10-year period. This particular finding is of considerable importance. Our study demonstrates that for the lower-class patients, outpatient treatment increases the likelihood that the patient will remain out of the psychiatric hospital, yet it is precisely this group which is least likely to receive such treatment.

As a final test of our second hypothesis, we examined the 1950 to 1960 treatment experience of the clinic patients. In support of our hypothesis, we found that more lower-class than middle- and upper-class patients were hospitalized during the 10-year period and were still hospitalized at the end of the follow-up period. While the use of psychiatric outpatient facilities do not vary greatly by social class for the clinic patients, the length and type of treatment are significantly related to social class. Upper- and middle-class clinic patients remain in outpatient care for longer periods and while in treatment are more likely to receive individual psychotherapy.

adjustment in the community

part three

In this part attention is shifted from the entire patient population to those persons not under hospital care in 1960. Chapter Six describes how the adjustment of former patients and their controls in the community was studied. The next three chapters analyze relationships between social class and three major aspects of community adjustment: psychobiological adjustment, economic role performance, and social participation.

social class and patient adjustment in the community

THEORETICAL ISSUES

The ability to remain out of a mental hospital is a basic measure of treatment outcome. As long as an individual is hospitalized, he is unable to perform the social roles expected of him by the members of society. Although mental health experts and laymen may disagree on certain aspects of psychiatric illness and treatment, they are in general agreement that the success of therapy is limited, indeed, if the patient cannot maintain himself in a noninstitutional setting. Consequently, for patients treated both in hospitals and in outpatient facilities, the ability to remain in the community and out of hospital treatment has commonly been used in follow-up studies as a measure of successful treatment outcome.[1] In fact, this is perhaps the most frequently used index in evaluating therapies and planning for additional inpatient psychiatric facilities.[2]

---

[1] See especially Howard E. Freeman and Ozzie G. Simmons, *The Mental Patient Comes Home*, Wiley, New York, 1963, p. 18. In this study a patient returning to the hospital within a year of discharge is identified as a failure. Similarly, Dinitz and his associates define as failures those hospital patients who return within six months of discharge; see Simon Dinitz, Mark Lefton, Shirley Angrist, and Benjamin Pasamanick, "Psychiatric and Social Attributes as Predictors of Case Outcome in Mental Hospitalization," *Social Problems*, 8, 322 (1961).

[2] See, for example, Benjamin Malzberg, "Cohort Studies of Mental Disease in New York State: 1943–1949," *Mental Hygiene* (reported in 10 parts), 40–41 (1956–57);

The ability to remain in the community, however, is only a minimal measure of successful treatment outcome. Nonhospitalized patients may or may not function in the social roles expected of them—earning a living, supporting a family, performing household tasks, rearing their children, participating in social and community activities, and so on. Even if they do perform these roles adequately, they still may be viewed as abnormal because of personality characteristics or symptomatic behavior. Consequently, in addition to community tenure, we need other measures of treatment outcome.[3]

Within the theoretical framework of the social scientist, an individual is considered a "normal," functioning member of the community if he can perform the societal roles expected of him.[4] Thus, posttreatment adjustment has been evaluated by social scientists primarily in terms of role performance. In contrast, the importance of intrapsychic functioning, as measured by mental status or psychological adjustment, has been emphasized by psychiatrists and other clinicians.[5] Despite the problems of reliability and validity in utilizing measures of mental status, according to this point of view intrapsychic functioning is considered the most

---

Aaron Mason, Eleanor Tarpy, Lewis J. Sherman, and Don P. Haefner, "Discharges from a Mental Hospital in Relation to Social Class and Other Variables," *Archives of General Psychiatry*, 2, 11 (1960); F. A. Mettler, A. Crandell, J. R. Wittenborn, K. Litten, E. H. Feiring, and M. B. Carpenter, "Factors in the Preoperative Situation of Schizophrenics Considered to be of Significance in Influencing Outcome Following Psychosurgery," *Psychiatric Quarterly*, 28, 549 (1954); Nathaniel S. Lehrman, "Follow-up of Brief and Prolonged Psychiatric Hospitalization," *Comprehensive Psychiatry*, 2, 227 (1961); and A. B. Baker, J. G. Thorpe, and V. Jenkins, "Social Status After Five Years in a Mental Hospital," *British Journal of Medical Psychology*, XXX, Pt. 2, 113 (1957).

[3] Freeman and Simmons, *op. cit.*, pp. 37–40, for example, view rehabilitation in two ways: community tenure (the ability to remain out of hospital treatment) and successful performance of instrumental roles.

[4] A number of studies in their measures of social or community adjustment have emphasized the ability of the individual to function in an occupational role. See, for example, Freeman and Simmons, *ibid.*; Dinitz, et al., *loc. cit.*; J. S. Bockoven, A. R. Pandiscio, and H. C. Solomon, "Social Adjustment of Patients in the Community Three Years after Commitment to the Boston Psychopathic Hospital," *Mental Hygiene*, 40, 354 (1956); George W. Brown, "Experiences of Discharged Chronic Schizophrenic Patients in Various Types of Living Group," *Milbank Memorial Fund Quarterly*, XXXVII, 105 (1959); and H. L. Hyman et al., "Follow-up Study of 317 Patients Discharged from Hillside Hospital in 1950," *Journal of Hillside Hospital*, V, 17 (1956).

[5] Holmboe's follow-up study, for example, deals only with *clinical syndromes*, and no information other than the clinical analysis is presented. R. Holmboe and C. Astrup, "Follow-Up Study of 255 Patients with Acute Schizophreni-form Psychoses," *Acta Psychiatrica et Neurologica Scandinavia*, 32, (Suppl. 115) (1957).

refined indicator of an individual's ability to adjust himself to society.

In extreme form, each of these theoretical positions assumes that its concept encompasses all dimensions of community adjustment. More commonly the implicit assumption is made that the various dimensions are highly interrelated and that the particular measure used is the most valid indicator of the total adjustment process. Although both role performance and mental status certainly measure social functioning, neither, by itself, seems to be a sufficient measure of the individual's adjustment to community life, for the two are not necessarily related at all points.

Epidemiological studies have shown that some individuals are psychiatrically incapacitated, yet they perform their social roles and they have never been treated for mental illness.[6] Mr. B., one of the control cases in our study, illustrates this point. Mr. B. is a diabetic and arthritic, class V male. Although a physician warned him at one time that he might suffer a mental breakdown, he has never been treated for mental illness. A member of a large family himself, he has successfully reared seven children. At present he works full time in a factory, supports his wife and one minor child, attends church regularly, and visits with friends and relatives. Despite his ability to work and perform his role as husband and father, meeting and discharging most of his social responsibilities, he possesses a number of psychological problems which differ little from classical symptoms of specific psychiatric disorders. Mr. B. maintains that he has been able to see and talk to Jesus since, at the age of 16, he encountered Him in a field, dressed in flowing robes, leaning on a golden gate with pearl doorknobs, and surrounded by 26 sheep. Although Mr. B.'s mother was called to the field she was unable to participate in this visitation. Since that time, Mr. B. claims he has been told in advance about everything that occurs; even flat tires on his car have been predicted. Mr. B. checks with Jesus before making any important decisions. Thus, he would not grant us an interview on our first visit to his home, but consented a week later when he believed he had received divine permission for the interview.

By any standard measure of mental status, Mr. B. would be judged

---

[6] In the Midtown Study, 73.3 per cent of the respondents classified as impaired had never been treated in a psychiatric facility. Leo Srole, Thomas S. Langner, Stanley T. Michael, Marvin K. Opler, and T. A. C. Rennie, *Mental Health in the Metropolis: The Midtown Manhattan Study*, Vol. I, McGraw-Hill, New York, 1962, p. 147. See also Dorothea C. Leighton, John S. Harding, David M. Macklin, Allister M. Macmillan, and Alexander H. Leighton, *The Character of Danger* (*The Stirling County Study*, Vol. III), Basic Books, New York, 1963, pp. 116–69.

as psychologically impaired; yet he is able to function in the community. Apparently, psychological measures of adjustment do not pick up the strengths of ego functioning as well as the weaknesses. In turn, while measures of social role performance may discern certain ego strengths, as in the case of Mr. B., such indices may overlook particular weaknesses detected by psychological measures.

Because of the complexity of the process, the position taken in our research is that community adjustment cannot be measured adequately by a single index. For this reason, we have divided community adjustment conceptually into two major dimensions—psychobiological functioning and social performance. These two dimensions of community adjustment may overlap and, empirically, there may be some association between them. Specifically, the individual incapacitated by a variety of psychosomatic problems might find it difficult to work in certain occupations in which physical strain is high. However, the somatic problem, reflecting some psychobiological malfunctioning, may not prevent him from holding other jobs and performing them adequately. Conversely, the individual who is unable to find a steady job as the result of a lack of education or discrimination might find it difficult to maintain a favorable self-image of himself. However, if the individual who lacks training and is unable to find a suitable job is able to view himself simply as part of a population which faces the same common problem he may maintain his ego integrity in spite of the problem. Failure to find a job then becomes the problem of the society and not of the individual.

Because there need not necessarily be an empirical link between psychobiological adjustment and social adjustment, it would be erroneous to utilize measures of one such area of adjustment as indicators of adjustment in other areas as well. A comprehensive evaluation of community adjustment must analyze measures designed to tap both dimensions.

In the materials presented in the following chapters, we deal with measures of both the psychobiological and the social areas. Since both dimensions of adjustment are multifactorial in their own right, the problems of measurement are complex. Moreover, it is difficult to make operational theoretical concepts in the social sciences since there are seldom single, unambiguous, and standard indices available. For only a few concepts, such as age, sex, and group size, are there close to standard and agreed upon operations. Even in these cases problems arise, but when we deal with more abstract concepts like adjustment the difficulties are multiplied. Therefore, it is frequently desirable to use multiple indicators of conceptual variables. We have done this by employing a variety of measures of each dimension of community adjustment.[7]

The measures of psychobiological adjustment used are related to those aspects which are most important for this study. Little attention, therefore, is paid to the physical health problems of patients, although at a general level of analysis this is a critical factor in the assessment of adjustment. However, since the focus of this study is on former mental patients, particular attention is paid to the assessment of the psychological and psychosomatic, rather than purely physical, aspects of adjustment. Specifically, in this study we employ as indices of the patient's psychobiological adjustment an index of mental status and family reports of symptomatic behavior.

In the second major area of community adjustment—the social—the individual's position in a matrix of interpersonal relationships is emphasized. It is assumed that behavior is evaluated within the context of a range of role expectations relevant to a given aggregate of individuals— men, women, old people, mother, father, and so on. Insofar as the patient is able to function within the framework of a set of normatively structured role demands, he is defined as being adjusted in the community.

In this study the social adjustment of the patient is measured by his ability to meet certain role requirements of society. Two general aspects of role performance have been selected to measure social adjustment: economic functioning and social participation.[8]

---

[7] In the absence of clear-cut measures of complex concepts, certain methodological advantages are gained through the use of a number of indices of the concept under consideration. See Richard F. Curtis and Elton F. Jackson, "Multiple Indicators in Survey Research," *American Journal of Sociology*, LXVIII, 195 (1962).

[8] These two aspects may be viewed as measures of instrumental and expressive role performance. Although every individual in the community performs a number of roles throughout his lifetime, according to Parsons two major classes of roles—instrumental and expressive—may be identified conceptually in terms of general functions. Instrumental roles are primarily task-oriented and directed toward fulfilling goal attainment and adaptive functions. Expressive roles, in contrast, emphasize integrative functions such as effective participation in groups. The instrumental-expressive distinction refers to major orientations of specific roles, and no single role need be solely instrumental or expressive. For example, the occupational role of an adult in a complex industrial society is essentially instrumental in that it is task-oriented and adaptive. At the same time, insofar as the individual, through the performance of his occupational role, is integrated into functional social groups—such as work cliques or unions—this role has certain expressive-integrative functions as well. The classification of roles, therefore, is either instrumental or expressive in terms of the *primary orientations*, i.e., the dominant functional orientations of the various roles. In this study economic roles may be considered instrumental, and social participation may be viewed as an index of expressive-integrative role performance.

For a more complete treatment of the theoretical distinction between instrumental

In any society adults are expected to perform essential economic roles which include the domestic activities of the housewife as well as the market activities of the wage earner. Because of the societal importance of these activities, we use economic role performance as the first measure of social adjustment.[9]

Individuals are also expected to participate in groups and situations beyond the occupational which require action on their part, but these are not defined precisely. In general, there is a minimal expectation that the healthy individual will participate in a range of social activities and will not regress and isolate himself voluntarily. Only under specified conditions, such as illness or disability, is failure to participate legitimized temporarily.[10] The individual's general performance in the community, therefore, may be measured by his ability to participate in various groups and organizations and to function as a friend, neighbor, or associate. This second measure of social adjustment is measured by a number of indices of social participation.[11]

To summarize briefly, community adjustment is conceptualized as a general term referring to how well the patient gets along in the community. The concept has two major dimensions—the psychobiological and the social. To measure psychobiological adjustment, we examine two indices of mental status. To measure social adjustment we examine two general aspects of role performance: economic adjustment and social participation.

METHODOLOGICAL ISSUES

In preceding chapters, the 1950 social-class position of patients was used to test the first two hypotheses on treatment outcome. The year 1950 was used as a base line to determine class influences on the patient's treatment and chances of discharge during the 10-year period. However,

---

and expressive actions, see Talcott Parsons, *The Social System*, The Free Press, Glencoe, Ill., 1951, pp. 79–88; and Talcott Parsons and Robert F. Bales, *Family, Socialization and Interaction Process*, The Free Press, Glencoe, Ill., 1955, pp. 310–12, 317–20.
[9] Several studies of former mental patients include measures of occupational performance as an index of adjustment. See Freeman and Simmons, *loc. cit.*, Brown, *loc. cit.*, Dinitz et al., *loc. cit.*, Bockoven et al., *loc. cit.*, and the U.S. Department of Health, Education, and Welfare, Vocational Rehabilitation Administration, *The Rehabilitated Mentally Ill*, Division of Statistics and Studies, U.S. Government Printing Office, Washington, D.C., 1955.
[10] See, for example, Parsons' discussion of the sick role; Parsons, *op. cit.*, pp. 287–88.
[11] Similar measures have been utilized in other follow-up studies of former mental patients; for example, see Freeman and Simmons, *loc. cit.*, Dinitz et al., *loc. cit.*, and Bockoven et al., *loc. cit.*

for the discharged patient who returns to the community the most immediately relevant class influences are those generated by the 1960 class position. For most patients, class position was the same in both years—1950 and 1960—so that either the 1950 or 1960 Index of Social Position could have been used. For the patient whose class position changed after discharge from treatment, we had to make a decision. We decided to use the 1960 class position to test the third hypothesis on community adjustment because, although the individual's entire social-class history affects his current behavior, the class factors associated with the patient's current position in the social structure are more relevant to understanding his posttreatment adjustment than his class position before he entered therapy.

As with patients, control cases were classified on the basis of their 1960 social-class status,[12] and some also had changed class position. For persons who changed class position there was generally little difference in the amount and direction of mobility between patients and controls, as indicated in Table 6.1. Although in class IV a higher percentage of patients than controls was downwardly mobile in the 10-year period, in total there were no substantial differences in the proportion of patients and controls who were upwardly or downwardly mobile.

Because of the use of the 1960 social-class position of the patients and controls in the following chapters, the number of patients in each class differs somewhat from the number of patients in the community as reported in Chapters 4 and 5.[13]

---

[12] The length of time patients had been discharged from treatment and were actually living in the community prior to the 1960 follow-up varied. Yet, for all practical purposes, it was only during this discharge period that shifts in mobility could occur for most patients because such shifts were brought about by occupational changes or changes in marital status in the cases of some female patients. Thus, all patients did not have the same opportunity in length of time to become mobile. Few patients, however, had the full 10-year period, since the majority were hospitalized some part of the time and many for at least several years. Considering the variations in length of time of patients in the community, we measured the mobility of the control respondents for 5 years, 1955 to 1960, as a basis for comparison to minimize and average this time variation.

[13] The actual difference in the number of cases in each class when classified by 1950 and 1960 social-class position is not great as indicated in Table 6.1, p. 122. The difference, however, does raise the question of whether it is legitimate to relate data on class differences in treatment to differences in adjustment and *vice versa*. Further detailed analyses of the data which are not reported here indicate that no major errors are introduced in this procedure. Data were analyzed separately for patients who were stable in their class position between 1950 and 1960 as well as for patients who were socially mobile. No evidence was found, for example, to indicate that the use of adjustment data to interpret differences in discharge was distorted by the change of classification procedures using the 1950 social-class position in Chapters 4 and 5 and the 1960 social-class position in Chapters 7, 8, and 9.

TABLE 6.1

**Social Mobility of Patients and Controls, 1950 to 1960, by
1950 Social Class (Per Cent)**

| | 1950 Social Class | | | |
	I–III [a]	IV	V	Total
A. Patients and Controls				
Stable				
Patients	75	63	90	74
Controls	86	75	93	84
Difference	−11	−12	−3	−10
B. Patients and Controls				
Upwardly Mobile				
Patients	6	7	10	8
Controls	—	11	7	7
Difference	6	−4	3	1
C. Patients and Controls				
Downwardly Mobile				
Patients	19	30	[b]	18
Controls	14	14	[b]	9
Difference	5	16	[b]	9

[a] Although classes I–III are combined in this table, mobility was defined as movement from one class to another.
[b] Not applicable.

In most follow-up studies the standard for the comparison of patient performance has been other patients. Former patients distinguished by some attribute, such as type of previous treatment, age, or sex, are compared with other former patients who differ with respect to these attributes. In other studies, the patients serve as their own "controls" in a "before-after" design. For example, studies of patients treated by lobotomy compare the work records of patients before hospitalization and after discharge to determine if their occupational performance is significantly influenced by the treatment received.[14]

In this research, the adjustment of patients is compared to that of their matched controls who have not been treated for mental illness. However, patients are not contrasted with their controls as a single group. Since the treatment agency itself is an important variable, the 1950

---

[14] See, for example, M. Greenblatt, E. Robertson, and H. C. Solomon, "Five-Year Follow-Up of 100 Cases of Bilateral Prefrontal Lobotomy," *JAMA*, 151, 200 (1953).

hospital patients and clinic patients are analyzed separately.[15] A crucial issue involved in this division by treatment agency, as discussed earlier, is that hospitalization removes the individual from the community. Therefore, the fact that some clinic patients were hospitalized during the 10-year period may contaminate the design. Of the 133 clinic patients studied, 32 (24 per cent) were hospitalized at some time during the 10-year period; 11 of these were hospitalized at follow-up or death, and five had died in the community before 1960, so these 16 were not included in the interview sample. Thus, only 16 of the 108 former clinic patients interviewed (15 per cent) had received some hospital treatment.

The hospital experience of these patients was quite different from that of the 1950 hospital group: 13 of the 16 were hospitalized for less than three months, while the other three patients were hospitalized for from three months to a year. Most of these patients had multiple hospitalizations so that the average length of time each individual was hospitalized was extremely short—24 days. In other words, the few clinic patients who were hospitalized were removed from the community only briefly, whereas all hospital patients were institutionalized for extended periods of time.[16]

The testing of Hypothesis Three—that social class is related to the former patient's adjustment *in the community*—is much more complicated than the testing of the first two hypotheses. The test of Hypotheses One and Two was limited to the patient population, and variations in the independent variable (social class) could be related directly to the dependent variable (follow-up status, treatment outcome, type therapy, etc.). However, the testing of the third hypothesis is not limited to the patient population. Since a control group is used, treated mental illness is itself a third major variable, along with social class and community adjustment, which complicates testing the hypothesis. Thus, the hypothesis contains two independent and one dependent variable, and requires some form of multivariate analysis.[17]

---

[15] See Chapter 4, pp. 76–78 for a discussion of the differences between hospital and clinic patients.

[16] The median length of inpatient care for hospital patients was 12 months, while the mean length was 45 months. Only 12 per cent were hospitalized less than one month.

[17] Some form of analysis of variance design might have been used to determine the independent and interaction effects of the independent variables. Unfortunately, because of measurement and sampling problems, analysis of variance tests or multiple and partial correlation and regression techniques cannot be used consistently. The discharged patients are not a random sample of all patients, but a biased sample—albeit the population of discharged patients—of the total treated-patient population. However, some multivariate solution to the problem must be used, since the hypothesis contains three terms—two independent and one dependent variable.

We employed standard multivariate techniques designed for survey research data to test Hypothesis Three, proceeding serially from our preliminary question of whether or not mental illness is related to adjustment to our more important question of whether or not *social class accounts for adjustment differences*, i.e., the differences which exist between the patients and their controls. The hypothesis is tested by determining whether the social class of patients accounts for any patient-control differences in adjustment and may be demonstrated in the following way:

First, we determine if patients and controls differ with respect to a given measure of adjustment. Next, we determine if there are class differences in adjustment among patients. Then we determine if class differences in adjustment are found among the controls. Finally, we cross-classify patients and controls by social class to determine whether or not patient-control differences are constant for each social class. If the patient-control differences at each class level are the same and therefore, by extension, the same as the differences for the total patient and total control groups, we must conclude that social-class differences do not make a difference in adjustment and that all differences are due to the treated mental illness itself. If, however, the patients and controls differ significantly at one class level, but do not differ significantly at other class levels, then we must conclude that social class is related to community adjustment.

SUMMARY

As an introduction to the test of the third hypothesis of the follow-up study, that *social class is related to the former patient's adjustment in the community*, we have introduced the concept of community adjustment. Community adjustment is conceptualized as having two dimensions—the psychobiological and the social. The psychobiological dimension is measured by an index of mental status and family reports of symptomatic behavior. The latter dimension, the social, reflects the ability of the individual to perform crucial social roles in the community. It is measured by work-role performance and participation in formal and informal groups.

The test of the third hypothesis involves certain methodological as well as theoretical problems. To begin with, 1960 social-class position is used. Next, the study design contrasts the adjustment of patients with that of controls and takes into account the differences in treatment agencies by examining hospital and clinic patients separately. Finally, methods of analysis designed to test the third hypothesis are examined.

adjustment in the community: I. the psychobiological dimension

In this chapter we shall make the initial test of our third hypothesis—
*that social class is related to the former patient's adjustment in the com-
munity*—by examining the psychobiological dimension of adjustment.
Two indicators of psychobiological adjustment are analyzed: an index of
mental status and family reports of patient behavior.[1]

---

[1] The psychobiological aspect of adjustment may itself be conceptualized as multidimensional including physical-biological and psychological functions. Because of the
nature of the problem under study, particular attention is paid to psychiatrically
identifiable symptoms and functions, including somatic symptoms generally considered to be psychosomatic. While data were collected on nonpsychological medical
problems and symptoms, the results of the analysis were essentially negative. Patients
and controls were little different with respect to physical problems and limitations.

To examine further the psychobiological adjustment of former patients, we adopted
and constructed a series of scales to measure 10 specific dimensions of personality,
such as suspiciousness and obsessive-compulsive ideations. While these scales support
the findings presented for our general measure of mental status, the problem of scale
construction and interpretation for 10 different measures is so great that presentation
of this material adds little to the substantive findings, in addition to introducing a
complex problem in interpretation which might be confusing to the reader. Therefore, the analysis presented in this chapter is restricted first to a general measure of
mental status and second to a report of symptomatic behavior of the patients by
family members.

THE INDEX OF MENTAL STATUS

Traditionally, mental status has been assessed through a clinical psychiatric examination designed to establish a global summary emphasizing higher-order adaptive, integrative, and discriminatory functions. Typically, the clinical evaluation relies upon responses to both structured and unstructured questions and to the interviewer's rating of the respondent's behavior during the interview process itself, with particular attention paid to attitudes, manners, gestures, gross motor behavior, and other evidences of thought and emotional processes.[2] For research purposes, however, clinical mental status examinations are not very satisfactory, as there has been so far little standardization or quantification of mental status evaluation. Generally, evaluations stress individual variation and are used to diagnose and treat the patient's unique psychological problems. Furthermore, they are lengthy and require a trained psychiatrist to administer, and when large numbers of cases are involved the cost becomes almost prohibitive even if sufficient psychiatric manpower is available.

As an alternative to the complete clinical examination for mental status, short, screening devices have been developed. Commonly, specific physical, psychological, or psychosomatic symptoms have been used as critical indicators of psychological impairment both in clinical settings and in research. A number of instruments have been developed which are self-administered by respondents, administered by interviewers, or administered by some combination of the two.

---

[2] Among the factors enumerated are: the respondent's general appearance and behavior (descriptive); the stream of talk (its amount, rate, rhythm, coherence, presence of idiosyncratic words or expressions, etc.); mood (depressed, elated, variations, appropriateness, worries, suicidal ideation, physical symptoms related to depression, etc.); content and expression of self-concept; presence of concreteness of thought; fears, dreams, etc.; and sensorium. The latter is an evaluation of mental grasp and capacity which employs, for the most part, simple structured questions of a clinical-psychological nature which evaluate: consciousness and orientation with respect to time, place, person, and situation; memory (remote and recent, and testing of immediate retention and recall); grasp of general information; calculation; reading, writing, and speech; judgment (ability to make reasonable plans and to give due value to practical considerations); and insight (realization of failures of memory or other capacities and appreciation of presence of disorder). Finally, in modern dynamic psychiatry, a central and underlying concern in the total evaluation is the presence of and variation in expression of anxiety. In sum, the clinician forms by direct examination a rather complex and more or less comprehensive picture of the individual's functioning.

The first widely employed mental-status screening instrument was the Neuropsychiatric Screening Adjunct developed during World War II.[3] As millions of men had to be screened by the armed services before induction, the necessity for securing a quick assessment of the mental status of large numbers of individuals was of paramount importance. Following World War II, other instruments were developed which could be readily administered in the field by nonpsychiatrists to a large number of individuals for epidemiological and community studies of mental illness. In the Nova Scotia studies, Macmillan developed a 16-item scale, the Health Opinion Survey (H.O.S.) which was based, in part, on the World War II Neuropsychiatric Screening Adjunct.[4] Rennie and Srole used a number of the same questions in the Midtown Study, as did Phillips in a recent study in New England, and, finally, Rogler and Hollingshead also used the H.O.S. scale in their Puerto Rican study.[5] Gurin and his associates modified the scale further and utilized it in a nationwide survey of mental health.[6]

Scales, such as those mentioned above, may not be notably successful in identifying a particular individual with a particular set of psychological problems, except for extremely disturbed or impaired individuals. Our interest, however, is primarily in groups of people not individuals, and research indicates that these mental-health scales or symptom inventories are reliable and valid in discriminating between groups of psychiatric patients and controls. In the Stirling County, Nova Scotia, Midtown, and Puerto Rican studies they differentiated between respondents diagnosed by psychiatrists as having psychiatric problems and respondents judged as not having such difficulties. More recently, Manis et al. have

---

[3] S. A. Stouffer, A. A. Lumsdaine, M. H. Lumsdaine, R. M. Williams, M. B. Smith, I. L. Janis, S. A. Star, and L. S. Cottrell, *American Soldier: Combat and Its Aftermath*, Vol. II, Princeton University Press, Princeton, N.J., 1949, Chapters 9, 13, and 14.

[4] Allister M. Macmillan, "The Health Opinion Survey: Technique for Estimating Prevalence of Psychoneurotic and Related Types of Disorder in Communities," *Psychological Reports*, 3, 325 (1957), and D. C. Leighton et al., *The Character of Danger*, Basic Books, New York, 1963, Chapter 7.

[5] Leo Srole et al., *Mental Health in the Metropolis*, McGraw-Hill, New York, 1962, especially Chapter 4 and Appendices E and F; Derek L. Phillips, "The 'True Prevalence' of Mental Illness in a New England State," *Community Mental Health Journal*, 2, 35 (1966); Lloyd H. Rogler and A. B. Hollingshead, *Trapped: Families and Schizophrenia*, Wiley, New York, 1965, pp. 22–27.

[6] Gerald Gurin, Joseph Veroff, and Sheila Feld, *Americans View their Mental Health: A Nationwide Interview Survey*, Basic Books, New York, 1960, pp. 175–205.

demonstrated that such a mental-health scale distinguished between groups of hospitalized patients and nonhospitalized individuals.[7]

While these scales can be demonstrated to be valid and reliable indices of psychiatric impairment, sometimes certain technical problems are encountered, and these should be recognized clearly. For example, social-class bias as well as interviewer bias may influence the reporting of symptomatic behavior. Such problems are common not only to these scales but to any interview or examination. In this study such problems were reduced as far as possible in standard ways: interviewer training, random assignment of interviewers to patients as well as to controls, rephrasing of questions where necessary to ensure understanding, careful editing to determine the internal consistency of the interview-schedule responses, and, in cases where questions arose, recontacting the respondent. As a result of the organization of the schedule and the structure of the interview, we find no reason to suspect that systematic biases influenced the responses to the mental-status scale or to any other interview-schedule item.

The instrument we selected to measure mental status is the 20-item symptom list used by Gurin and his associates. It includes specific psychological, physical, and psychosomatic symptoms which are diagnostic indicators of psychological distress. The index measures selected aspects of the individual's physical health, psychological and physical anxiety, and psychological symptomatology. The wording of two questions from the original scale has been modified slightly, but this does not impair the basic structure of the scale.[8] The questions used in the scale, the response categories, and the weights assigned to each response category are presented in Appendix 4.

Scoring of the responses is consistent with the scoring used by Gurin and his associates. Briefly the scoring system is as follows: For each individual answering the 20 questions the response weights, as indicated in Appendix 4, are totaled, providing a single numerical score to represent the mental status of the individual. For example, *1* indicates the continuous presence of a given symptom and *4* the complete absence of the symptom. If an individual gave a response of "unknown" to three or fewer items, the average score for the balance of items actually answered by the respondent was assigned to the one, two, or three items which the respondent did not answer. If the respondent was not able to or did not answer more than three items, the total scale score was not computed

---

[7] Jerome G. Manis, Milton J. Brawer, Chester L. Hunt, and Leonard C. Kercher, "Validating a Mental Health Scale," *American Sociological Review*, 28, 108 (1963).
[8] The two changes were made to clarify terms, as noted in Appendix 4.

and the individual respondent was dropped from this section of the analysis. Because of this procedure, scores were not computed for 18 (6 per cent) of the patients who were interviewed in the community.[9]

The total scale scores range from *24* to *80*. An individual with a score of *24* is maximally impaired, that is he has indicated that all 20 of the symptoms of stress indicated by the questions are present nearly all the time. A score of *80* would indicate the total absence of symptoms.[10] The results of other studies demonstrate that relatively low scores identify individuals with major psychological problems and that a cut-off point may be selected which will distinguish this group with a high degree of psychological impairment.[11] The cut-off point used in this study is based on the procedure followed by Jackson in his analysis of Gurin's data,[12] and the distribution of scores indicates a clustering above and below the cut-off point. Individuals with numerical scores of *66* or less are assigned to the "psychologically impaired" group, i.e., their symptoms are greater in number and/or severity than those with scores of *67* or above.[13] We pre-

---

[9] In addition, two young adolescent patients were excluded since we did not interview controls for them as indicated in Chapter 2. The characteristics of the 20 respondents for whom scores were not computed are as follows: *sex:* male, 13 (65%), female, 7 (35%); *social class:* I–III, 3 (15%), IV, 7 (35%), V, 10 (50%); *marital status:* unmarried, 13 (65%), married, 3 (15%), single, divorced, widowed, 4 (20%); *religion:* Catholic, 13 (65%), Protestant, 6 (30%), Jewish, 1 (5%); *agency:* hospital, 11 (55%), clinic, 9 (45%); *age:* 34 or less, 12 (60%), 35–44, 2 (10%), 45–54, 1 (5%), 55–64, 3 (15%), 65 or more, 2 (10%); *diagnosis:* neurotic, 10 (50%), schizophrenic, 2 (10%), affective, 5 (25%), other psychotic, 3 (15%).

[10] A score of 80 is technically a legitimate score, but in practice it is unlikely that many individuals are totally free of all symptoms indicated in the mental-status scale. Only 17 nonpatients and 3 patients have such scores, and careful examination of the cases indicates that these respondents have few psychological problems. It is evident that symptoms indicated in the check list are so infrequent as to be disregarded consciously by these respondents as problems. While technically competent individuals such as professional workers are more likely to indicate some health problems, it is not surprising to find that of 603 respondents for whom scores could be completed 20 are healthy enough to view themselves as being free from symptoms. The range of test scores is approximately the same for patients (36 to 80) and controls (39 to 80), but the patients are more likely to have low scores.

[11] For example, see Srole et al., *loc. cit.*, and Manis, et al., *loc. cit.*

[12] See Elton F. Jackson, "Status Consistency and Symptoms of Stress," *American Sociological Review,* 27, 469 (1962).

[13] Since the mental-health scale combines the number and frequency of symptoms into an ordinal scale, operationally we can interpret any given score as indicating a greater degree of psychiatric impairment than any higher-order score. While the rank-order statistics for analysis could be used, we decided instead to dichotomize the respondents as described. Thus, the tests will be more conservative though less sensitive, and the presentation will be simplified.

sent two cases to illustrate the severe psychological problems of persons classified as "psychologically impaired" (scores of 66 or less).

Mr. H., a class V clinic patient, has a Gurin score of 56. His last contact with a psychiatrist was in 1955 when he was diagnosed as psychoneurotic with somatic reaction. At present he describes himself as without energy, unable to sleep, and bothered by recurrent pains, ailments, and headaches. Ill health has forced him to change his job recently. Although he works regularly he claims that a full day's work is possible only because of the "energy pills" prescribed by a local general practitioner and because he avoids all social contacts and outside activities to conserve his energy. Other than his regular work he does nothing. He is, according to his wife, a completely apathetic person. He would like to return to the psychiatric outpatient clinic he attended formerly, but with his low income, heavy debts, and family responsibilities he feels he cannot afford to pay for both his "energy pills" and "talks with the psychiatrist."

Mrs. G., a class IV housewife, has a variety of psychiatric problems which are reflected in her Gurin score of 54. Diagnosed as a schizophrenic, paranoid type, she was treated in a state hospital until 1952. Since then she has been rehospitalized once and has been in outpatient clinic treatment on two occasions. She takes vitamin pills regularly for her health and has been on maintenance dosages of tranquilizers at times. Mrs. G. describes herself as nervous and unable to "get going" and to sleep or eat properly; the year before we interviewed her she lost 14 pounds in three weeks from nervous vomiting. Recently she has had extreme difficulty in getting up in the morning. She worries unduly about her children's school grades and is afraid she may have a nervous breakdown because of them. She complains that no one appreciates her and that people keep watching her. Her feelings are hurt easily and she cries often. During the study interview she broke down and cried several times.

The percentage of hospital and clinic patients and their matched controls with scores in the impaired range are presented in Table 7.1. As we might expect, more of the hospital patients are "impaired" than their matched controls, as measured by the index of mental status; the outpatient clinic patient-control difference in the proportion with scores in the impaired range is equally striking.

Readers may be surprised at the large percentage of former clinic patients with scores in the impaired range, but it must be remembered that we are dealing with former patients, none of whom are hospitalized at present although some are in outpatient treatment. Also the nature of the institutional treatment for clinic and hospital patients may help to

TABLE 7.1

Patients and Controls with Mental-Status Scores in the Impaired Range

	Hospital		Clinic	
	%	n	%	n
Patients	40	193	49	99
Controls	20	193	17	99
Difference	20 [a]		32 [a]	

1950 Treatment Agency (spanning Hospital and Clinic)

[a] Patient-control difference, χ^2 test, $p < .05$.

account for the slightly higher rate of impairment among the former.[14] Clinic patients are seldom legally committed for treatment as are most hospital patients so that they do not need to show any significant degree of improvement in their psychological condition in order to be released from treatment. Stated another way, the requirements for discharge for those committed to a hospital may be higher than for those in clinic treatment. In fact, previous studies show that frequently it is the failures who are discharged early from outpatient treatment in clinics or who quit at their own volition.[15] In contrast, the return of the hospital patient to the community involves serious readjustment problems, and the decision to discharge him is not made lightly. Because of legal considerations alone, failures are less likely to be discharged from hospital than from clinic care.

Another possible reason for the higher degree of impairment among clinic patients may be that the mental-status scale is sensitive to diffuse anxiety. Frequently, such anxiety is directly indicative of the specific types of psychiatric problems more common to clinic patients who are predominantly neurotic than to hospital patients who are predominantly psychotic. However, the fact that we are dealing with *former patients* is probably the critical point. Rogler and Hollingshead who studied individuals with no previous psychiatric treatment utilized a similar type of scale and secured a professional psychiatric diagnosis for each respondent. Their study indicated that in a previously untreated sample those subsequently diagnosed as schizophrenic were the "sickest" according to the

---

[14] For a fuller discussion of this point, see Chapter 5.
[15] Jerome K. Myers and Frank Auld, Jr., "Some Variables Related to Outcome of Psychotherapy," *Journal of Clinical Psychology*, XI, 51 (1955).

H.O.S. scale, those diagnosed as neurotic were next, and those adjudged to have no mental illness were the least sick.[16] This schizophrenic-neurotic distinction corresponds closely to the diagnostic differences between our former hospital and former clinic patients, yet in dealing with a previously treated group the order of impairment is reversed, suggesting thereby that institutional differences in discharge may, in part, account for our findings that a higher proportion of former clinic patients than former hospital patients have mental-status scores in the impaired range. (We will return to this line of argument later in this chapter since the explanation is relevant to the differences found among the various social classes.)

While it is clear that a higher proportion of former patients than their matched controls are psychiatrically impaired, the crucial issue in our research is whether or not the degree of patient and nonpatient impairment in the community is related to social class. It is to this issue which we now turn.

SOCIAL CLASS AND MENTAL STATUS: HOSPITAL PATIENTS

In this section, data are presented on the relationship between social class and mental status of the former hospitalized patients. In examining community adjustment, classes I, II, and III are combined to provide enough cases for statistical calculations. In order to present the findings as clearly as possible, percentages are used in all tables in the remainder of the book when patients and controls are compared. The actual numbers are presented for the interested reader in Appendix 2.

Findings concerning the relationship between social class and mental status for the hospitalized patients are presented in Table 7.2. By reading the row labeled "Controls" in Table 7.2, it becomes clear that social class is related to mental status: the lower the class the greater the proportion of individuals with impaired mental status. The percentage of controls psychologically impaired jumps from 6 in classes I–III through 21 in class IV to 25 in class V. This inverse relationship between social class and mental status is consistent with epidemiological studies which have been carried out in a variety of settings.[17]

Shifting attention from these base-line data to the percentage distribution of former hospitalized patients with scores in the impaired range, we find that the expected inverse relationship does not exist. Indeed, the highest-class patient group, classes I–III, had the greatest proportion of

---

16 Rogler and Hollingshead, *loc. cit.*
17 For example, see Srole et al., *op. cit.*, pp. 230–34; D. C. Leighton et al., *loc. cit.;* and Phillips, *op. cit.*

TABLE 7.2

Hospital Patients and Controls with Mental-Status Scores in the Impaired Range (Per Cent) [a]

	Social Class			
	I–III	IV	V	Total
Patients [b]	56	33	39	40
Controls [b]	6	21	25	20
Difference	50	12 [c]	14	20

[a] Unless otherwise stated, social-class and patient-control differences, x^2 test, $p < .05$.
[b] Differences by social class, x^2 test, $p < .10$.
[c] Patient-control difference, x^2 test, $p < .20$.

persons with scores in the impaired range, 56 per cent, followed by class V with 39 per cent and class IV with 33 per cent.

The reversal in the relationship between social class and impaired mental status, as we move from controls to patients, indicates that social class is indeed related to the mental status of the former hospital patients. This is confirmed further by examining the patient-control differences. The greatest patient-control difference, 50 percentage points, is found in classes I–III. In contrast, the proportion of patients with impaired mental status is only 12 per cent more than for the controls in class IV and 14 per cent more than in class V. Thus, social class is related to the mental-status differences which exist between patients and controls. The patient-control difference in the proportion of cases with scores in the impaired range is greatest at the class I–III level and is least at the class IV and V level. Stated in another way, compared to their matched controls, former upper- and middle-class patients are less well-adjusted than patients at other class levels according to the mental-status index.

To determine whether other factors account for these class differences, we controlled sequentially for the biological, social, and psychiatric variables used in previous chapters, omitting race since very few nonwhites were discharged and living in the community in 1960.[18] In addition, we

---

[18] Since the patients and controls were matched on the basis of age, sex, race, marital status, and religion, these factors do not account for the patient-control differences in mental status at any one class level. However, the variations which arise in the comparison of patient-control differences between classes, classes I–III and class IV, for example, might be influenced by these variables since the difference may be traced to class variation within the patient population itself. For example, assume that mental-status impairment is related to age for patients but not for controls; older

included two variables unique to the experience of the discharged hospital patients, length of time discharged from hospital prior to June 1, 1960 and 1950 to 1960 type of psychiatric treatment. The procedure followed in controlling was similar to that used in previous chapters.[19]

---

patients who have been mentally ill may be more likely to be psychologically impaired than younger former patients. If the former upper-class patients are on the average significantly older than former lower-class patients, we would expect to find that class I–III patients are more impaired but that the difference is not due to class but rather to age differences. Thus, the high proportion of classes I–III with impaired mental status could be caused by the fact that this group differs markedly in age from the class IV and class V groups, for example, if this factor were related to mental status.

[19] Detailed cross-classifications for the patients and controls were made, contrasting patient and control relationships between social class and mental status within more refined categories. To eliminate any influence of sex difference between social classes, for example, the relationship between social class and mental status was examined for males; then the relationship was examined only for females. Because of the smaller number of cases than in Chapters 4 and 5 some control categories had to be combined with others or eliminated. Therefore, the controlling procedure was carried out for the following categories: (a) sex—male, female; (b) age—44 years of age or less, 45 years and over; (c) religion—Protestant, Catholic; (d) marital status—single, married, separated–divorced–widowed, in 1960; (e) length of hospitalization—entered hospital 1949 or 1950, entered hospital 1948 or earlier; (f) previous psychiatric hospitalization—hospitalized previously, not hospitalized previously; (g) major 1950 psychiatric treatment—psychotherapy, organic therapy, custodial care; (h) type hospital by sponsorship—state, veterans–private; (i) diagnosis—schizophrenic-paranoid, affective psychotic; (j) length of time discharged from hospital prior to June 1, 1960—in the community five years or longer, in the community less than five years; (k) major 1950 to 1960 psychiatric treatment—psychotherapy, somatotherapy, drug therapy, custodial care. Although analyses were not made for race because of the small number of Negroes, all previous tests have shown no class differences by race.

In this and the following two chapters, whenever control variables are introduced for former hospital patients and their controls, the above variables and categories are utilized unless otherwise indicated. As the number of cases may be too small with the detailed cross-tabulations to analyze every category, we simply indicate the total number of analyses made for the possible 26 categories. Summary results are reported and any exceptions to the expected pattern which appear systematically are presented. Since we are interested in social-class patterns of patient-control differences, we cannot use the chi-square test as in previous chapters where we were interested only in patient differences by class. Therefore, in each instance, we determine the exact class pattern of patient-control differences and set the control standards accordingly. The expected pattern is considered present in this case if the patient-control difference is greatest in classes I–III and is at least 10 percentage points higher than the next greatest difference. In 25 of the 26 tables generated by the controlling procedure, class I–III patients are more impaired than other patients and the greatest patient-control difference is found at this class level.

The results of the control analyses may be summarized as follows: The original relationship between social class and posttreatment adjustment as measured by the index of mental status is not accounted for by the control variables. While the greatest degree of impairment is in classes I–III, the least degree of impairment fluctuates between classes IV and V, and consequently the patient-control difference is minimal about as often for class IV as for class V. This lack of a clear-cut difference between the two lowest classes of patients in the degree of mental-status impairment is not unexpected in view of the minimal overall difference between these two groups, as noted in Table 7.2.

The finding that former patients in classes I–III are more likely to be psychologically impaired than patients in other classes but still remain in the community seems to reflect a number of class-related factors. First, as we have indicated in previous chapters, upper- and middle-class patients are more likely to use outpatient treatment facilities following hospital discharge. Second, we have found also that these patients are more likely to receive the support and assistance of family members. Third, upper- and middle-class patients are more likely to have access to a variety of resources—family, economic, and community—which assist them in coping with their psychological impairment. Finally, it may be that the upper- and middle-class former hospital patients are better able to cope with their psychological problems because they possess more insight into them. Such factors are clearly evident in the following cases presented as illustrations.

In 1950 Mr. B., a class I, married man, was discharged from a private hospital where he had been diagnosed as a schizophrenic, catatonic type. Following his discharge he resumed his career as an attorney but found his independent practice too demanding. Through his professional and personal contacts he was able to find a position in the legal department of a large organization. Several years later he changed to his present governmental position and has been active in a variety of local, national, and international professional associations, assuming responsibility for organizing and conducting professional meetings and activities. Beyond his professional activities, he takes part in a variety of community social groups and actively participates in a number of sports. He has been able to provide a comfortable life for his wife and three children. Despite his success in these areas, he still has a number of psychological complaints which, from time to time, make it difficult for him to be as active as he wishes to be. His major complaints to date are "tension and insomnia." More specific complaints are reflected in his Gurin score (55): feelings of nervousness, inability to work efficiently, headaches, nightmares, and dizziness; additional complaints are "tiring easily," "disturbed potency," and "recurrent ulcers." To cope with these complex psychobiological problems, Mr. B. has remained in private outpatient treatment. Although in 1960 he spent over $1000 for therapy, sedatives, and tranquilizers, his income is sufficiently large so that the cost of his continuous treatment does not create any financial hardship for him or his family.

Mr. C. is a 32-year-old, class III male with a diagnosis of schizophrenia, paranoid type. Since his discharge from a private hospital, which his lower-middle-class parents insisted on using despite the financial hardship, he has married, had two children, and secured a position with a large business firm. Although he frequently finds it necessary to use paid sick leave because of his "nervous condition," he is a relatively stable employee and has received the normal promotions we would expect of any other worker in a similar organization. Socially, Mr. C. is active, visiting family and friends as well as participating in a variety of other informal and formal social and religious groups.

The psychological problems of Mr. C. to which he refers as his "nervous condition," are reflected not only by his periodic absences from work, but also by his complaints of restlessness and his worries about his health, fear of another "nervous breakdown," and inability to make decisions. Consistent with his diagnosis at discharge, he worries about "personal enemies" and feels that "people are against me with no good reason." Specific psychosomatic complaints include inability to sleep, headaches, loss of appetite, weight loss during periods of acute anxiety, and cold sweats.

The private hospital in which Mr. C. was treated in 1950 specialized in organic therapy. He views the electroshock therapy he received as the one thing which "cured" him and which continues to be a viable form of therapy when it becomes difficult to cope with the "nervous condition." Again as a result of a certain level of insight, Mr. C. is able to recognize the signs and symptoms which preceded his earlier hospitalization. When these conditions arise, he uses a day of his company's paid sick leave to get an electroshock treatment in an outpatient clinic, returning to work the next day.

SOCIAL CLASS AND MENTAL STATUS: CLINIC PATIENTS

As is the case of former hospital patients, at each class level a higher percentage of clinic patients than controls has impaired mental status scores (see Table 7.3). Furthermore, the same general relationship between social class and impaired mental status is found among controls; the largest proportion of impaired individuals is found in class V. However, among clinic patients the largest group with impaired mental status

TABLE 7.3

Clinic Patients and Controls with Mental-Status Scores in the Impaired Range (Per Cent) [a]

	Social Class			
	I–III	IV	V	Total
Patients	41	38	75	49
Controls [b]	16	13	25	17
Difference	25	25	50	32

[a] Unless otherwise stated, social-class and patient-control differences, χ^2 test, $p < .05$.
[b] Differences by social class, χ^2 test, $p > .20$.

scores (75 per cent) is in class V instead of classes I–III, as with hospitalized patients. Thus, the same relationship between social class and mental status characterizes both clinic patients and their controls.

The patient-control difference is also greatest in class V, 50 per cent as compared to 25 per cent in the other classes. The magnitude of the differences at the various class levels indicates quite strongly the high degree of impairment to be found among the lower-class patients who were treated in 1950 outpatient agencies.

To determine whether or not these class differences are influenced by other factors, we followed the same control procedure as previously described for the hospital cases. Not all of the variables are relevant in the case of clinic patients, however, so we used only 12 control categories.[20] Although the introduction of these control variables reduces

---

[20] The following variables are not included here for the reasons cited: (a) 1950 treatment is not included because psychotherapy was the only treatment received by most clinic patients; (b) 1950 to 1960 treatment is not included for the same reason; (c) type of hospital is excluded since all patients were in outpatient clinics; and (d) length of time out of treatment is excluded because most patients were in the community during any treatment period. Some other categories are also dropped because of insufficient cases. Wherever the number of cases was sufficiently great we tested for the following seven control variables divided into 12 categories: (a) *sex*—male, female; (b) *age*—44 or less, 45 or more; (c) *religion* —Catholic, Protestant; (d) *marital status*—married, other than married; (e) *length of previous treatment*—entered treatment in 1949 or 1950; (f) *previous psychiatric treatment*—some, none; (g) *diagnosis*—neurotic. These seven categories will be used in the controlling procedure followed in the analysis of clinic patients in each of the following two chapters. Summary results will be presented and exceptions to

markedly the number of cases within each category and within each social class, the same general pattern found for the total clinic patients obtains: class V former clinic patients have the greatest proportion of cases in the impaired range, and the patient-control differences are generally greatest at the class V level.[21]

In brief, the greatest degree of impairment is found among class V clinic patients. These patients, when compared both to patients at other class levels and to their controls, show severe mental-status impairment. This finding is in marked contrast to the relationship found for the hospital patients in which class I–III former patients are more likely to have scores in the impaired range and differ most from their matched controls.

FAMILY EVALUATION OF SYMPTOMATIC BEHAVIOR

So far in this chapter, psychobiological adjustment has been measured by an index of mental status based upon psychological, physical, and psychosomatic symptoms reported by patients and their controls. On the basis of respondents' perceptions and reports of their behavior, significant social-class differences are found in the degree of psychological impairment. To test further this relationship between social class and psychobiological adjustment, data were gathered to determine if patients' reports of impaired behavior were confirmed by others in the household.[22]

In this section we focus specifically on the patient's psychological impairment as perceived by members of his family. The informants were presented a list of behavioral items considered symptomatic of psychiatric illness and were given a choice of three degrees of frequency of patient behavior: frequently, occasionally, or never. These items have been used in a number of previous studies and range from such relatively innocuous

---

the expected pattern which appear systematically will be presented. The expected pattern is considered present in this instance if the patient-control difference is greatest in class V and is at least 10 percentage points higher than the next greatest difference.

[21] In 11 of the 12 tables generated by the controlling procedures, class V patients are more impaired than other patients and the greatest patient-control difference is found at this class level.

[22] No attempt was made to secure comparable data for the controls by interviewing a member of the control's family. It is clear that the availability of data from a family respondent would have been useful to analyze the dynamics of psychological impairment in the control group in contrast to a former patient group. While the advantage of such data was foreseen in the construction of the research design, the cost involved in interviewing a family member of a control respondent precluded the inclusion of such a group. Eighteen household informant interviews are not included in the analyses because of insufficient information.

questions as "Does (the patient) appear nervous?" to items indicating severe adjustment problems such as attempted suicide or indecent exposure.

All the questions used to measure symptomatic behavior were included in the Boston follow-up study by Freeman and Simmons.[23] They found that these items distinguished between former patients who had to be rehospitalized and those who were able to remain out of treatment during the period covered by their study.

The problem of perceptual biases of family informants in reporting patient behavior is a crucial issue in the measurement of symptomatic behavior by this method. Freeman and Simmons point out that family reports may incorporate the systematic perceptual biases of the informants. Since the response categories of *frequently*, *occasionally*, and *never* represent judgments that informants make according to their own ideas of normal frequency, such reports may not be consistent with the evaluations of others. However, Freeman and Simmons present evidence that family-informant responses are reliable when viewed as a test-retest situation.[24]

The responses of household informants are presented in Table 7.4. The categories *frequently* and *occasionally* are combined as positive responses which reduces the problem of judging frequency. The first point to note is that the rank order of responses is very similar to that found by Freeman and Simmons.[25] The next point concerns differences between hospital and clinic cases. Although the rank order is somewhat similar for these two groups, there are important differences related to the severity of the symptoms. Former hospital patients were reported more frequently as exhibiting symptoms characteristic of psychosis: stays by self, talks without making sense, talks to self, appears in a daze, thinks people are talking about him/her, and hears voices. In contrast, clinic patients more frequently were reported to be nervous and to drink too much of alcoholic beverages.

Turning now to our main interest, we determined social-class differences in the frequency with which individual symptomatic behavior was reported. Following our usual procedure, 1950 hospital and 1950 clinic cases were analyzed separately. The procedure utilized in the examination of the reports of symptomatic behavior was as follows: we examined

---

[23] H. W. Freeman and O. G. Simmons, *The Mental Patient Comes Home*, Wiley, New York, 1963, pp. 61–67.

[24] *Ibid.*, p. 62.

[25] *Ibid.* Freeman and Simmons report only the proportions who respond *frequently* to the item presented, but they note that the findings hold for the *occasional* category as well.

TABLE 7.4

Symptomatic Behavior Exhibited by Patients, according to Household Informant (Per Cent) [a]

	1950 Patients		
	Total	Hospital	Clinic
Appears nervous	60	56	67 [b]
Worries or complains about his/her problems	40	38	42
Argues with family members	39	40	38
Stays by self	30	34	22 [c]
Thinks things look hopeless and his/her life is unhappy	29	30	27
Talks senselessly	24	30	13 [d]
Talks to self	23	29	12 [d]
Forgets to do important things	22	22	23
Appears in a daze	21	25	14 [c]
Fails to keep a time schedule	17	17	18
Thinks people are talking about him/her	15	17	11 [b]
Drinks too much of alcoholic beverages	11	8	17 [d]
Gets in debt by foolish buying	11	9	13
Curses when strangers are around	10	9	10
Tries to hit or hurt someone	8	8	8
Damages or wrecks things	7	7	9
Hears voices	8	11	3 [d]
Gets into arguments with neighbors	7	7	5
Cannot dress or take care of self	4	5	3
Tries to commit suicide	3	4	3
Exposes self indecently	—	1	0
$n =$	229	151	78

[a] In the chi-square test made between frequency of occurrence for hospital and clinic cases, $p > .20$ unless otherwise specified.
[b] $p < .20$.
[c] $p < .10$.
[d] $p < .05$.

each individual item to determine if the relationship between class and the reporting of the presence of a given symptom is consistent with the expected relationship. For hospital patients, we expected to find that the higher the social class of the patient, the more frequently the family respondents would report the presence of symptomatic behavior. A given item was adjudged to be consistent with the expected findings if there were order of magnitude differences greater than 10 percentage points in the expected direction. For example, among hospital patients the expected pattern was considered confirmed if the symptom was reported most frequently in classes I–III and was 10 percentage points higher than in class IV. Thus, 50 per cent of classes I–III but only 37 per cent of class IV and only 36 per cent of class V household respondents reported that the patient worries and complains about his/her problem. Therefore, these findings are adjudged to be consistent with the patient reports of mental-status impairment.

Because of the distribution of reported symptoms by class, the above procedure was used since there were frequently not enough cases in a cell to use tests of significance for each of the individual items. An approximate test was made by considering the total group of reported symptoms. If there were no systematic class differences in the reports of symptomatic behavior, we would expect no class variations in the reports, and if symptomatic reports were randomly distributed, class I–III patients would be reported to display more specific symptomatic behavior than patients in other classes for about one third, or seven, of the questions. The results of the test show, however, that informants reported the highest proportion of positive responses for former hospitalized patients in classes I–III for 12 symptoms, in class V for one symptom, in class IV for one symptom, and no difference by class for seven symptoms. Using the binomial theorem assuming order of magnitude differences of 10 per cent and random variation, the chances of finding 12 out of 21 symptoms in this predicted direction is less than .05.

The relationship between class and positive responses is the opposite among former clinic patients. The highest percentage of positive responses reporting symptomatic behavior occurred in class V for 14 symptoms, in classes I–III for only three symptoms, and no class difference for four symptoms. In no case was the highest proportion in class IV. Again, the probability of this distribution (14 out of 21) occurring by chance is less than .05. Thus, the reports of household informants concerning the presence of individual symptoms supports the hypothesis that social class is related to the psychobiological adjustment of former patients and reconfirms the relationship found for both hospital and clinic patients.

As an alternative test of the data and in order to reduce the responses to the individual symptoms to a more manageable form, a factor analysis was undertaken. Five items are loaded heavily and approximately equally on a single factor which accounted for most of the variation; these may be used as an overall index of reported symptomatic behavior. The percentage of positive responses on these items are as follows: (1) Patient appears nervous, 60 per cent; (2) patient worries and complains about his problems, 40 per cent; (3) patient thinks things look hopeless and life is unhappy, 29 per cent; (4) patient drinks too much of alcoholic beverages,

TABLE 7.5

		Social Class (Per Cent)			
		I–III	IV	V	Total
Symptom level [a]					
High symptom level		33	15	18	19
Low symptom level		67	85	82	81
	$n =$	21	52	78	151

$$\chi^2 = 3.35; \ df = 2; \ p < .05 \ \text{(one-tailed test)}$$

[a] Scores 3–5 represent high symptom levels and 0–2 low symptom levels.

12 per cent; (5) patient tries to hit and hurt people, 8 per cent; ($n = 229$). These five items were combined into a single scale by assigning for each item a score of *0* to a negative response and a score of *1* to a positive response (*occasionally* or *frequently*). For purposes of discussion, we refer to this measure as an index of symptom levels.

The relationship between the symptom level reported by family informants and social class for hospital patients is shown in Table 7.5.[26]

It is clear that family informants in the household of former class I–III hospital patients are more likely to report high symptom levels, while the family informants in the household of working- and lower-class patients report low symptom levels. Thus the relationship between symptom levels reported by family informants and the social class of former hospital patients is consistent with the relationship between social class and patient-reported mental status: the higher the class, the greater the degree of psychiatric impairment.

In contrast to the findings for former hospital patients, the class pattern is just the opposite among former clinic patients as shown in Table 7.6: the lower the class, the higher the proportion of patients with high symptom levels.[27]

In summary, the data on the patients' symptom level as reported by household informants strongly confirm the findings based on patients'

---

[26] Since these data were employed to evaluate mental status as reported previously by the patients, we were able to predict the direction of difference and thereby use a one-tailed test of significance.

[27] Since these data were employed to evaluate mental status as reported previously by the patients, we were able to predict the direction of difference and thereby use a one-tailed test of significance.

TABLE 7.6

		Social Class (Per Cent)		
		I–III	IV	V	Total
Symptom level [a]					
High symptom level		24	23	43	30
Low symptom level		76	77	57	70
	$n =$	25	30	23	78

$\chi^2 = 2.66$; $df = 2$; $p < .10$ (one-tailed test)

[a] Scores 3–5 represent high symptom levels and 0–2 low symptom levels.

mental-status scores. Social class is related to the degree of psychological impairment for both hospitalized and clinic patients but in opposite directions.

DISCUSSION

In this chapter we have looked in two ways at the relationship between social class and the level of psychological impairment of the former hospital and clinic patients. First, we examined differences in mental status as measured by the Gurin index, based upon the responses of the patients and their controls to a series of 20 items, and, second, we examined symptomatic behavior exhibited by patients, as reported by household respondents.

According to the mental-status index, at each class level a higher proportion of former patients than controls have scores in the impaired range. Among controls, there is, in general, an inverse relationship between social class and mental status: the lower the class, the higher the percentage impaired. There are also significant relationships between social class and mental status among former patients. However, the direction of the relationship differs according to treatment agency. Like their controls, the proportion of former clinic patients with impaired mental status is greatest in class V. Equally important, the difference in the percentage of patients and controls with impaired scores increases from the highest to the lowest class. In marked contrast not only is the proportion among former hospital patients in the impaired range greatest in classes I–III, but patient-control differences also are greatest at that level. Reports of symptomatic behavior by family respondents confirm these class differences.

In part, the reversal in the direction of association between social class and psychiatric impairment for former hospital and clinic patients may be because of the same differences in the institutional structuring of the treatment processes which we have earlier suggested account for hospital-clinic patient differences in mental-status impairment. From a social point of view, the mental patient's role in American society may be viewed as deviant, and psychiatric treatment agencies and practitioners, therefore, function in part as social-control agents. As control agents, psychiatrists or other practitioners may act in a variety of ways which range between two types. They may attempt to "reform" or rehabilitate the deviant by "curing" or "improving" him or they may remove him from society by hospitalization.

These two methods of handling deviant behavior are not mutually exclusive. Hospitalization, for example, may be not only a method of protecting society against the deviant but also a means of rehabilitation. However, if hospital therapy fails to produce significant improvement in the patient's symptoms or changes in his ability to function as a member of the community, institutionalization becomes in time primarily a means of isolating the patient from the rest of society. In fact, in some cases such removal, even initially, is the primary purpose of hospitalization.

These alternate approaches to social control available to the psychiatrist, however, are related to the institutional role played by psychiatrists or other practitioners. The psychiatric staff of the mental hospital not only may treat the patient but also restrict his range of movement in order to prolong treatment or to prevent his return to the community. In the clinic the role of the practitioner is limited to treating the patient, and, in general, the clinic psychiatrist has severely limited legitimate means of keeping the patient or guaranteeing that he will remain in treatment. Because of the different alternatives available to the hospital psychiatric staff, we may conceive of the staff as playing not only the role of a treatment agent but also that of gatekeeper—one who restricts the movement of the deviant out of the treatment agency into the community, as well as into the agency for treatment.

The impact of this additional role played by the staff of the psychiatric hospital may be one of the crucial factors accounting for the social-class differences in mental status for the hospital and clinic patients. Before a hospital patient is discharged from treatment it is generally necessary for the gatekeeper to make a decision about the advisability of his release. Patients must reach a minimal level of psychological and social functioning before discharge is considered. This level is not a rigid line, however, and psychological functioning alone is not a sufficient criterion for discharge. After the decision has been made that the appropriate minimal level of functioning has been reached, an equally important decision must be made on actual discharge. At this point, social factors become increasingly important. Consideration is given to the relevant effects of past factors related to the patient's attainment of the minimal level of functioning and also to factors which will operate in the family and community once he is released.

On the basis of available evidence, the staff may assume, and rightly so as we have indicated in Chapter 5, that upper- and middle-class patients are more likely to continue their treatment in outpatient agencies, whereas lower-class patients are less likely to do so. Moreover in abrogating the control role by releasing the patient the staff transfers the responsibility for the control of further potential deviance on the part of the patient to other individuals or agents in the community. If further treatment is required as the result, say, of psychological deterioration, the staff may take it for granted that the family of the higher-class patient will most likely assume the responsibility of returning the patient to treatment. In contrast, the lower-class patient goes back to a subculture in which the population is not likely to seek professional assistance for deviant behavior; such behavior may continue until it becomes so extreme that intervention by formal control agencies such as the police or courts becomes necessary. Evidence presented in Chapter 5 indicates that this is precisely what happens with former hospital patients: class I–III patients are more likely to be returned directly or indirectly by their family or through self-referral, while lower-class patients are more likely to be returned by the police or by court order.

Finally, giving due consideration to the welfare of the discharged patient, the gatekeeper probably assumes that the higher-status patient will have access to a variety of resources and facilities in the community, such as the availability of protected and less stressful employment and more social activities. Because of these class differences in the access to and use of treatment facilities, the process of readmission in the case of future deviant behavior, and the access to family and community resources, the gatekeeper probably requires for discharge of a lower-class patient a fairly high level of psychological functioning as compared to other patients. It is, therefore, not surprising to find that among the former hospital patients a smaller proportion of lower-class than higher-status patients are impaired psychologically.

Since former patients had been discharged from treatment for varying lengths of time when mental status was evaluated in the research interview, we do not know whether or not there had been significant changes in their mental status since discharge. Although we have no direct evidence of mental status at discharge, we do have data to indicate no class differences in the changes which did occur. We asked household informants to compare the patient's mental condition at the time of interview with his condition when he was released from the hospital or left treatment. Most informants felt the patient's mental condition was better—66 per cent for hospital cases and 68 per cent for clinic cases; few felt the patient was worse—8 per cent for hospital and 4 per cent for clinic; the remainder believed the patient's mental condition to be the same. More important from our viewpoint, there are no significant class differences in the responses for either improvement, worsening, or no change in the patient's mental status since discharge. Since two thirds reported an improvement, most patients at all class levels are probably more impaired at discharge than when studied, but probably the relative class distribution is the same as at interview.[28]

Additionally, the fact that length of time since hospital discharge does not change the class pattern of patient-control differences in mental-status scores on the Gurin index supports our position. Whether patients had been discharged five years and more or less than five years at interview, the higher the class the greater the proportion of patients with scores in the impaired range. Patient-control differences follow the same pattern. In fact, the more recently patients were discharged, the greater the patient-control difference in the higher classes. The difference increased from 14 percentage points in class V to 37 in classes I–III for patients discharged more than five years but from 13 to 62 points, respectively, for those out of hospital less than five years.

In contrast to the institutionalized control mechanisms operating in the hospital, the clinic staff control role is limited to treatment and even then essentially on a voluntary basis. While formal agencies may recommend that the individual seek treatment, there are no institutionalized means of guaranteeing that the patient will remain in treatment. Mr. Z., for example, a former class V clinic patient was sent to the state prison for a three-year period during the time of the Follow-Up Study as the result of conviction on a charge of attempted rape. At the time of release, the parole officer urged Mr. Z. to seek treatment at the local psychiatric outpatient clinic. Mr. Z. followed the instructions of the parole officer by appearing for a single visit at the clinic but he never returned.

Since clinic treatment is, in general, voluntary and no simple mechanisms are available to channel patients directly into outpatient treatment

---

[28] The percentage of patients by class reported to have a better mental condition for hospital cases is: I–III—58, IV—70, and V—66, $\chi^2 = 1.32$, $df = 2$, $p > .20$; for clinic cases: I–III—79, IV—66, and V—66, $\chi^2 = 2.10$, $df = 2$, $p > .20$.

agencies, it is not unusual to find that the relationship between social class and mental status for clinic patients is similar to that for the nonpatient population, that is, the lower the class the greater the proportion of respondents with mental status scores reflecting psychological impairment. What requires explanation, however, are the relative patient-control differences at the various class levels. Why do the patient-control differences in the percentage impaired systematically increase from the highest to the lowest class?

Among the many factors probably involved, the following seem to be some of the more important ones: First, because of class differences in the use of psychiatric facilities, it may be that lower-class persons who enter outpatient-clinic treatment are initially more severely disturbed psychiatrically than higher-status patients. As a consequence of differences in attitudes and feelings of stigma, upper- and middle-class patients are more likely to seek psychiatric treatment for less serious emotional disturbances than lower-class patients, and they are also more likely to remain in treatment. Lower-class patients who come into contact with psychiatric outpatient treatment agencies are more likely to be referred by formal agencies of social control which have become involved as a result of the patients' aberrant behavior. This lower-class pattern of "delay" in seeking medical treatment for a variety of illnesses has been demonstrated in a number of studies.[29]

As an extreme example of situations which lead to psychiatric treatment in outpatient agencies for lower-class patients, the case of Mrs. P. is illustrative. Mrs. P., a class V female, entered a common-law marriage some years ago with a man 20 years her junior. As described by Mrs. P.'s daughter by a previous legal marriage, the disparity created some uncomfortable circumstances, frequently climaxing in quarrels of increasingly violent proportion. An "accident" occurred when at the height of one dramatic skirmish, the young man "fell on a knife," a mishap which produced his unpremeditated death. As a result, Mrs. P. was sentenced to serve time in the state prison. While there, she received treatment from the prison psychiatrist and, upon parole, was referred to an outpatient agency.

---

[29] See, for example, Odin W. Anderson and Jacob J. Feldman, *Family Medical Costs and Voluntary Health Insurance: A Nationwide Survey*, McGraw-Hill, New York, 1956; Health Information Foundation, "The Increased Use of Medical Care," *Progress in Health Services*, October (1958); Odin W. Anderson, "The Utilization of Health Services," in H. E. Freeman, S. Levine, and L. G. Reeder (eds.), *Handbook of Medical Sociology*, Prentice-Hall, Englewood Cliffs, N.J., 1963.

Since the parole was not conditional upon continuance of psychiatric treatment, she soon terminated her treatment. At the end of the parole period, she left her job, which *was* a condition of the parole, and established another common-law alliance.

Certainly not all lower-class patients come into contact with psychiatric outpatient agencies under such dramatic circumstances or as the result of referral by some formal agent or agency of social control. However, even in the case of voluntary admission the lower-class patient is less likely to remain in treatment. On the one hand, the costs of psychiatric outpatient treatment, while low, still constitute a significant drain on his limited resources. On the other hand, the perceived stigma associated with mental illness apparently is related to a desire on the part of the lower-class patient to avoid formal identification as a mental patient. It is not uncommon to find that lower-class patients attempt to "hide" their treatment or "forget" that it ever occurred. Mrs. C., for example, entered treatment in a clinic in 1950 while involved in a severe marital conflict. Following treatment which was of short duration, she divorced her husband although she was a devout Catholic and remarried without the sanction of the Church. An extremely anxious and fearful woman, she expressed concern during the interview that her new husband might discover that she had been treated in a psychiatric clinic. To date, she has never admitted this to him because, "He wouldn't understand." (Owing to her concern, we did not interview her husband.) Because of this fear she has not sought further psychiatric treatment although she admits to being nervous, taking tranquilizers prescribed by a general practitioner, and being unable to sleep or carry out most of her household responsibilities effectively. She feels that she is apt to have a "nervous breakdown." During the interview her anxiety became evident and by the end of it she was shaking noticeably. Despite her psychological problems, Mrs. C. prefers to forget about her former treatment and has not sought further psychiatric treatment.

SUMMARY

In this chapter we have examined data relevant to our hypothesis that social class is related to the former patient's adjustment in the community. Focusing on the psychobiological dimension of community adjustment, we examined an index of mental status based on patients' self-reports and family reports of symptomatic behavior.

For both measures of psychobiological impairment, we find significant social-class differences which vary by the history of institutional treatment. Among former hospital patients, the upper- and middle-class patients, classes I–III, are more impaired psychologically than other hospital patients and their matched controls. Among outpatient clinic cases we find that the class V patients are the most severely impaired psychologically compared to other outpatient clinic cases and their matched controls.

adjustment in the community: II. economic role performance

chapter
eight

We now begin the examination of the second major dimension of community adjustment—the social—by analyzing several measures of economic role performance. Although roles tend to become increasingly diversified in an industrial society, certain common classes of role expectations exist for adult members of such societies. Among these, none is considered more important than work.[1] In this chapter we examine a number of indicators of occupational adjustment and certain corollaries of work performance, specifically the economic adjustment of former patients. As in the chapters dealing with other dimensions of adjustment in the community, the questions to be answered are: (1) Does the work performance and economic adjustment of the former patients differ significantly from that of their matched controls? (2) If so, is social class related to these patient-control differences?

OCCUPATIONAL ADJUSTMENT

The concept of work performance, which in an industrialized urban community is most directly concerned with market activities, does not

---

[1] For a discussion of economic-role performance and its place in the analysis of posttreatment adjustment of mental patients, see Chapter 6, p. 120.

apply to all former patients, many of whom are not currently employed in market-oriented activities. This, however, does not indicate a significant degree of impairment, as married women and men past the age of 65 are often and normally not employed, while other women, such as divorcees or widows with young chlidren, may not be working for reasons other than those associated with mental illness. In order to take into account these factors in the analysis of work performance the patients have been divided into two groups: workers and nonworkers.[2]

To distinguish between the two groups, we have made use of information on the patients' work performance in 1960 and during the five-year period preceding the interview or since hospital discharge. Operationally, we distinguish between *workers* and *nonworkers* on the following basis: Patients who are retired, housewives, or full-time students are defined as *nonworkers;* a few of these patients, for one reason or another, are currently employed but only on a temporary or emergency basis. All others are defined as *workers*. Analysis of the differences between worker and nonworker patients indicates that this classification closely approximates the distinction made when using traditional definitions of labor force, as utilized by the U.S. Department of Labor in its monthly surveys or the U.S. Census Bureau in its reports.[3] The nonworker group is composed of those individuals who traditionally would be classified as "not in the labor force." We found, for example, that of the 25 nonworker males, 19 were age 65 or over and were retired; of the six males between the ages of 21 and 64 years, five were early "retirees" under industrial and business pension plans, while one was not and never had been a member of the labor force. The balance of the nonworkers generally consists of older women, married women, and students. The workers are made up disproportionately of males in the normal working years of life and females

---

[2] The terms used here were selected to avoid confusion with traditional labor-force analysis terminology.

[3] The U.S. Census, for example, defines *the labor force* as all individuals 14 years of age and over who are either employed or unemployed but looking for work. Those not in the labor force include individuals under the age of 14 and those over 14 years of age who are doing only incidental unpaid family work, including students, housewives, retired workers, or seasonal workers who are enumerated during the off-season and those not actively seeking work. The focus, however, is on current performance *only*. See U.S. Bureau of the Census, *United States Census of Population: 1960, General Social and Economic Characteristics, United States Summary*, PC (1)–1C, pp. XXVII and XXVIII, Washington, D.C.

who are currently not married (single, separated, divorced, or widowed).[4]

WORK PERFORMANCE: INDICES

The analysis of occupational performance is based upon three measures of work performance, including a general index as well as more specific measures of employment and unemployment. The general and major measure of occupational performance is the occupational index which is reproduced in full in Appendix 5.[5] This scale covers a five-year period

---

[4] The characteristics of the workers and nonworkers is as follows:

	Workers (Per Cent)		Nonworkers (Per Cent)	
	Hospital	Clinic	Hospital	Clinic
Social Class				
I–III	11	28	25	41
IV	32	41	35	41
V	57	31	40	18
Marital Status				
Unmarried	54	32	13	27
Married	25	52	52	65
Separated or divorced	14	8	12	5
Widowed	7	8	24	3
Age				
Younger than 20	0	8	0	24
20–64	96	92	65	68
65 and older	4	0	35	8
Religion				
Catholic	66	48	58	46
Protestant	24	37	37	24
Jewish	10	15	6	30
Diagnosis				
Neurotic	13	69	9	77
Alcoholic	3	14	1	14
Schizophrenic	60	10	49	3
Affective	17	3	33	3
Other psychotic	7	4	7	3
Sex				
Male	58	75	14	35
Female	42	25	86	65

[5] We modified for our use the Adler Scale of Occupational Adjustment, an index developed for a follow-up study of mental patients in Arkansas and subsequently utilized in other studies. See L. M. Adler, J. W. Coddington, and D. D. Stewart, *Mental Illness in Washington County, Arkansas: Incidence, Recovery, and Posthospital Adjustment*, University of Arkansas, Research Series No. 23, Fayetteville, Arkansas (1952); and H. E. Freeman and O. G. Simmons, *The Mental Patient Comes Home*, Wiley, New York, 1963, pp. 48–54.

of work performance and is based on the frequency and duration of employment and unemployment during that period of time. A person who has been self-employed continuously for a five-year period receives a scale score of *1*, while a person continuously unemployed for five years receives a scale score of *9*. Thus, the lower the numerical scale value, the better the work record of the patient. The two more specific measures examined are: employment at the time of the interview and unemployment for a period of one week or more during the year preceding the interview. The occupational index is the most comprehensive of the three measures and covers a five-year period; the others relate to either current occupational status alone or the experience of the past year.

WORK PERFORMANCE: HOSPITAL PATIENTS

Good work performance (or adjustment) is operationally defined by occupational index types 1, 2, and 3. Index types 1 and 2 include persons regularly self-employed or employed since release from hospital or for the past five years, while index type 3 includes persons who worked more than half time the six months preceding the interview and all of the preceding four years or since discharge, whichever is the longest period. Detailed analysis of total index values and distribution is consistent with the abbreviated data presented in this and the following tables.

In Table 8.1, data are presented indicating the proportion of worker former hospital patients and their matched controls who are given the rating *good work performance*. It is evident that the former patients as a group are significantly less well-adjusted occupationally than their

TABLE 8.1

Hospital (Worker) Patients and Controls with Good Occupational-Adjustment Scores (Occupational Index) [a]

	Social Class (Per Cent)			
	I–III	IV	V	Total
Patients [b]	67	57	44	50
Controls [c]	100	94	84	89
Difference	−33[c]	−37	−40	−39

[a] Unless otherwise stated, social-class and patient-control differences, χ^2 test, $p < .05$.
[b] Differences by social class, χ^2 test, $p > .20$.
[c] χ^2 test inappropriate because of small expected frequencies.

matched controls. Fewer former hospital patients have good work performance scores. Former hospital patients are more likely to have been continuously unemployed or to have experienced major periods of unemployment during the period of study. Only 50 per cent of the patients have good occupational adjustment as defined by the index, but 89 per cent of their matched controls have scores in the same range.

The proportion of patients and nonpatients with scores in the range indicating a stable work record decreases from the highest to the lowest classes; regardless of the class position, however, the patient-control difference is striking at each class level albeit the difference does increase from the higher to the lower classes.

To specify the nature of the occupational problems encountered by the former patients, we examined two additional measures dealing with more recent work performance. The percentage of patients employed full time at a regular job when interviewed declines from 69 in classes I–III to 62 in class IV and 47 in class V; the corresponding percentages for controls are 92, 92, and 77 respectively (see Appendix 1, Table A1.4). Thus, at each class level, fewer patients than controls are employed full time, and since employment declines as social-class status decreases, class V patients are less likely to be employed full time than any other group. The patient-control differences are least in classes I–III (23 per cent) but are equally great in classes IV and V, 30 per cent.

The next question extends the period under examination to the year preceding the interview. The proportion of patients who were unemployed and without an earned income for at least one week during the year preceding the interview increases from 31 per cent in classes I–III to 52 per cent in class V; the corresponding percentages for controls is 8 and 23 (see Appendix 1, Table A1.5). Although class variations in patient-control differences are not great, they increase steadily from 23 per cent in classes I–III to 25 per cent in class IV and 29 per cent in class V. When unemployment does occur for the patients, it usually is lengthy—an average of 35 weeks in classes I–III, 31 weeks in class IV, and 37 weeks in class V.

Securing and holding a job appears to be a long-term, major problem faced by most former hospital patients. When asked to compare the amount of unemployment experienced during the past year with the amount experienced in the preceding four years, 84 per cent indicated that the recent amount of unemployment was the same or less than that experienced previously. Similarly, 87 per cent of the controls gave the same response. Thus the record of frequent unemployment is relatively constant for patients and the record of infrequent unemployment is relatively constant for the controls.

As a further measure of the unstable employment of the former hospital patients, an index of job stability was computed for the male former hospital patients and their controls in the working force. The index of job stability is simply an average of the number of job changes occurring during the past five years or since discharge. A lay-off and return to the same job was not counted as a job change. Contrasting these patients and their controls, we found that 25 per cent of the patients but only 7 per cent of the controls had changed their jobs on the average of once or more each year during the preceding five years.

While employment problems are widespread among the former hospital patients, they are relatively greater among the class IV and V patients. This fact is documented by the story of Joseph B., a 42-year-old, class IV, married man who was diagnosed as schizophrenic while in a state mental hospital in 1949. After treatment by electroshock he was discharged in 1951. In 1953 he returned for a two-month stay and then received psychotherapy in an outpatient clinic for six months.

At the time of Mr. B.'s original hospitalization, he was a tool-and-die-maker. Following his initial discharge, he worked at his trade for two brief periods, but in both cases he was "laid-off." He told us: "Nobody wants me as a tool-and-diemaker. You can't get a job as a tool-and-diemaker when you are an ex-mental patient." Apparently, however, Mr. B. has found it difficult to hold any job. During the 10-year period of the Follow-Up Study, he worked as an assembler, gas-station attendant, gardener, house painter, shipping-room clerk, and machine operator (on three different jobs including the present one). He quit three of the jobs voluntarily, but in every other case he was "laid-off." He has been in his current job for two years.

While Mr. B. has had difficulties in retaining a job following his hospital treatment he has adjusted fairly satisfactorily in other respects. He gets along well with his family and participates in a variety of extra-familial social relationships. However, he has never been able to go back to his original occupation of tool-and-diemaker and is able to support himself and his family only by working at a less-skilled occupation. Even in this area, he has had difficulty in securing and holding a job for a prolonged period of time.

To summarize briefly the findings concerning occupational performance among the employable hospital patients and their matched controls, the following patterns are found for the index of occupational adjustment as well as for the other more specific measures: Collectively, the hospital patients are less likely than the nonpatient group to be employed in full-time jobs or to have a stable work record in the years immediately preceding the interview. For each of the three measures of occupational performance, class V patients have poorer work records than patients in class IV. While the patient-control differences are striking at every class level, in each case the patient-control difference is least in classes I–III. Compared to their controls, class IV and V patients experience the major employment problems.

The next step in the analysis was to control for a second variable in addition to the control for the treatment agency. We controlled for the 11 variables indicated in Chapter 7, footnote 19, p. 134. Fewer analyses could be made than in previous chapters because of small numbers, since we are dealing only with patients classified as workers. However, the analyses which were possible continue to support the class pattern found: patient-control differences in occupational adjustment generally were least in classes I–III.[6] The greatest patient-control difference was found just as frequently in class IV as in class V, depending upon the particular occupational-adjustment index used and the specific control variable being analyzed.

The reasons for these social-class differences in patterns of occupational adjustment are probably to be found in the economic and occupational structure of society.[7] Former hospital patients in class IV, as well as in class V, have difficulty in securing and holding a job. Class IV occupations tend to be highly rationalized, requiring stable workers with regular work habits. Employers tolerate little deviant behavior in the skilled and semiskilled factory jobs available to working-class people. Consequently such jobs are difficult to maintain for the class IV ex-patient who is psychiatrically incapacitated to some degree. In class V, the jobs available to workers are frequently marginal and unstable so that unemployment

---

[6] The 11 control variables were divided into the same categories as in Chapter 7 except in the case of marital status where single, separated, divorced, and widowed respondents were combined. In addition, eight categories were dropped because of too few cases: (1) veterans and private hospitals; (2) in psychotherapy in 1950; (3) entered treatment before 1949; (4) in custodial care, 1950; (5) in psychotherapy, 1950 to 1960; (6) in drug therapy, 1950 to 1960; (7) in custodial care, 1950 to 1960; (8) affective psychosis. Thus, analyses could be made for each of the three occupational-adjustment indices for 17 categories instead of the 26 utilized in Chapter 7. The class pattern was considered confirmed in this chapter if hospital patient-control differences were least in classes I–III. In all but eight of the 51 possible analyses this expected finding was confirmed, with no other variables systematically eliminating the class differences.

[7] For a discussion of these factors for schizophrenic patients, see Lee L. Bean, Jerome K. Myers, and Max P. Pepper, "Social Class and Schizophrenia: A Ten-Year Follow-Up," in A. B. Shostak and W. Gomberg, (eds.), *Blue Collar World*, Prentice-Hall, New Jersey, 1964.

is common. Former hospital patients, however, experience even more work problems than other persons at this social level.

In contrast to the employment opportunities available to class IV and V persons, the occupations open to class I–III individuals are such that personal variations in mood and affect can be accepted more readily. Even absence from such jobs, if sufficiently irregular, does not affect the person's position, because paid sick leave is generally available. Thus, in the middle- and upper-classes, where perception of the legitimate sick role more likely includes emotional disturbance, a worker can withdraw from the job for a few days, when under stress, without fear of losing his position. Additionally, because of the differential access to the power structure of the economic world, class I–III families are better able to guarantee regular employment for members of their families who are patients. They are more likely to own or control a business, or have a friend who does, where the former patient can work. Thus, variations in the demands of occupational roles at each class level are probably related to the adjustment patterns which are found at different class levels.

In brief, the analysis of several indices of occupational performance for the former hospitalized patients supports our hypothesis that community adjustment is related to social class. Despite the common work problems of all patients, as indicated by the large patient-control differences, the class I–III patients, compared to other patients and their controls, generally have fewer problems in securing and retaining employment in the community. While the maximum problems in the area of work adjustment appear in either class IV or class V, depending upon the measure of adjustment examined and the control variables introduced, it seems that class IV and V patients are relatively similar in this one particular area of adjustment. Both class IV and class V patients have problems in finding and holding full-time paid employment. For these two social classes, unemployment and reliance upon part-time and irregular work is a common feature of their posttreatment behavior in the community.

WORK PERFORMANCE: CLINIC PATIENTS

The evaluation of the occupational adjustment of former clinic patients is based upon the same three indices utilized for the hospital patients, and the analysis is similarly restricted to the worker clinic patients.

Data for occupational adjustment over a five-year period of time, as measured by the occupational index, are presented for the employable clinic patients and their controls in Table 8.2. As found in the analysis of material for the hospital patients, a smaller percentage of clinic patients

TABLE 8.2

**Clinic (Worker) Patients and Controls with Good Occupational-
Adjustment Scores (Occupational Index)** [a]

	Social Class (Per Cent)			
	I–III	IV	V	Total
Patients	83	95	57	78
Controls [b]	100	95	89	95
Difference	−17 [b]	0 [b]	−32	−17

[a] Unless otherwise stated, social-class and patient-control differences, χ^2 test,
$p < .05$.
[b] χ^2 test inappropriate because of small expected frequencies.

than controls is well adjusted occupationally. Class differences in work
performance among patients are striking. A much smaller percentage of
patients in class V than in the higher classes has a good work record over
the years, as measured by the occupational index. However, the highest
proportion of steady employment is found in class IV, rather than in
classes I–III.

The employment picture for clinic patients, as indicated by the occupational index, is strongly confirmed by each of the other two indices of
occupational performance. The percentage of patients employed full-time
decreases from 89 in classes I–III to 57 in class V, while the corresponding figures for controls are 84 and 81 (see Appendix 1, Table A1.6). The
greatest patient-control difference is found in class V (−24 per cent),
while differences at the other class levels are minimal and approximately
the same (I–III—5 per cent; IV—7 per cent).

The percentage of patients who experienced some unemployment
during the year preceding the interview increases by class as follows:
I–III—22, IV—29, and V—76; for controls, the corresponding percentages
were 6, 21, and 24 (see Appendix 1, Table A1.7). Not only are lower-
class patients more likely to be unemployed than other patients and controls, but their unemployment extends over a much longer period of
time. For those patients who were unemployed during the preceding
year, the average length of unemployment is only 3 weeks in classes I–III,
but 15 weeks in class IV and 25 weeks in class V. These class differences
in unemployment did not develop only in the preceding year. At all class
levels approximately the same percentage of patients indicates that the
degree of unemployment in that year was the same or less than in the

preceding four years: 90 in classes I–III, 92 in class IV, and 92 in class V. Thus, frequent job changes and long-term periods of unemployment mark the employment history of the class V clinic patients alone.

The instability of the lower-class clinic patients is further evidenced in the case of males in the working force by the average number of job changes during the preceding five-year period. While none of the class I–III clinic males have made a job change on the average of once per year, 6 per cent of the class IV patients but 46 per cent of the clinic class V patients have averaged a job change each year during the preceding five years. The proportion of control cases with similar frequencies of job changes is 8 per cent in classes I–III, none in class IV, and only 7 per cent in class V.

In brief, the three measures of occupational adjustment indicate that substantially more patients than controls in class V or than patients or controls at any other class level are poorly adjusted occupationally. Patient-control differences at this level are substantial for all three measures ranging from 25 per cent to 54 per cent. In contrast, the patient-control differences at other levels are minimal.

We next controlled for the same seven variables utilized in the previous chapter to determine if other variables were affecting our findings. Because of small numbers some categories had to be dropped from the analysis. However, all the analyses made confirmed the original finding that patient-control differences in occupational adjustment are greatest in class V.[8]

The pattern of irregular work found among class V clinic patients is reflected in the job history of Mr. C., a 36-year-old male, who was treated in an outpatient clinic in 1950 and discharged with a diagnosis of "chronic alcoholism, undefined; psychoneurotic disorder, obsessive-compulsive reaction." In the intervening years, Mr. C. served a two-year term in the state prison for attempted rape. Mr. C. apparently cannot remain in one job for an extended period of time. Prior to the interview he had worked at five unskilled and semiskilled jobs, holding none for longer than two years. In each case, according to his report, he "quit" the job voluntarily. At the time of the interview he had been employed full-time

---

[8] See Chapter 7, footnote 20, pp. 137–138 for the variables controlled and the categories utilized. The three categories dropped are: (1) age 45 and older, (2) females, and (3) previous psychiatric treatment. Thus 9 categories were used, and 3 occupational-adjustment indices were examined for a total of 27 tests. The class pattern was considered confirmed in this chapter if clinic patient-control differences were at least 10 percentage points greater in class V than in the next highest class.

as an unskilled factory worker for 12 months. In response to a direct question as to whether or not he would like a different job, he said, "Sometimes, but nothing in particular. I just don't like sticking to a job for too long."

INSTRUMENTAL PERFORMANCE: HOMEMAKERS

The concept of work performance in the sense of marketplace activities does not apply to female patients who are normally housewives or homemakers. However, specific expectations concerning household chores as economic activities are relevant for this group of patients.

The identification of a female as a housewife or homemaker does not necessarily indicate that the patient is currently married, although this notion is implicit in the term *housewife*. Separated, divorced, and widowed females commonly perform the role of the homemaker or housewife as their major activity and are not employed in market-type activities. Moreover, it is not uncommon to find that single females act as "homemakers" for parents or siblings employed outside the home. This pattern, however, is more frequently found among working- and lower-class families. Therefore, to avoid the ambiguity introduced in the term *housewife*, we use the term *homemaker* to refer to females who are not regularly employed in market-type activities, but who function primarily within the home in the performance of instrumental roles.[9]

To determine if the household performance of the homemakers reflects lowered activity levels, a number of questions were asked concerning a variety of activities generally performed by females in the household. The respondents were asked to indicate if these activities were performed (1) alone or (2) with the assistance of others, or (3) if other individuals in the household performed the tasks alone. The following seven activities were cited: (1) preparing meals, (2) doing the grocery shopping, (3) handling the grocery money, (4) cleaning the house, (5) taking care of the laundry and mending, (6) dressing and bathing small children, (7)

---

[9] This definition is somewhat arbitrary since many females, who normally work outside the household are also, if married, expected to perform household duties, or, if living alone, have no recourse but to perform these duties. Such females, however, have as their major economic role that of the employee in a market-type activity and have been included in the discussion of employment. In this section, the focus is upon those females whose major instrumental activity is that of housewife. Included in this group are females who are normally homemakers but do work outside the home on a part-time basis. In this one sense there is an overlap with the category of worker females. The inclusion of this group is based upon our interest in the ability of the former patient to perform any economic roles.

making sure the children get to school on time.[10] The responses to these questions indicate that the majority of former patients, both hospital and outpatient clinic patients, who are classified as homemakers are able to perform household chores. Moreover, there are no major differences by social class and treatment agency or between the patients and controls.[11]

The proportion of class I–III patient-homemakers who indicate that they perform the above tasks alone ranges from 75 per cent for doing the housecleaning (83 per cent for controls) to 100 per cent for dressing and bathing small children in the home (100 per cent for controls); for class IV patients the positive responses range from 74 per cent for doing the grocery shopping (70 per cent for controls) to 100 per cent for dressing and bathing small children (100 per cent for controls); for class V patients the proportion of positive responses ranges from 60 per cent for doing grocery shopping (61 per cent for controls) to 100 per cent for dressing and bathing small children (100 per cent for controls). In general, the women who do not perform the above activities alone are women living in a household with other adult females who share the responsibility of maintaining the household. Only three women are so incapacitated psychologically that they are unable to carry out household responsibilities—one each in classes I–III, IV, and V.

In order to determine the validity of these self-reports, questions were asked of other household members. First, the family members were asked to indicate whether or not they expected the household tasks listed above to be performed by the former patient; the findings corroborate the self-reports. If family members reported that they do not expect the patient to perform certain activities it is because there were others in the household to whom the tasks were assigned for reasons other than incompetent performance on the part of the former patient. One man, for example, did not expect his wife to prepare meals because he enjoys cooking himself. In another case, an elderly woman, recently widowed and now lonely, "rescued" her 74-year-old second cousin from the state hospital after 32 years of continuous hospitalization. In this household, a rather efficient division of labor has been worked out, so that the negative responses reflected simply a sharing of the household tasks.

Second, husbands of former patients were asked to evaluate the housekeeping of their wives and to compare the current housekeeping with

---

[10] These items were included in the Freeman and Simmons study; see Freeman and Simmons, *op. cit.*, p. 54.

[11] Hospital and clinic cases were combined since they did not differ from one another for any measure of household activity.

that of the early years of their marriage and the period immediately following discharge from treatment. Only four husbands (3 in classes I–III and 1 in class V) indicated that their wives are poor housekeepers. No husband indicated that his wife's housekeeping is worse now than when she left treatment, and only 3 (1 class III and 2 class IV) husbands indicated that their wives' housekeeping is worse now than when they were first married.

The evidence on performance of household chores indicates that, with few exceptions, former female patients were able to carry out expected household chores. This high performance level is undoubtedly due to a number of factors. Household chores, while they may be physically strenuous, are not as demanding as a job in the community or the market. The nature of the relationship between the housewife and other members of her role-set is quite different from that found in the role-set of the marketplace worker. In the household, familial relationships tend to be more flexible and diffuse and less rigorous, while in an employer-employee relationship impersonal specific demands govern work performance. Although family members may expect some adequacy on the part of the patient, expectations as to the quality of the performance may be adjusted to take into account the reduced capacity of the patient. Therefore, while patients may be doing the household chores, the quality of the work, a dimension we are not in a position to measure precisely, may have been reduced.

Again, former female patients who have major psychological problems may be able to "buy" family support by performing instrumental activities in the household at a high level. Family members may accept deviance in other areas of behavior—verbal aggression or failure to participate socially, for example—as long as the "house is kept up." It is possible that good instrumental performance in the household may be a minimal requirement for family support of a patient's discharge from treatment. If a female is so incapacitated that she is unable to fulfill family expectations of her performance of household tasks, the family may hesitate to support her discharge from treatment. The ability to take care of children in the home appears to be a critical factor. In particular, the married male with school-age children may find it an intolerable burden to have his wife in the household when she is incapable of maintaining the home and caring for the children. For those patients in the community with young children, we did not find one case in which the female did not care for the children. The importance of the woman's ability to perform such tasks is demonstrated by a negative case in which failure to perform household chores led first to rehospitalization and finally to divorce.

Mrs. Z., a class IV married female, diagnosed as schizophrenic, paranoid type, was first discharged from a state hospital in 1951. She was returned to the hospital in 1952 by her husband who complained that she did not care for the home or their two young children. Her husband reported that she simply sat in front of the television set all day, eating. Following two subsequent discharges and readmissions and a prefrontal lobotomy, she returned home and again neglected the housework, was unable to control the children, and, according to her brother, "raised hell in the house." By 1955 Mr. Z. had given up on his wife and on the psychiatric treatment agencies. Rather than send her back to the hospital, he sold his chicken farm, deposited his wife at the driveway to her father's farm, and moved to Florida with his two children. He later obtained a divorce.

Whatever the reasons involved, it is clear that instrumental performance is high for the female former mental patients now living in the community and functioning as homemakers. Few are unable to perform required household chores, although the *quality* of the performance may be lower than would be found among a group of nonpatients.

OCCUPATIONAL PERFORMANCE: JOB SATISFACTION AND WORK RELATIONS

The next phase in our analysis of work performance was to determine the extent to which social class and mental illness are related to work relations. Several questions were included in the interview dealing with job satisfaction and relations with other workers on the job. Although patients, and lower-class patients in particular, experience problems in securing and retaining work, on the job there is little to distinguish patients from nonpatients in terms of the way the job is viewed or the way in which respondents view their relations with fellow employees.

Hospital patients and controls were asked how satisfied they were with their current or last position. Most patients and controls, 85 and 88 per cent, respectively, reported that they were satisfied or very satisfied with their jobs. Indeed no marked differences are found between patients and controls at any class level. While class I–III patients were more likely to be satisfied and class V patients less likely to be "very satisfied," the class differences for both patients and controls are small. The high proportion of hospital patients and controls indicating job satisfaction is reflected by the low proportion of patients and controls who expressed a desire for a different job. Only 33 per cent of the former hospital patients and 30 per cent of the hospital controls indicated that they would like a different job. While the class V patients and controls were more likely to prefer another position, the class differences and patient-control differences are negligible. Further evidence of relative satisfaction with working conditions is found in the question dealing with the ability to get along with fellow workers; 86 per cent of the hospital patients and 93 per cent of the hospital controls stated that they got along well or very well with their fellow workers. Controlling singly for the variables used in the previous phases of the research results in no systematic changes in these findings. Regardless of the control variables, hospital patients and their controls were apparently satisfied with their working conditions and appeared to get along amicably with their fellow workers.

Clinic patients in general viewed their jobs and work relations in somewhat the same fashion as hospital respondents, although there is one significant difference. While the majority of clinic patients and controls, 84 per cent and 94 per cent, respectively, were satisfied with their current jobs, substantially more clinic patients than controls would have liked a different job; 48 per cent of the patients but only 24 per cent of the controls indicated that they would like to change jobs. Among the clinic patients, a greater proportion of class V patients than patients at any other class level wanted another job; 58 per cent responded that they frequently desire another job, while only 15 per cent of the class V control respondents answered in this manner. Thus, class V patients differ markedly from their controls and other patients in wanting another job.[12]

The desire of class V clinic patients to change to another job is not due, apparently, to disharmony in work relations. While fewer patients at each class level reported that they got along well with fellow workers, the differences are not large. At the class V level, 78 per cent of the patients reported that they got along well or very well with their fellow workers.

The general picture which emerges from the analysis of items dealing with job satisfaction indicates no significant problems for former patients at particular class levels. The one exception found—the significant proportion of class V clinic patients who would like another job—appears, at first glance, contradictory and inconclusive since the majority of class V clinic patients were satisfied with their present jobs and class V hospital patients did not indicate that they would like other jobs. The explanation is found in the values of class V, the structure of the employment market, and the differences in treatment history. Class V individuals who are faced with interminable financial problems believe that their problems can be solved if they can secure a better job. However, both class V clinic and hospital patients experienced problems in finding and holding a job.

---

[12] Controlling for other relevant variables does not eliminate this difference.

Given the difficulty in finding work and recognizing that employment opportunities are limited, they appeared to be satisfied to have any job.

Class V individuals who were hospitalized, however, faced certain problems not experienced by the clinic patients. Hospital patients had to secure a discharge from a psychiatric institution and find a job in the community where they were labeled by themselves and others as former patients. Moreover, hospital patients are in general older than the clinic patients and therefore also faced the same problem that other older unskilled individuals have in securing work. Thus, they are more content to simply "hang-on" once they secure any type of employment. On the other hand, the class V clinic patients were not removed from the world of work as a result of psychiatric treatment; they remained in the community, and employment interruptions may be attributed to lack of opportunity as well as psychiatric problems. In addition, being somewhat younger than the hospital patients they were often in the process of moving to find a more permanent job. The clinic patients may have had difficulty in finding work and, thus, recognized that employment opportunities at their skill level are limited. Although they appeared to be satisfied to have a job, this does not prevent them from wishing for something better. In part, these patients are happy with what they have but believe they can improve themselves, once they resolve their own personal problems.

THE ECONOMICS OF ADJUSTMENT

An additional aspect of community adjustment is the financial position of the former patient. Although we may question the use of finances as an index of adjustment, financial status reflects the success of the former patient in the job market and the extent of the burden of patient care and treatment on the family. The financial position of the patient is important for other reasons. First, should the need arise, possession of funds often determines the availability of medical and psychiatric facilities in the community and the type of facilities which may be utilized. Second, financial burdens and problems may generate strains and stresses which impede successful posttreatment adjustment of former patients.

The relevance of financial problems is clearly indicated in the case of Mrs. X., a working-class female. Mrs. X. sought psychiatric help for depression over mounting debts incurred when the family moved to an expensive home in the suburbs which they later lost through foreclosure. At the time of the interview, she was still severely depressed, and her husband felt that further psychiatric help was warranted but he could not

TABLE 8.3

Hospital Patients and Controls with Savings (Per Cent) [a]

	Social Class			
	I–III	IV	V	Total
Patients	97	82	56	72
Controls	100	95	88	93
Difference	−3 [b]	−13	−32	−21

[a] Unless otherwise stated, social-class and patient-control differences, χ^2 test, $p < .05$.
[b] χ^2 test inappropriate because of small expected frequencies.

convince his wife to continue her weekly clinic visits. She felt the money was better used to pay the family debts.

Financial Resources

To determine the availability of financial resources, a number of questions dealing with income, expenses, savings, and debts were included in the interview schedule. The first items examined deal with savings and debts. By *savings* we mean the availability of cash resources as well as capital and convertible securities. Included in the check list of items are the following: savings and checking accounts, stocks and bonds, real estate, insurance, and homeownership. The responses to the general question of availability of savings reflect the responses for all specific items, so we therefore present findings for the general question of possession of *any* savings.

The availability of financial resources in the form of savings, as defined here, is closely related to social class. Among the former hospital patients and their matched controls, we find, as indicated in Table 8.3, that the lower the class the smaller the proportion of respondents with any available savings. The absence of savings is compounded in the case of the former patients, and patient-control differences increase markedly as class decreases. Controlling for the standard variables utilized in previous sections, we find that patient-control differences in the availability of savings are always greatest in class V.[13]

---

[13] The 11 control variables were divided into the 26 categories utilized in the analyses for hospital cases in Chapter 7.

The relative lack of resources among class V patients apparent in the data presented in Table 8.3 is found for every type of savings for which we were able to secure data. Savings accounts and cash reserves are negligible, when not entirely absent. Equity in homeownership is almost unknown, and stocks and bonds lay beyond the grasp of these patients. Financial resources are not accumulated, or what available resources may have been available have been depleted by past treatment or expended to maintain the patient and his family during the periods of unemployment or irregular work which are common to these class V patients.

The marginal financial condition of these patients apparently does not prevent them from securing access to the credit market which is an integral part of the American family economic picture. The indebtedness of the former patients and their matched controls reflects not only home purchases but also installment buying of major items such as automobiles, furniture, and household appliances, particularly in classes IV and V. The pattern of installment purchasing has become increasingly widespread and, apparently, previous psychiatric treatment does not affect the access of the former patient to the credit market, nor does past treatment increase the degree of indebtedness of the patients. It seems that medical expenses incurred among the patients are offset by higher consumptive standards in other areas for the nonpatients. Therefore, when debts are considered without reference to type, there is no difference between the patients and controls: 33 per cent of patients and 38 per cent of controls have some debts. Class I–III patients and controls are more likely to have debts than lower-class patients and controls, but these debts are often in terms of home mortgages rather than installment payments for cars or appliances.[14] Evidently, lower-class patients who lack savings or who have an unstable work history either do not offset their financial limitations through the utilization of credit resources or, because of their employment history, they are regarded as poor credit risks.

Among the former clinic patients, the same pattern as among former hospital patients is found for responses to the question dealing with savings. Data presented in Table 8.4 indicate that while slightly fewer clinic patients than controls have savings, noticeable class differences are found among patients. Not only do fewer class V patients have such financial resources available, but also, in contrast to their controls, substantially

---

[14] The percentage of hospital patients with debts by class is as follows: I–III–50, IV–27, V–31; the corresponding percentages for controls are 42, 40, and 36. This pattern of minimal class and patient-control variation in debt remains consistent when the relevant control variables are held constant.

TABLE 8.4

Clinic Patients and Controls with Savings (Per Cent) [a]

	Social Class			
	I–III	IV	V	Total
Patients	91	98	44	82
Controls [b]	91	90	88	90
Difference	0 [b]	8 [b]	−44	−8 [c]

[a] Unless otherwise stated, social-class and patient-control differences, χ^2 test, $p < .05$.

[b] χ^2 test inappropriate because of small expected frequencies.

[c] Patient-contol differences, χ^2 test, $p < .20$.

fewer have any savings. In contrast, patients in all other classes are just as likely as their controls to have savings.[15]

Former clinic patients are more likely to have current debts than hospital patients and at each class level they are more likely than their controls to have debts. However, class V patients are more likely to have debts than any other group, and patient-control differences are twice as great in class V as at any other class level.[16] The greater degree of indebtedness among the clinic patients reflects, in part, the relationship between installment-buying and the life cycle. As indicated earlier, clinic patients are somewhat younger than hospital patients and, therefore, are at the life stage at which installment buying is necessary to furnish and maintain a household.

For both hospital and clinic patients, the employment difficulties previously described in terms of work performance are reflected directly in terms of the relative scarcity of economic resources in the form of savings. In particular, a sizeable number of former class V patients exist in a state of abject poverty. Mr. P., who was described in Chapter 2, subsists on his gleanings from the city refuse heaps. He has been unable to work since his hospital release which is officially recorded as an awol discharge. Although Mr. W. has an income from a Veterans Administra-

[15] This pattern of maximal patient-control differences in class V is found for each of the 12 control categories used in the analyses for clinic cases in Chapter 7.

[16] The percentage of clinic patients with debts by class is as follows: total—74, I–III—73, IV—73, and V—77; the corresponding percentages for controls are 58, 61, 61, and 52. Again, these differences are not changed by the introduction of the different control variables.

tion pension, by the end of each month he is reduced to near starvation as a result of poor financial planning. When interviewed in the late fall of 1961, he had no food in his home and would have no money until the arrival of his disability check in ten days. The day before the interview, he had spent his remaining few dollars for an aluminum Christmas tree to brighten his garage apartment for the coming holiday season. Another patient, Mrs. M., was discharged from a state mental hospital in 1951 with a diagnosis of psychoneurotic disorder, depressive reaction, and was abandoned by her husband in 1953. Unable to secure work, she lived with her mother until the latter's death in 1955. She then moved into a cold-water flat with her widowed sister who has assumed complete responsibility for the patient. In recent years, Mrs. M. has deteriorated, requiring more care. The sister left her job and took a position as a cleaning woman, working at night while Mrs. M. sleeps. The job change reduced the family income to $2100 a year, a figure considerably lower than that recently established for poverty margins.

In contrast to this compounding of economic problems of the lower class is the picture of upper- and middle-class patients who have succeeded financially "in spite of it all." Mr. J., for example, is a class III, 36-year-old male who was diagnosed as a schizophrenic, catatonic type. After six years of continuous hospitalization he was discharged in 1955. With his partial college training, he secured a position as a market-development salesman in a small local firm, continuing his college career at the same time. While Mr. J. has remained in outpatient care since his discharge, he has been able to move through a series of better-paying positions, finally accepting a job in a large metropolitan center which allows him sufficient flexibility so that he can return to New Haven whenever he feels the need to visit his psychiatrist. His current income is in excess of $8000 a year, with good prospects for further increments. He is able to meet the expenses of his psychiatric treatment out of current income and still carry out an active social life.

Income

Work-performance differences found among patients and controls are reflected dramatically in income differentials. As seen in Table 8.5, hospital patients have lower incomes than their matched controls, reflecting the poorer work performance of the patients when compared with their controls. For both patients and controls, yearly income decreases from the highest to the lowest class. The class differences are increased, however, among the former patients; consequently patient-control differences are strongly associated with social class: In classes I–III there is little differ-

TABLE 8.5

Mean Annual Individual Income for Hospital (Worker) Patients and Controls (Dollars) [a]

	Social Class			
	I–III	IV	V	Total
Patients	5645	2327	1645	2288
Controls	6167	4311	3142	3851
Difference	−522 [b]	−1984 [c]	−1497 [c]	−1563 [c]

[a] Only worker patients and controls are included.
[b] Patient-control difference, t-test, $p > .20$.
[c] Patient-control difference, t-test, $p < .05$.

ence in individual income for patients and nonpatients, whereas in class IV and class V the mean income for patients is much less than for controls.

When we control for the standard variables, we continue to find the same class pattern in income. Regardless of the control variable, patient-control differences in mean income are strikingly large in classes IV and V but minimal in classes I–III.[17]

The patient-control differences in income by social class are of particular interest. While the income differentials are generally consistent with the employment histories of the patients and controls, as measured by a variety of indices, the magnitude of patient-control differences is accentuated in the case of income. The slightly greater difficulty of securing and retaining a job in the case of class IV and V patients, compared with class I–III patients, results in much greater financial hardships. The class I–III hospital patients' movement back into the community and the world of work and their employment problems do not appear to have introduced any financial penalty, while serious financial disability is associated with the type of work to which hospital patients in classes IV and V returned. The financial problems associated with employment were particularly intensified for class IV patients, since the jobs which they were able to secure and hold were those involving some financial loss

---

[17] There is one exception to this pattern: patients receiving psychotherapy in 1960 do not differ from their matched controls at any class level. Otherwise, patient-control differences are least in classes I–III when control analyses are made for the 17 categories listed in footnote 6 of this chapter.

in comparison with other jobs held by class IV individuals in the community.

This pattern of reduced income for class IV hospital patients is illustrated by Miss C., a class IV, single female, employed as a secretary prior to her hospitalization during which she was diagnosed as schizophrenic, catatonic type. After her discharge, the only secretarial job she could secure was on a part-time basis. In order to increase her income she left the part-time position to take a full-time job as a sewing-machine operator. She has kept this job for five years, earning $2600 a year. In another case, Mr. B., a class IV male, separated from his wife, has been able to retain his same type of job but not his same earning power. Since his discharge from the state hospital where he was diagnosed as schizophrenic, paranoid type, he has worked over a 10-year period in about 50 jobs as a journeyman toolmaker in several eastern and midwestern cities. In each case he lost the job because of drinking or excessive absenteeism. Possessing a skill in short supply, he has been able to secure a new position each time, but it has meant working for smaller companies which frequently operate with a low-profit margin, forcing the use of marginal workers. Consequently, Mr. B. now works at a job for which his average income is $100 weekly, while the average income for a journeyman toolmaker working under the union scale is normally $150 weekly.

Although hospital patients in classes IV and V, in relation to their controls, adjusted occupationally nearly as well as those in classes I–III, they were not able to adjust as well financially; nearly as many had regular jobs but lower-paying ones. Despite the less stable work history of class I–III patients, their income was the same as that of their controls.

This class difference in financial adjustment is reflected also in savings. In brief, financial problems of hospital patients in classes I–III were no greater than those of their controls, whereas in classes IV and V such patients experienced financial and occupational problems greater than their controls. In general, it appears that working- and lower-class former patients are forced to take lesser-skilled, lower-paying jobs than is the norm at their class level. Apparently the stigma and personal problems of having been a mental patient in a hospital handicap individuals in class IV as well as in class V. Moreover, financial problems were actually as great, if not greater, for class IV as class V patients and seem to be related to the economic and occupational structure of society for the reasons indicated earlier.

For clinic patients and their matched controls, income differentials by class reflect occupational-adjustment differences. As in the case of occupational performance, patients in classes I–III and class IV differ

TABLE 8.6

Mean Annual Individual Income for Clinic (Worker) Patients and Controls (Dollars) [a]

	Social Class			
	I–III	IV	V	Total
Patients	6311	4943	2376	4500
Controls	5888	5192	3980	4984
Difference	423 [b]	−249 [b]	−1604 [c]	−484 [b]

[a] Only worker patients and controls are included.
[b] Patient-control difference, t-test, $p > .20$.
[c] Patient-control difference, t-test, $p < .05$.

little from their controls (see Table 8.6). Class V patients, in contrast, had considerably smaller average incomes than their controls. When the standard set of relevant control variables is introduced, the same findings obtain. The class V clinic patients were worse off financially than their controls or other patients.[18] In brief then, the finances of posttreatment performance reflect the occupational performance of both clinic patients and controls.

The incomes of worker patients and of their matched controls reflect the earning capacity of the individual but do not necessarily reflect the financial condition of the entire family. Furthermore, such data reveal nothing about the economic condition of families in which the patient is not working. Therefore, we analyzed data on family incomes.

Social-class differences in family income for both former hospital patients and their matched controls follow the same class pattern as for individual income. For patients, mean family income declined from $8122 yearly in classes I–III to $4714 in class IV and $3795 in class V; for controls, the comparable figures are $9315, $7300, and $5925. Patient-control differences, therefore, are much less in classes I–III ($1193) than in classes IV ($2586) and V ($2130).[19]

Among clinic cases, class differences in family income also follow the same pattern as for individual income. The average annual family income for patients by class was: I–III—$10,088, IV—$6996, and V—

---

[18] Cross-tabulations were made holding constant the control variables listed in footnote 8 of this chapter. No changes were found in the expected pattern of greatest patient-control differences in class V.
[19] The level of significance for patient-control differences by class when a t-test was made is as follows: I–III—$p > .20$, IV—$p < .05$, and V—$p < .05$.

$4382; for controls, I–III—$9723, IV—$8291, and V—$6347.[20] It is interesting that annual family income was $365 higher for patients than for controls in classes I–III, whereas in class IV controls had substantially higher income ($1295). This is in contrast to individual income and occupational adjustment for which patients and controls are similar in classes I–III and IV. However, the family income of patients in class V was again much lower than that of controls, $1965 per year.

FAMILY EXPECTATIONS

In the interviews with relatives of the former patients, a number of questions were included about the role performance of patients. The class differences in the responses to these questions reflect the occupational-performance differences found for the patients.

For the former hospital patients, the following information was secured from their relatives: 61 per cent of the relatives of the classes I–III patients but only 53 per cent of the relatives of class IV patients and 51 per cent of the relatives of class V patients told us they currently expected the patient to be working full time. Relatives of some patients expected an improvement in work performance over time, but the proportion is related to social class; only 55 per cent of the relatives of class V patients but 61 per cent and 75 per cent, respectively, of relatives of class IV and class I–III patients expected full-time work on the part of the patients six months hence.

Similarly, families of class V clinic patients were less likely to expect the patient to be working full time. To the question concerning present expectations, 84 per cent of classes I–III, 87 per cent of class IV, and 75 per cent of class V family respondents answered that they expected the patient to work full time. For future expectations, the proportion expecting full-time work is 88 per cent in classes I–III, 88 per cent in class IV, and 75 per cent in class V. Thus, in terms of employment, family respondents of class V patients were less likely to expect full-time employment of the patient currently or in the future. It appears that the employment expectations of the family members are related directly to the actual work performance of the patient.

SUMMARY

In this chapter we have examined a variety of measures of economic-role performance. In general, the findings support the hypothesis that

---

[20] The level of significance for patient-control differences by class when a t-test was made is as follows: I–III—$p > .20$, IV—$p < .20$, and V—$p < .10$.

social class is related to the adjustment of former mental patients in the community.

For those normally identified as workers—members of the labor force —former patients are considerably less likely to work regularly or be able to retain a steady job. Unemployment and the inability to find a full-time job or any job are common problems for the former patients. In the case of the hospital patients at each class level, problems of adjustment are found relative to the work-performance records of the control cases. Consistently, however, it is the class IV and V patients who are most likely to have poor work records, as compared with their controls.

Among the clinic cases, it is only the class V former patients who experienced major periods of unemployment or who relied upon part-time and irregular work. Class I–III and class IV former clinic patients had few employment problems, when compared with their controls.

Consistent with the employment history of the patients, financial standing, as reflected in income, savings, and debts, indicates that class is a significant factor in the economic adjustment of former patients. However, patients and their families in classes I–III were able to compensate financially for their occupational problems: the proportion of patients without savings and with lower incomes or higher debts at this class level is no higher than the proportion of controls. In contrast, for both clinic and hospital cases, class V patients were less likely to have savings and are more likely to have a lower income, individually and within the family. Reflecting the occupational history, the financial adjustment of class IV patients is related to institutional treatment history: class IV former hospital patients had fewer savings than their controls and significantly lower incomes; class IV former clinic patients did not differ financially from their matched controls to any great extent.

Essentially negative results are found in the examination of two areas: First, for homemakers the ability to perform household tasks did not differ between patients and controls, and no significant social-class variations are found. Second, no significant variation is found for the degree of job satisfaction, although class V former clinic patients were more likely to express a desire to change to another type of job.

Briefly, poor role performance is found among those patients who are normally expected to perform a productive work role in the community. Occupational performance and concomitant financial problems, however, are a function of social class as well as institutional treatment history.

adjustment in the community: III. social participation

Data are presented in this chapter on the relationship of social class to community adjustment for the final test of the study's third hypothesis. The variables examined encompass a variety of roles performed by the patient following his discharge from treatment. Specifically, in this chapter we investigate social-role performance through a number of measures of patient participation in informal and formal groups and organizations. The questions we examine are whether or not the ability to participate effectively in a variety of groups as friend, colleague, associate, or relative is influenced by mental illness and if social class is related to such participation.

The inability of an individual to establish viable interpersonal relationships and to participate socially with his fellowmen has long been used as an indicator of psychopathology. The individual who is without friends may be psychologically unable to relate effectively to others or may lack the social skills to do so; if he has the ability to relate, he may withdraw voluntarily and isolate himself because he fears the responsibility of friendship. On the other hand, the absence of friends and associates may, in itself, contribute to personal disintegration so that personal and social isolation can be important stress-inducing mechanisms.

The problems engendered by personal and social isolation have helped produce some of the recent changes in the organization of psychiatric treatment facilities in which attempts have been made to minimize the

175

separation of the patient from his family, friends, and associates during his course of treatment. Increasingly, small, community treatment facilities are being substituted for the massive state hospitals, often located far from population centers and, thereby, minimizing the contact between the patient and his own community. Indeed, the importance of social participation and the danger of personal and social isolation is embodied directly in the concept of the community mental-health center which reduces spatial restrictions on interaction between the patient and his relatives or friends and emphasizes a new concept of psychiatric service. The patient is offered not only direct services but also indirect ones through community groups that may serve him. A consultation model has been developed in which the mental-health center works with agencies and groups who, in turn, can help support the patient not only while he is in treatment but also after he has been discharged. Central to the concept of psychiatric services is the assumption that patients need to be integrated into social groups in the community.

Previous studies have found that the extent and rate of participation in formal and informal associations is related significantly to social class: the lower the class, the less likely the individual is to have friends and to participate in informal and formal organizational activities.[1] However, the extent of the effect of mental illness on such social participation and the uniformity of that effect for each social class remain unknown phenomena and are the focus of the research findings presented in this chapter.

HOSPITAL PATIENTS

Informal Social Participation

The first measures of social participation relate to informal interpersonal relationships and friendship patterns. Two areas of participation are examined: association with neighbors and friendships in general.

The degree of participation in informal neighborhood activities and groups is measured by the number of close friends [2] in the neighborhood and the frequency of exchanging house visits with neighbors. The

---

[1] See, for example, Charles R. Wright and H. H. Hyman, "Voluntary Association Memberships of American Adults: Evidence from National Sample Surveys," *American Sociological Review*, 23, 284 (1958); Joseph A. Kahl, *The American Class Structure*, Rinehart, New York, 1957, pp. 137–38; Peter H. Rossi, *Why Families Move, A Study in the Social Psychology of Urban Residential Mobility*, The Free Press, Glencoe, Ill., 1955, pp. 34–40.

[2] *Close friend* is defined as "one to whom you can tell anything which is on your mind."

percentages indicated in Table 9.1 refer to the negative aspects of participation, the failure to interact with others in the immediate neighborhood. In this sense, the materials may be interpreted as the degree of social isolation of the patients and controls and therefore emphasize the problematic aspects of participation. For each measure examined, the former patients are consistently more isolated than their matched controls. The extent of isolation, however, is not the same at all class levels. Among both patients and controls, the lower the class the higher the proportion of persons who are isolated socially in the neighborhood. Moreover, the increase is greater among patients so that patient-control differences in social participation and interaction in the neighborhood are greatest in class V and least in classes I–III. In terms of frequency of participation, the number of friends or visits made increases as the social-class position of patients becomes higher. Patient-control differences in neighborhood participation also follow the same class pattern.

Friendships and informal social participation outside the neighborhood were measured by four indices (see Table 9.2). First, patients and controls were asked whether they had any close friends, not necessarily persons in the neighborhood. As seen in Table 9.2, Section A, few of

TABLE 9.1

Social Isolation of Hospital Patients and Controls from Neighbors (Per Cent) [a]

| | Social Class | | | |
	I–III	IV	V	Total
A. No Visits Exchanged with Neighbors				
Patients	26	53	60	52
Controls	10	33	40	33
Difference	16 [b]	20	20	19
B. No Neighbors Regarded as Close Friends				
Patients [b]	48	62	68	63
Controls [c]	35	44	45	43
Difference	13 [c]	18	23	20

[a] Unless otherwise stated, social-class and patient-control differences, χ^2 test, $p < .05$.
[b] Social-class and patient-control differences, χ^2 test. $p < .20$.
[c] Social-class and patient-control differences, χ^2 test, $p > .20$.

TABLE 9.2

Social Isolation of Hospital Patients and Controls from Friends and Relatives (Per Cent) [a]

| | Social Class | | | |
	I–III	IV	V	Total
A. No Close Friends				
Patients [b]	15	26	34	28
Controls [c]	6	8	12	10
Difference	9 [d]	18	22	18
B. Does Not Receive Visits from Friends				
Patients	25	49	65	53
Controls [e]	9	20	32	24
Difference	16 [e]	29	33	29
C. Does Not Visit Friends				
Patients	28	41	61	48
Controls [e]	16	27	33	28
Difference	12 [c]	14 [e]	28	20
D. Participates Socially with Friends or Relatives Less than Once a Month				
Patients [c]	21	27	34	29
Controls [c]	15	17	22	19
Difference	6 [c]	10 [b]	12 [e]	10

[a] Unless otherwise stated, social-class and patient-control differences, χ^2 test, $p < .05$.
[b] Social-class and patient-control differences, χ^2 test, $p < .20$.
[c] Social-class and patient-control differences, χ^2 test, $p > .20$.
[d] χ^2 test inappropriate because of small expected frequencies.
[e] Social-class and patient-control differences, χ^2 test, $p < .10$.

the controls at any class level are without close friends, and there are no class differences among them. Among the patients, the percentage with no close friends decreases consistently from class V to classes I–III. At every class level more patients than controls have no close friends, but the patient-control differences increase from the highest class to the lowest class. Thus, lower-class patients are not only more isolated in the neighborhood, but fewer have any close friendships.

It may well be that in defining *close friend* in such a rigid fashion we are overstating the degree of isolation experienced by class V patients. Since it is possible for persons to interact socially with other than close friends, we allowed the matter of definition of *friend* to remain with the respondent and examined visiting patterns in general by asking two questions about visiting patterns. The respondents were asked if they had been visited in their homes by friends (Table 9.2, Section B) or had visited in the homes of friends (Table 9.2, Section C) during the month preceding the interview. The answers are consistent with the previous findings on participation. Class V patients and controls are less likely to visit or be visited by friends, and patient-control differences at this level are considerably greater than at other class levels. About three fifths of patients in class V neither visit nor are visited by friends, in contrast to about one third of controls.

Since some respondents may have differentiated rigidly between friends and relatives, we tried to determine the amount of social interaction outside the immediate household by asking how frequently the patients and their matched controls got together with either friends or relatives to visit in each other's home or to go out together socially (Table 9.2, Section D). No distinction was made between friends or relatives and no attempt was made to determine the different types of activities which might be undertaken jointly by friends and relatives. Analysis of these general visiting patterns shows that in frequency of socializing there are no great class differences among controls. Among patients, however, the proportion who visit infrequently increases as social class declines so that patient-control differences in social participation are greatest in class V.

In brief, when various measures of informal social participation are examined, patients as a group are found to be more isolated than their matched controls. Among patients, a consistent pattern of class differences is found: the lower the class, the greater the proportion of socially isolated individuals. Among controls, the class differences are not as consistent; in some instances the same pattern holds as for patients, while in others there are only minimal class differences; in no instance, however, is the class pattern reversed. The relationships between social class, treated mental illness, and social isolation become clear when patient-control differences are examined at each class level. These differences demonstrate that the lower the class, the less the degree of social participation and the greater the degree of social isolation. For every measure the differences are greatest in class V.

To determine if any of the control variables account for these class differences, we tested in the same manner as in Chapter 7.[3] The results

---

[3] The same 26 categories listed in Chapter 7, p. 134, footnote 19, were used in the analysis. The expected class pattern for hospital patient-control differences in this chapter was considered confirmed if these differences were greatest in class V by 5 or more percentage points.

indicate that there are no systematic variations to the pattern of class differences found.[4]

Participation in Formal Organizations

In highly urbanized communities, such as those in which the patients and controls reside, associations and formal organizations are available and may be substituted for the traditional informal and extended family systems of interpersonal relations. Thus, an individual's social isolation may be reduced if he is integrated into the community activities through participation in formal organizations in which he meets with others of like outlook and interests.

To determine the extent to which patients utilize and participate in formal organizations and to determine if such participation is linked to social class, we examined a number of measures dealing with such organizations. The respondents were asked several questions concerning their participation in religious organizations and several questions concerning participation in other formal organizations, such as clubs, lodges, unions, and fraternal groups.

Concerning religious organizations, respondents were asked to indicate their affiliation with a religious group (church or synagogue) and whether or not they attended religious services. If they were affiliated with a religious group they were asked if they belonged to any church-sponsored organizations such as the Holy Name Society, a men's club, couples' club, mothers' circle, board of trustees, or missionary society. The responses to these questions are summarized in Table 9.3.

For each item we found that patients are less likely than controls to identify with and to participate in a religious organization. For patients, class differences in participation are striking: the lower the class the greater the proportion of those unaffiliated religiously, never attending church services, and unaffiliated with church-organized activity groups. For controls, the class patterns, while in the same direction, are not as strong or as clear-cut.

The patient-control differences, however, are consistent with the

---

[4] We made 26 analyses for six measures of social adjustment and found 123 instances of confirmation, 15 instances of nonconfirmation, and 18 instances in which there were too few cases to analyze. The six measures are: (1) visiting with neighbors, (2) neighbors as close friends, (3) number of close friends, (4) visiting at friends' homes, (5) receiving visits from friends, and (6) social occasions with friends and relatives less than once per month. In the 15 cases which failed to support the original findings, no single variable consistently resulted in contradictory findings for the various measures of social participation.

TABLE 9.3

Lack of Participation of Hospital Patients and Controls in Religious Organizations (Per Cent) [a]

	Social Class			
	I–III	IV	V	Total
A. Not Affiliated with Church or Synagogue				
Patients [b]	30	36	50	42
Controls [c]	15	27	30	27
Difference	15 [d]	9 [c]	20	15
B. Does Not Attend Religious Services				
Patients [b]	21	29	40	33
Controls [c]	9	14	16	14
Difference	12 [d]	15	24	19
C. Does Not Belong to Church Organizations				
Patients	48	74	96	77
Controls	64	58	80	69
Difference	−16 [c]	16 [d]	16	8 [d]

[a] Unless otherwise stated, social-class and patient-control differences, χ^2 test, $p < .05$.
[b] Social-class differences, χ^2 test, $p < .10$.
[c] Social-class and patient-control differences, χ^2 test, $p > .20$.
[d] Patient-control difference, χ^2 test, $p < .20$.

other findings concerning isolation. In every instance a significantly greater number of patients than of controls in class V did not participate and the difference is as great as or greater than at any other level. Interestingly, we find that if we compare the patient-control differences in classes I–III with those in class V, the size of the disparity between these two differences increases as the degree of personal involvement or participation increases in intensity. In terms of simple nonaffiliation with a church or synagogue, the difference in class V (20 per cent) is 5 percentage points more than in classes I–III (15 per cent) (see Table 9.3). For nonattendance at religious services, the corresponding percentage point difference between classes V and I–III is 12, and for nonaffiliation with organizations within the church it is 32. Thus, we find that the greater the degree of personal involvement required in a religious activity, the greater the proportion of class V patients who do

TABLE 9.4

Participation of Hospital Patients and Controls in Formal Organizations (Per Cent)[a]

	Social Class			
	I–III	IV	V	Total
A. No Membership in Formal Organizations				
Patients	38	67	80	68
Controls	31	50	66	55
Difference	7 [b]	17	14	13
B. Although Affiliated, Does Not Attend Meetings				
Patients	30	18	61	35
Controls [b]	27	18	32	26
Difference	3 [b]	0 [b]	29	9 [b]

[a] Unless otherwise stated, social-class and patient-control differences, χ^2 test, $p < .05$.

[b] Social-class and patient-control differences, χ^2 test, $p > .20$.

not participate, as compared with patients and controls at other class levels.[5]

As we examine the responses to questions about participation in other formal organizations, the isolation of class V former patients is again demonstrated. The respondents were asked to indicate membership in clubs, lodges, unions, or other formally organized groups, and when they indicated such membership they were asked if they regularly attended meetings of the organization. The responses to these two questions, summarized by social class for the patients and the controls, are presented in Table 9.4. It is clear that generally more patients than controls do not belong to formal organizations, and if they do belong they are less likely to attend meetings regularly. Among patients, the proportion not participating increases greatly from classes I–III to class

---

[5] We tested to determine if any of the control variables account for the class differences we have found. The results show that they do not. The control variables were divided into the same 26 categories and analyses made for each of the three items in Table 9.3. Thus there were a total of 78 analyses. In 66 instances the expected class differences were found; in five instances there were too few cases to test; and in only seven instances did the class differences disappear but with no other variables systematically eliminating these differences.

V. Among controls, the pattern differs for membership and attendance; the proportion who are not members increases from classes I–III to class V, but, among members, lack of participation is about as great in classes I–III as in class V. When patient-control differences are examined they are always minimal in classes I–III. In terms of nonmembership, the relative isolation of patients is as great in class IV as in class V, but in terms of the more intimate involvement of attendance the greatest patient-control differences are found in class V in which 61 per cent of the patients who belong to formal organizations do not attend meetings regularly in contrast to only 32 per cent of controls.[6] Again we find that as the degree of personal involvement increases, the disparity between the patient-control differences in classes I–III and V increases from 7 percentage points for simple membership in formal organizations to 26 percentage points for attendance at meetings.

In brief, lower-class patients participate less than higher-status patients in informal and formal organizations, and these class differences increase as a result of treated mental illness. While few differences are perceived between class I–III patients and controls, consistently substantial differences are found between class V patients and controls. Class IV patients tend to be intermediate to these two groups, and the patient-control differences are not consistently significant. Whether the class IV patients differ from their controls depends upon the particular activity under examination.

Changes in Patterns of Participation

The materials presented so far demonstrate that proportionately more patients in class V than at any other social-class level are isolated, both in relation to other patients and to their matched controls. Moreover, the patient-control differences become greater in class V as the degree of personal involvement and participation becomes more intense.

In order to determine when this isolation began, we asked the respondents several questions about changes in informal and formal social participation. As measures of informal participation we studied visiting patterns and number of friends. Participation in formal organizations and attendance at religious services were examined as the formal aspect of social participation. The base line for patients is the period before

---

[6] In controlling for other relevant variables, analyses were made for the two items in Table 9.4 for each of the 26 control categories. In 40 instances the expected class differences were found; in four instances there were too few cases to analyze; and in eight instances class differences disappeared but with no other variables systematically eliminating these differences.

TABLE 9.5

Changes in Social Participation of Hospital Patients and Controls (Per Cent) [a]

	Social Class			
	I–III	IV	V	Total
A. Visits Less Frequently				
Patients [b]	22	45	43	40
Controls [c]	22	35	24	28
Difference	0 [c]	10 [c]	19	12
B. Has Fewer Friends				
Patients [c]	24	42	38	37
Controls [c]	9	15	8	11
Difference	15 [b]	27	30	26
C. Participates Less in Formal Organizations				
Patients [d]	30	18	50	32
Controls [c]	36	24	19	26
Difference	−6 [c]	−6 [c]	31	6 [c]
D. Attends Fewer Religious Services				
Patients [b]	24	33	45	37
Controls [c]	6	20	17	16
Difference	18	13 [b]	28	21

[a] Unless otherwise stated, patient-control difference, χ^2 test, $p < .05$.
[b] Social-class and patient-control differences, χ^2 test, $p < .10$.
[c] Social-class and patient-control differences, χ^2 test, $p > .20$.
[d] Social-class and patient-control differences, χ^2 test, $p < .20$.

the illness for which they were being treated in the original study. For controls we used a base line of five years ago. The answers to these questions are presented in Table 9.5.[7]

Most patients indicate that, in comparison to the period of time before their psychiatric illness, either there has been no change in their rate of participation or they participate more. Over one third, however, visit less frequently, have fewer friends, participate less frequently in formal organizations, or attend religious services less often. Generally, there is an inverse relationship between class and increased isolation among patients, but the differences are not always consistent or especially great.

---

[7] See previous discussion of this base line for mobility, Chapter 6, p. 121, footnote 12.

TABLE 9.6

	Social Class (Per Cent)		
	I–III	IV	V
Visited regularly	83	82	53
Corresponded regularly	42	31	26
Sent packages	75	56	43
Consulted hospital authorities about patient's discharge	60	44	41

However, patient-control differences vary significantly at the different class levels. Without exception, the greatest differences are always found at class V in which proportionately more patients than controls become more isolated over the years both in informal and formal associations. Generally, the least difference is in classes I–III, with class IV occupying an intermediate position. This pattern of increased isolation in class V cannot be accounted for by other variables.[8]

This pattern of increasing isolation as we move from classes I–III to class V began during the period of hospitalization. We asked a series of questions of the household informant covering the family's contacts with the patient while he was hospitalized. The proportion who maintained contact by class is given in Table 9.6.

Although most families maintained contact with the hospitalized patients, there are consistent class differences in the proportions: the higher the class, the greater the proportion of family members who visited, wrote, sent packages, and consulted with hospital authorities. Thus, even before discharge lower-class patients are more likely to be cut off from contacts with persons outside the hospital, and, upon discharge, class V patients are more likely to be isolated socially than persons at other class levels.

Focusing on patients at home, we asked household informants two questions about social expectations: Do you expect the patient to help you entertain at home? Do you expect the patient to go to parties and other social activities? The results are given in Table 9.7. It is clear that the families of lower-class patients expect less of them socially

[8] The four items in Table 9.5 were used and the same 26 control categories for a total of 104 analyses. Expected class differences were found in 82 instances; there were too few cases to test in 16 instances, and class differences disappeared in six instances but with no other variables systematically eliminating these differences.

TABLE 9.7

	Social Class (Per Cent)		
	I–III	IV	V
Patient not expected to help entertain at home now	25	22	41
Patient not expected to help entertain at home six months from now	25	19	35
Patient not expected to go to parties and other social activities now	12	29	35
Patient not expected to go to parties and other social activities six months from now	12	20	31

since the proportions replying negatively are considerably greater in class V than at other class levels. Perhaps more important, the same class differences are found in terms of future expectations. More than one third of lower-class household informants do not expect the patient to be active socially at the time of the interview or even six months in the future.

In this section we have examined a number of measures dealing with the social adjustment of former hospital patients: the extent to which the former patients have been able to establish or reestablish viable interpersonal relationships with neighbors, friends, and relatives living outside the immediate household; their participation in religious organizations; and their other formal organizational activity. Further, we have examined a series of questions determining the degree to which the patients' patterns of participation in formal and informal activities and groups have changed. The results of these analyses are consistent with our findings on other measures of social adjustment—occupational and work performance. Patients, as a group, are more isolated socially than their matched controls. Previous psychiatric treatment is reflected in fewer friends and less frequent participation in formal and informal activities and organizations.

Treated mental illness does not affect the patients uniformly, however. The patient-control difference is strongly linked to social class (see Appendix 1, Table A1.8). Treated mental illness is not consistently or significantly associated with increased isolation or high levels of isolation among class I–III patients. In most cases, we find that in classes I–III patients differ little from their matched controls. In contrast, patients in class V are more isolated than at any other social level. Moreover, they differ consistently from their matched controls by a significant margin. The patient-control difference for the measures examined is almost always at a maximum in class V.

When class IV patients are compared to their matched controls, they are generally intermediate to patients in classes I–III and class V. They are not as active socially as class I–III patients, and, in many instances, substantially many more are isolated than their matched controls; patient-control differences, however, are generally much smaller than in class V.

Many class V patients would be almost totally isolated socially, save for the fact that they have relatives living nearby with whom they interact. A sizeable number live alone, have no friends, belong to no social clubs, attend no church, and seldom, if ever, participate with other individuals except for the process of acquiring the basic needs to sustain life. Those patients at this class level who are married and do not live alone are frequently just as isolated.

The extent of social isolation is illustrated by the story of Joseph D., a class V male schizophrenic, catatonic type. Hospitalized early in the 1950's, Mr. D. was discharged in 1952. Eighteen months later he married, and at the follow-up interview he was 34 years old and had a five-year-old son. He has worked regularly as an unskilled laborer with the same company for eight years. Mr. and Mrs. D. never discuss his hospitalization or his mental illness with others, and they are concerned if the subject of mental illness comes up in any conversation lest they say something to "give us away." They were fearful that our study might betray them to someone.

Mr. D. has three brothers and a sister living in the immediate community. He sees them usually a few times a year, although he had seen none of them during the three months previous to the interview. Both he and his wife told us that in case of an emergency no relative would loan them money. Mr. D. is acquainted with two families in the neighborhood but never visits them. He has neither visited nor been visited by anyone during the past month. Throughout the year Mr. D. gets together socially less than once a month with friends or relatives. He told us that he has no close friends except his wife. Mr. D. belongs to no clubs or organizations, and although he is affiliated with the Catholic Church he attends only a few times per year at most. He reads daily and Sunday newspapers but little else. His main leisure-time activity is watching television which consumes at least two or three hours every night and most of the weekend. Both he and his wife like to watch television because they find it "very relaxing."

In contrast to this social isolation in class V, patients in classes I–III are just as active socially as their matched controls. Mrs. S., a class III, married woman with five children ranging in age from 1 to 12, is an example. Diagnosed as schizophrenic, unclassified, at hospitalization, she was discharged in 1952 and moved with her family into a new, single-family home in a lower-middle-class housing development. Mrs. S. and her husband, a manager in a large organization, like the area very much. They know more than a dozen neighbors and visit back and forth regularly with three couples. They hire a baby-sitter once a week so they can go out together or visit friends. Mrs. S. tries to attend church each week, and she participates in numerous social activities, many of which are organized around her children; she is active in the Parent-Teacher Association, is a den mother for the Cub Scouts, and assists with a Brownie troop; she is also a member of a women's group in her church and of the alumnae association of the junior college she attended. Her husband frequently takes care of the children in the evening so she can go to her various meetings.

Neither Mrs. S. nor her husband feels that they should hide the fact of her hospitalization. Although they generally do not make a point of discussing it with others, if the subject of mental illness arises they usually mention Mrs. S.'s successful treatment. Mrs. S. is satisfied with her social activities and believes that they have helped her regain and maintain her emotional stability.

CLINIC PATIENTS

The same analyses just described for former hospital patients were made also for former clinic patients. Therefore, the presentation here does not need to be as detailed.

Social Participation

Table 9.8 presents summary data concerning relationships between social class, treated mental illness, and social participation of clinic patients. More detailed data are presented in Appendix 1, Table A1.9. The first important point is the general similarity to the hospital cases for the indices of informal social interaction. Among clinic patients, class is inversely related to isolation: the lower the class, the higher the percentage of persons who do not participate socially. Class differences among controls are less pronounced and not as consistent. However, the pattern of clinic patient-control differences at the various class levels is even more striking than that of hospital patients: the lower the class, the

TABLE 9.8

Informal Social Interaction and Lack of Participation in Formal Organizations for Clinic Patients and Controls (Per Cent)

Patient-Control Difference [a]	Social Class			
	I–III	IV	V	Total
Informal				
No visits exchanged with neighbors	−9	13	30	9
No neighbors regarded as close friends	7	7	38	14
No close friends	0	15	32	14
Does not receive visits from friends	7	3	17	7
Does not visit friends	−10	2	13	1
Participates socially with friends or relatives less than once a month	−3	2	21	5
Formal				
Not affiliated with church or synagogue	−3	5	21	6
Does not attend religious services	6	10	16	11
Does not belong to church organizations	−14	33	−4	9
No membership in formal organizations	−12	7	12	3
Although affiliated, does not attend meetings	0	4	35	5

[a] See Appendix 1, Table A1.9 for the percentages for patients and controls.

more isolated the patients, compared to their matched controls. Without exception, for every measure of informal participation the largest proportion of socially isolated individuals is found among class V patients.[9]

---

[9] Using the same control procedure described in Chapter 7, we tested for the influence of other factors. The six Informal items in Table 9.8 were analyzed for each of the 12 control categories described in Chapter 7, pp. 137–138, footnote 20. The expected class pattern for clinic patient-control differences in this chapter was considered confirmed if these differences were greatest in class V by 5 or more percentage points. Class differences in the expected direction were found in 63 instances; in seven cases there were no class differences, but no other variables systematically eliminated these differences; and in two instances there were too few cases in a cell to analyze.

TABLE 9.9

Changes in Social Participation of Clinic Patients and Controls (Per Cent)

| Patient-Control Differences [a] | Social Class | | | |
	I–III	IV	V	Total
Visits less frequently	−3	−18	8	−7
Has fewer friends	−14	−6	20	−1
Participates less in formal organizations	−29	−7	27	−13
Attends fewer religious services	21	20	12	19

[a] See Appendix 1, Table A1.10, for the percentages for patients and controls.

Class differences among patients and controls are not as pronounced for participation in formal organizations as for informal social interaction. Patient-control differences, however, are uniformly greater in class V than at any other social level except for participation in church-affiliated organizations. With the exception of this activity, in which a larger proportion of patients than controls in class IV does not participate, class V patients include a larger proportion of socially isolated individuals than is found at any other class level for patients or for controls.[10]

Changes in Patterns of Participation

Summary findings on changes in the amount of social participation from a period before the psychiatric illness for the clinic patients and five years ago for the controls are shown in Table 9.9. More detailed data are presented in Appendix 1, Table A1.10. For three of the four measures, the proportion of patients who withdrew from participation over the years increases from classes I–III to class V, while for one measure—attendance at religious services—there are no such class variations. Among controls there are no class differences in decreasing social interaction. Patient-control differences in increasing isolation, however, are greatest in class V for all measures except attendance at religious services.

---

[10] When we control for the influence of other factors, class differences in the expected direction remain in 49 instances and disappear in four cases but with no other variables systematically eliminating these differences; in seven instances there are too few cases to make an analysis.

It should be noted that patient-control differences in class IV are similar to those in classes I–III. In other words, the class relationship is not linear, but class V differs from the other social levels in terms of an increase in the proportion of patients not participating in formal organizational activities.[11]

SUMMARY AND DISCUSSION

In summary, relationships between social class, treated mental illness, and social participation are similar for former hospital and clinic patients. Generally, among patients there is a strong inverse relationship between class and social isolation: the lower the class, the higher the proportion of socially isolated persons. Class differences in social participation are not as pronounced among controls but do follow the same pattern. Patient-control differences in social isolation, however, are striking by social class, increasing consistently from classes I–III to class V. With few exceptions, a much larger proportion of patients than controls are socially isolated in class V than in any other class.

Class differences in social participation among patients reflect, to some degree, differences found among controls: the lower the class, the less likely the individual to participate in formal, organized, social activities. More persons in class V than at any other social level are outside the mainstream of community life.[12] Not only are they less likely to participate in formal social organizations, including the church, but also they have fewer friends and do less informal visiting. In general, they have few positive, social, group experiences or rewarding interpersonal relationships. Leisure-time activities in class V are mostly passive—viewing television, sitting around the house, going to the movies, and so on.

Lower-class persons have more difficulty in establishing friendships outside the neighborhood than persons of higher social status. They do not have the same opportunities as middle- and upper-class persons to find friends among colleagues or work associates, as social interaction is constricted in the types of jobs open to them. Spatial movement also is more limited than at other social levels, especially for older persons who depend more upon public transportation. The lack of household help and baby-sitters frequently restricts the movement of mothers and even

---

[11] To determine if other factors might be influencing these class differences, we controlled as previously for relevant factors. Class differences are as expected in 38 instances and disappear in only two cases; in eight instances there are too few cases to analyze.

[12] See Jerome K. Myers and Bertram H. Roberts, *Family and Class Dynamics in Mental Illness*, Wiley, New York, 1959, pp. 172–198.

couples with young children. Yet, lower-class patients are less able than higher-status individuals to find friends in the neighborhood, since the suspicion and distrust of lower-class persons toward authority figures carry over into their interpersonal relationships, especially under the conditions of congestion and lack of privacy in tenement slum living.

Many of the conditions of lower-class life which give rise to social isolation are magnified for former mental patients. Class V patients are less likely than nonpatients to have even the limited opportunities to make friends on the job because fewer are employed regularly, as described in Chapter 8. The poor economic or financial condition of former patients means also that they have less money available than their matched controls to pay for organizational activities. Some are even hesitant to go to church because they do not have enough money for the collection plate.

A higher percentage of patients than controls in class V live alone in large rooming houses or tenements where it is difficult to get to know neighbors.[13] Because of their emotional problems, interpersonal relations for former patients are especially brittle and they are probably affected more than controls by the tensions arising from congestion and lack of privacy in their living arrangements.[14]

In brief, the very conditions of lower-class life which help to produce social isolation reinforce the patients' difficulties in performing their expressive-integrative roles and lead to further isolation. Two additional factors, the perceived stigma attached to mental illness and family expectations for former patients, also differ by class and help to account for the differences in social participation which we have found.

Previous research indicates that the lower the class the greater the degree of perceived stigma attached to treatment for mental illness.[15]

---

[13] See Chapter 5, p. 89.

[14] The lack of privacy and constant visibility of the lower-class patient may, indeed, be an important stress-inducing factor. Robert K. Merton, for example, suggests that the need for privacy is, to some degree, universal. Furthermore, he suggests that the need to live constantly up to the demands of ever-present individuals would be unbearable and, in "a complex society, schizophrenic behavior would become the rule rather than the formidable exception it already is." See Robert K. Merton, *Social Theory and Social Structure*, The Free Press, Glencoe, Ill., 1957, p. 375. For a further discussion of the pressure arising from lack of privacy, see Lloyd H. Rogler and August B. Hollingshead, *Trapped: Families and Schizophrenia*, Wiley, New York, 1965.

[15] For example, see Charles D. Whatley, "Social Attitudes Toward Discharged Mental Patients," *Social Problems*, 6, 313 (1959); and J. L. Woodward, "Changing Ideas on Mental Illness and Its Treatment," *American Sociological Review*, 16, 443 (1951).

Rather than subject himself to potential ridicule or avoidance on the part of friends and neighbors, the lower-class patient may rationally limit his involvement. On the other hand, the upper-class patient can expect a greater degree of sympathy and understanding from his more enlightened peers, so he does not tend to isolate himself socially for this reason. Our data strongly support this position. We asked former patients whether a former mental patient should keep secret from friends and acquaintances his psychiatric hospitalization or outpatient treatment (whichever the case might be). The answers in Table 9.10 demonstrate that the lower the class the higher the proportion of respondents who believe treatment for mental illness should be kept secret.

TABLE 9.10

	Social Class (Per Cent)		
	I–III	IV	V
Hospital Patients			
Keep secret from friends	20	44	57
Keep secret from acquaintances	34	52	69
Clinic Patients			
Keep secret from friends	15	24	40
Keep secret from acquaintances	32	46	67

A similar class pattern is found when household informants (usually family members) were asked the same questions. Apparently lower-class persons are more afraid than higher-status individuals that relations with friends and acquaintances will be damaged if the patients' treatment for psychiatric illness is known. The answers given by household informants are given in Table 9.11.

Although we are dealing with perceived stigma and do not know whether such stigma actually exists in the community, the very fact that former patients and their families believe that it does influences their behavior. Moreover, lower-class patients do encounter such stigma often enough to give credence to their beliefs. Miss M., a class V, single, former hospital patient, would like more friends but feels that people avoid her because she has "been up to the state mental hospital." She claims that the friends of her family have not treated her the same since her return. Her sister, with whom she lives, is embarrassed by the thought

TABLE 9.11

	Social Class (Per Cent)		
	I–III	IV	V
Hospital Patients			
Keep secret from friends	17	28	34
Keep secret from			
acquaintances	26	44	53
Clinic Patients			
Keep secret from friends	27	29	38
Keep secret from			
acquaintances	40	48	62

of the psychiatric hospitalization. She reports that since the patient's return, family members are less willing to invite friends to their home and sometimes avoid their friends because they are embarrassed.

Frequently, the lower-class individual's behavior is interpreted differently if he is identified as a former mental patient. For example, aggressive and physically violent behavior is not at all uncommon at this level of society, but such behavior is viewed as much more dangerous if the person has been hospitalized for mental illness. Several class V men have life-time histories of such behavior which was not considered at all unusual before their hospitalization. Since their discharge, however, similar behavior is viewed as dangerous by their families and friends and considered an indication of their "insanity." Consequently, people avoid these former patients as much as possible.

In contrast, higher-status persons more frequently overlook the eccentricities of former patients. A more conscious effort is made to accept the patient socially and incorporate him into regular activities. One socially active woman of higher status is well known among her friends for her eccentricities which are accepted as part of her personality and do not interfere with her participation in numerous clubs and a multitude of social activities. No one in her circle of friends and acquaintances is surprised if she attends a cocktail party in the middle of the summer in a full-length fur coat or appears at a formal afternoon tea wearing sneakers and a sport dress. Similarly, the friends of one class II man are amused by his tendencies (after a few drinks at a party) to pinch or pat the ladies' posteriors and make other advances. It is the subject of amiable conversation, and newcomers are apprised of the situation.

In other studies family expectations for former patients have been

TABLE 9.12

Class	Hospital Patients		Clinic Patients	
	Now	Six Months from Now	Now	Six Months from Now

Expected to Help Entertain at Home (Per Cent)

Class	Now	Six Months from Now	Now	Six Months from Now
I–III	78	81	92	88
IV	75	75	97	92
V	59	65	70	60

Expected to Go to Parties and Other Social Activities (Per Cent)

Class	Now	Six Months from Now	Now	Six Months from Now
I–III	88	88	96	96
IV	71	80	93	92
V	65	69	80	74

shown to be related to successful community adjustment.[16] We asked our household informants a series of questions about social expectations for patients at present and for the future. Their answers appear in Table 9.12.

Although most patients are expected to be socially active, there are important differences by class: the lower the class, the less socially active the patient is expected to be. When these class differences in expectations are added to the differences in perceived stigma and in life conditions, it becomes clearer why the social isolation of patients increases as social class decreases. Thus, the social participation of patients in class V is less than that of patients or controls at any class level. Morever, compared to other patients and to controls, a higher proportion of class V patients have become increasingly isolated since the termination of their psychiatric treatment.

It is interesting to note the influence of treatment agency on this class pattern in social participation. We would expect that former hospital patients, in relation to their controls, would be more isolated socially than former clinic patients because of their absence from the community and the more serious psychiatric difficulties which led to their hospitalization. This is true, however, only in class IV. In classes I–III former

---

[16] Howard E. Freeman and Ozzie G. Simmons, "Social Class and Posthospital Performance Levels," *American Sociological Review*, 24, 345 (1959).

patients are no more isolated socially than their matched controls regardless of treatment agency. There is little difference ($p > .20$) between hospital or clinic patients and their controls in class III for most measures of social participation studied (see Appendix 1, Table A1.11).

In contrast, both clinic and hospital patients in class V are more socially isolated than their matched controls for most indices of social participation. Thus, treatment agency makes little difference in classes I–III and in class V. Upper- and middle-class patients are just as active socially as their matched controls, whereas lower-class patients are substantially more isolated regardless of institutional history.

In class IV, social activity falls between that in class V and in classes I–III, and treatment agency, itself, is an important factor in the degree of social isolation. A substantially greater percentage of hospital patients than their controls are socially isolated according to 9 of the 11 measures of social participation. In contrast, clinic patients are less active than their controls for only 2 of the 11 measures.

When we examine the relationships between social class, treatment agency, and the perceived stigma attached to mental illness, we find a clue to the differences just described (see pp. 193–194). In class IV, the proportion of former hospital patients and their families who believe psychiatric hospitalization should be kept secret is substantially higher than in classes I–III and approaches the figures for class V. Although the corresponding percentages for clinic cases in class IV are also higher than in classes I–III, they are more like those in classes I–III than those in class V. Apparently in class IV the stigma attached to psychiatric hospitalization is relatively more important than that attached to outpatient treatment and than that at other class levels. There is less stigma attached to outpatient treatment as long as the person can continue to perform the usual social roles expected of him. If an individual is institutionalized and removed from the community he is clearly identifiable as being mentally ill, whereas outpatient treatment can be hidden easily or presented as medical treatment since it does not interfere with the patient's usual activities. Thus, former hospital patients in class IV may participate in social activities less than former clinic patients in an attempt to ensure the secrecy of their hospitalization.

Other factors that may also be involved include: adverse attitudes toward psychiatric illness and its treatment operating on the part of others in their social interaction with former patients (the patient may wish to participate but be handicapped because of the attitudes of his peers) and a break in community living brought about by hospitalization (the social relations of clinic patients are never broken like those of the individual under hospital care). Reestablishment of social relationships in class IV may be more difficult than their continuation, especially if negative attitudes toward psychiatry are held by the patient's friends and acquaintances. Economic factors may also be more important for hospital than clinic patients at this class level. If a mother with small children has been hospitalized, her husband probably has had additional expense in caring for the children. Therefore, upon her return, there may not be enough money to hire someone to care for the children to free the patient to be active socially. Furthermore, the husband himself may have become increasingly isolated during his wife's hospitalization. A man returning from hospitalization might find an even more difficult situation at home.

There are class differences also in family expectations for patients according to the treatment agency involved (see pp. 195–196). About the same proportion of families of clinic patients in class IV as in classes I–III have high expectations for them, whereas a substantially smaller proportion of class V families expect as much from the patients. In contrast, the proportion of families of hospital patients in class IV with high expectations falls between those in classes I–III and in class V. Thus, differences in expectations may also help to account for clinic-hospital differences in the extent of social participation in class IV.

In summary, the data presented in this chapter support the study's third hypothesis that social class is related to the former patient's adjustment in the community. An examination of various measures of social-role performance demonstrates that the lower the class, the higher the proportion of socially isolated patients. Patient-control differences in social participation are equally striking, decreasing consistently from classes I–III to class V. This general class pattern is characteristic of hospital and clinic patients alike, although there are some differences in its details for the two groups.

summary and conclusions

part four

This part presents a summary of the major findings and some suggestions for future reseach. It also raises certain questions about psychiatric practice and its future development.

final
considerations

chapter
ten

This research was undertaken to determine whether or not social class is related to the outcome of psychiatric treatment and to the adjustment of former patients in the community. It grew out of previous studies of social class and mental illness conducted in New Haven in the 1950's. The earlier studies dealt with the development, manifestations, distribution, and treatment of diagnosed mental illness. The current research extends the focus of attention to later stages in the career of mental patients.

In the research we examine three hypotheses to determine the relationships between social class and treatment outcome: (1) *Social class is related to treatment status in 1960 at follow-up;* (2) *Social class is related to the patient's 1950 to 1960 treatment and readmission experience;* (3) *Social class is related to the former patient's adjustment in the community.*

To test these hypotheses the original group of 1563 patients from greater New Haven who were in hospital or clinic treatment between May 31 and December 1, 1950 were followed over a 10-year period to June 1, 1960 through their various courses and terms of treatment. Patients not hospitalized and living in the community on June 1, 1960 were interviewed along with a family or household member. A matched control group of never-treated individuals also was interviewed to provide a base line for comparison of performance of patients in the community.

201

The data collected from institutional records and from the series of interviews were analyzed separately for patients who were in hospital treatment in 1950 and for those in outpatient clinic treatment for a number of reasons. First, hospitalized patients are more frequently diagnosed as psychotic while outpatient clinic patients are more frequently diagnosed as neurotic. Second, hospitalized patients are, in general, older than clinic patients. Finally, the nature of the institutional treatment is different: hospital patients are removed from the community while in treatment, whereas clinic patients experience no such community isolation during their treatment.

The many systematic tests made on the three hypotheses support the general proposition that social class is related to the outcome of psychiatric treatment and adjustment in the community no matter how they are defined or measured. Beginning with the first hypothesis that *social class is related to treatment status in 1960 at follow-up,* we find that for both hospital and clinic patients the higher the class, the less likely the patients were to be hospitalized 10 years after the original study. Among persons living in the community in 1960, the opposite relationship is found between class and treatment: the higher the class, the greater the proportion in outpatient treatment, either in a clinic or private practice. Class differences in treatment status are similar for those who died during the 10-year period: the higher the class, the more likely the persons to be living in the community at the time of their death. In general, class is found to be related to death rates and age at death: the higher the class, the lower the age-specific death rates and the older the age at death.

Three separate analyses were made to test the second hypothesis that *social class is related to the patient's treatment and readmission experience during the period from 1950 to 1960:* (1) the 10-year discharge and readmission history of 1950 hospital patients; (2) the 1950 to 1960 treatment experience of 1950 hospital patients and its relationship to follow-up status; and (3) the psychiatric treatment experience of 1950 clinic patients.

The results of the analyses show that the chances of hospital discharge are greater for higher-status persons not only for first discharge but also for each subsequent discharge following a readmission. In turn, the chances of readmission are just as high, and in some cases higher, for lower-status as for higher-status persons. Thus, there is a piling-up of patients in the hospital as social-class status decreases. In terms of the type of hospital treatment received, the higher the class, the greater the proportion of patients receiving therapies associated with higher discharge rates—psychotherapy or somatotherapy. Moreover, the higher the class of the patients receiving such therapies, the greater the proportion discharged. In contrast, as the social status of patients decreases they are more likely to receive drug therapy and custodial care. Among 1950 clinic patients, class is related to treatment and its outcome in several ways. Upper- and middle-class patients remained in outpatient care for longer periods than lower-class patients, more frequently received individual psychotherapy, and were more likely to be receiving outpatient care at follow-up in 1960. Lower-class clinic patients, on the other hand, were more likely to be hospitalized for their psychiatric illnesses during the 10-year follow-up period.

The third hypothesis examined was that *social class is related to the former patient's adjustment in the community*. In testing this hypothesis, the patient's performance in the community is compared with that of a matched control group consisting of individuals who had never been treated for mental illness. Adjustment is divided conceptually into two dimensions: (1) the psychobiological which is measured by indices of mental status impairment, and (2) the social which is measured by the ability of the patient to perform certain economic roles and to participate in a variety of formal and informal organizations and groups.

In summarizing the data relating to the third hypothesis, we present a composite profile of the patient's adjustment in the community at each class level.

COMMUNITY ADJUSTMENT: A SOCIAL-CLASS PROFILE

Classes I–III

When class I–III patients in the community are compared with patients at other class levels and with their matched controls, important differences are discovered in the psychobiological adjustment of those treated in hospitals and in clinics in 1950. A substantially higher proportion of class I–III former hospital patients than persons at other class levels is psychologically impaired. In contrast, among former clinic patients, patient-control differences by class in the degree of psychological impairment are reversed, being least in classes I–III and greatest in class V. Thus, relative to other patients and their controls, hospital patients in classes I–III are the most impaired psychologically and clinic patients the least impaired. It should be noted that former clinic as well as hospital patients show a greater degree of psychological impairment than their matched controls at all class levels.

In the first measure of social adjustment, hospital and clinic patients in classes I–III also differ in economic-role performance but not to the same degree as in the case of psychobiological adjustment. Occupationally and economically, former clinic patients differ little from their matched controls at this level, having comparable records of employment stability and approximately equal incomes. Hospital patients in classes I–III, in contrast, are less likely than their matched controls to be regularly employed in full-time jobs and more likely to have experienced longer periods of unemployment. The employment difference results in only slight variations in individual income, however, and does not produce any substantial decrease in family income. The higher level of psychological impairment found among class I–III hospital patients thus is reflected in employment but not in financial problems. However, the actual patient-control difference in regularity of employment in classes I–III is less than at other class levels.

In the second area of social adjustment examined (social participation), no major patient-control differences are found between hospital and clinic cases in classes I–III. At this social level all patients participate as frequently as their matched controls in social activities and in the same variety of informal and formal organizations. No evidence is found to indicate that middle- and upper-class patients experience any unusual degree of social isolation following their psychiatric treatment.

To summarize briefly, the upper- and middle-class patients may be characterized as follows: Clinic patients are well adjusted as judged by the performance of their matched controls. They experience no greater social isolation, have no greater employment and financial problems, and (while functioning psychologically at a lower level than their controls) are, in fact, functioning at as high (if not higher) a level psychologically as any other patient group. Hospital patients are well adjusted in one area: they participate in formal and informal organizations in a manner similar to their matched controls. They are more likely to experience employment problems, but financial hardships are minimal and they function at a much lower level psychologically than their matched controls.

Class IV

In terms of psychobiological adjustment, patient-control differences in psychological impairment in class IV are as small as, or less than, at any other class level. Among former hospital patients these differences are less in class IV than in classes I–III and about the same as in class V. Among clinic patients, they are the same in class IV as in classes I–III and much less than in class V.

In other areas of performance in the community, class IV patients generally fare less well than class I–III patients, but their relative success varies with treatment agency. Hospital patients are hard pressed to secure and retain work in the community, particularly at their previous level of skill. Despite their higher level of psychological functioning, their occupational performance is poorer than that of class I–III patients and is reflected in lower incomes. Clinic patients are relatively much more successful in their work roles. Compared to their matched controls and to patients at other class levels, they have no greater problems in securing and retaining employment nor do they suffer more financially.

In addition to their employment problems, class IV hospital patients are more likely than their matched controls and class I–III patients to be socially isolated and to participate less in formal and informal organizations, while clinic patients do not differ in the degree of social participation from their matched controls nor are patient-control differences any greater than in classes I–III.

In general, the same pattern of adjustment in the community characterizes clinic patients in class IV as in classes I–III, but a different pattern is found for class IV hospital patients. Clinic patients are no more impaired psychologically than class I–III patients and, like the upper- and middle-class clinic patients, experienced no major difficulties in employment, income, or social participation. Class IV hospital patients function psychologically at a higher level than upper- and middle-class former hospital patients but experience greater economic and social problems when compared to their matched controls.

In summary, the adjustment of class IV patients in the community is generally intermediate between classes I–III and class V. At this level, the treatment agency itself is more directly related to the patient's social and economic adjustment than it is at higher or lower levels in the class system.

Class V

Adjustment in the community is the most difficult for lower-class patients. In only one instance are patient-control differences minimal in class V: in the analyses, former hospital patients in class V are found to function at a higher level psychologically than patients at other social levels and with only slightly more impairment than their matched controls. In contrast, former clinic patients in class V are substantially more impaired psychologically than such patients at other class levels, and patient-control differences are maximal.

Despite the difference between class V hospital and clinic patients in mental status and symptomatic behavior, no similar difference distinguishes these groups with respect to any measure of social adjustment. Both clinic and hospital patients in class V encounter more problems in securing and retaining employment than other patients and their matched controls, and their dependence upon part-time and irregular work is reflected in extremely low incomes which are not offset by earnings of other family members. Thus, the higher level of psychological adjustment among class V former hospital patients is not reflected in their work performance.

In terms of social participation, both clinic and hospital patients in the lower class are extremely isolated when compared to other patients and to their matched controls. Regardless of treatment agency or level of psychological performance, the class V individual who has been treated for mental illness is isolated from formal and informal groups in the community.

In brief, mental illness is apparently catastrophic for the lower-class patient and his family. The social and economic problems which characterize this class level in our society are magnified for the former mental patient. If hospitalized, the chances are less than at higher social levels that he will return to the community. If the patient does return or is treated in outpatient facilities, the impact of his illness is maximal, resulting in serious employment and financial problems and a high degree of social isolation.

UNDERSTANDING TREATMENT OUTCOME: SOCIAL CLASS AND MENTAL ILLNESS IN RETROSPECT

The class differences observed in treatment outcome in this study reflect the way in which social factors influence certain aspects of the career of the mental patient. These findings not only extend our knowledge about later stages in the patient's career but also throw light on studies which have dealt with earlier stages, particularly the period of treatment.

The original 1950 study of social class and mental illness in New Haven found striking social-class differences in the prevalence rates of treated mental disorders: the lower the class, the higher the rates of psychoses and the lower the rates of neuroses. Since there is a strong association between diagnosis and treatment agency, it was found that the lower the class, the more likely the patients were to receive hospital care and the less likely to receive outpatient treatment. Other studies generally support these findings.[1]

The original work of Hollingshead and Redlich suggests that the higher prevalence rates of total illness in class V are due, in part, to a

---

[1] See, for example, Leo Srole et al., *Mental Health in the Metropolis: The Midtown Manhattan Study,* Vol. 1, McGraw-Hill, New York, 1962, p. 241.

piling-up of lower-class psychotics in the mental hospital.[2] This view was supported in the 1950 study by the finding that social-class differences in the prevalence of treated psychosis are markedly higher for those individuals in continuous treatment than for those entering treatment for the first time or reentering treatment. Thus, the large class differences in prevalence rates for hospitalized psychotic patients were interpreted to be due, in part, to the fact that lower-class patients remain in inpatient facilities for longer periods.

Findings on treatment outcome reported in this study confirm the following conclusions: Lower-class patients are, in fact, less likely to be discharged and thus remain in treatment for longer periods. Once discharged, class V patients are just as likely, if not more so, to be readmitted to the hospital. Once rehospitalized, substantial class differences in rates for subsequent discharges continue. Thus, lower-class patients are less likely to be discharged from the hospital but are, if discharged, equally or more likely to return to inpatient treatment, where they again face the greater probability of continuing in treatment. The differential discharge rates thus produce a differential rate of aggregation, multiplying at any given point in time the number of lower-class patients in treatment. This piling-up process, in conjunction with differences in type of treatment received in the hospital, helps to account for the large class differences in hospital prevalence rates found in the original study.

Similar processes account for the higher rate of treated prevalence for upper- and middle-class neurotics found in the New Haven and other studies.[3] Among the clinic patients we followed who were predominantly neurotic, the higher the class, the more likely the patient was to receive lengthy outpatient treatment during the 10-year period and to be under such care in 1960. Moreover, lower-class patients originally in clinic treatment, more frequently than higher-status individuals, move into hospital care where they then face the problem of securing a discharge. In contrast, higher-class hospitalized patients, upon discharge, moved into outpatient treatment more frequently than lower-status persons. The greater use of outpatient facilities by upper- and middle-class patients again results in a piling-up process which is class related.

The current study not only documents the class differential in the

[2] August B. Hollingshead and Fredrick C. Redlich, *Social Class and Mental Illness*, Wiley, New York, 1958, especially Chapters 7, 8, and 9.
[3] *Ibid.*, Chapter 8.

piling-up of patients in hospitals and clinics but also suggests reasons for this process. Beginning with hospital patients, we find that the type of treatment received is related significantly to the patients' chances of discharge from 1950 to 1960, and the lower the class, the more likely the patient to receive a type of treatment—custodial care or drug therapy—associated with a low probability of discharge. Since no standard information is available concerning the degree of psychological impairment at the time of hospital admission in the original study, it might be assumed on the basis of the class differences in prevalence rates found in epidemiological studies that class V patients were "sicker," i.e., more impaired psychologically, upon admission to the psychiatric hospital.[4]

If lower-class patients were indeed more impaired upon entry, this might account for their more frequent assignment to custodial care or drug therapy. The staff, which continually faces the problem of maximizing the efficient use of limited treatment facilities, might consider the lower-class patient a poorer risk and therefore a waste of limited resources. The assignment of the lower-class patient to forms of therapy which are associated with low rates of discharge might, therefore, not indicate any direct class bias but only the fact that many class V individuals upon entering treatment are past the point at which "success" therapies can be applied.

This assumption—that the class V hospital patient is more impaired psychologically upon entry to the hospital—if correct, may help to explain differences in types of treatment, but, in view of the evidence concerning discharge rates and class differences in adjustment in the community, it does not fully explain the piling-up of lower-class patients in the hospital. Whatever the differences in the degree of impairment at presentation, the lower-class patient apparently must demonstrate a higher level of psychological functioning than the higher-status individual before he can be discharged. Moreover, his chances of discharge are substantially less than those of higher-status persons even when he receives psychotherapy or somatotherapy, both of which are associated with high discharge rates.

The patient is subject to a variety of control mechanisms which operate in different ways in psychiatric inpatient and outpatient facilities. The psychiatric staff operating in hospital facilities, particularly in state mental hospitals, may be viewed as control agents or gatekeepers who

---

[4] See Chapter 7; Srole et al., *op. cit.*, Chapter 12; and Dorothea C. Leighton et al., *The Character of Danger* (The Stirling County Study of Psychiatric Disorder and Sociocultural Environment, Vol. III), Basic Books, New York, 1963, Chapters IX and X.

formally, and until recently in most cases legally, are empowered to control patient flow in and out of the hospital. Indeed it is this formal control function only which is legally recognized. Patients are not legally committed *to* treatment *per se* nor released *from* treatment. Rather, patients are legally committed to *hospitalization*. While patients are legally in institutions, the treatment *per se* is not at issue in the legal basis for commitment. Through the commitment process the power to decide whether or not the patient may be released from hospitalization (and not necessarily from treatment) is transferred to the psychiatric staff of the hospital. Although the more frequent use of voluntary admissions will reduce the tendency of the psychiatric staff to function as legal agents of control, the staff did function in this capacity during the period of our study.

The decision to release patients from hospitals depends upon a variety of factors, only one of which is the level of psychological functioning. Other factors range from broad social conditions at one extreme, such as economic conditions influencing job availability, to specific factors, such as the availability of family members willing to accept the patient upon discharge. Conditions which would affect the patient differentially in the community influence the psychiatric staff as well in determining the probability of discharge. Lower-class patients who face the prospects of returning to a community without friends, sufficient income, and adequate housing may not be motivated to seek a discharge. If the patient is motivated, the staff may be reluctant to return him to such a setting.

Our examination of patient performance in the community suggests conditions which may influence the psychiatric staff's decision to discharge. Few patients are completely successful in reassuming and securing jobs in the marketplace, but problems increase as social-class position decreases. Moreover, the consequences of these problems are compounded for lower-class patients, further reducing their prospects for successful community tenure. Financially, patients at any class level may be unable to maintain an income commensurate with their skill level, but the failure of the patient to maintain such an income is less likely to be offset by other family members or by savings in the lowest class. At this level, patients often live alone and cannot depend upon a family to supplement their income as at higher class levels; even if family members are available, they are seldom able to compensate for the lowered income of the patient. The hospital staff are aware also that lower-class patients will more likely suffer from social isolation in the community.

In addition to the work problems and social isolation of lower-class patients, other factors probably influence the decision of the psychiatric staff to discharge the patient. For example, class differences in use of out-patient facilities mean that, upon discharge, higher-status patients are more likely to continue in treatment. If psychological deterioration occurs following discharge, lower-class patients may lack the insight or social support necessary to seek and remain in treatment; friends and relatives may ignore the behavior of the patient until it becomes violent, when formal agents of control—the police or the courts—enter the process.

Hence, the decision to release the patient from the hospital depends upon a variety of factors, only one of which is the level of his psychological functioning. Given the facts concerning class differences in the use of outpatient facilities and access to family, social, and community resources, the evidence indicates that lower-class hospitalized patients must be functioning at a high level psychologically before the decision to discharge is made by the hospital agents of social control—the psychiatric gatekeepers. These control agents have the responsibility not only of treating or rehabilitating the mentally ill but also of controlling their very movements. Apparently, hospital authorities are extremely careful in discharging lower-status patients who might exhibit behavior which is unmanageable in the community.

In summary, the piling-up of lower-class patients in the mental hospital may be traced to the differential decisions made by the psychiatric agents which reflect, in part, social conditions in the community. The psychiatric treatment system and other community and family resources apparently provide more adequate aftercare for the upper- and middle-class patients than for those lower in the social structure. Differences may exist also in the abilities of patients at various class levels to readjust to community living, especially in view of the different resources available.

In contrast to the control functions vested in hospital psychiatric agents, no similar power to control deviant behavior is found in the clinic. Admission is generally voluntary, although other agents of social control such as the police or courts may recommend treatment. As indicated in other studies, the decision to seek treatment is more often delayed in the lower class, and the clinic staff has no formal or legal means to retain the patient.[5] In addition, lower-class patients who withdraw voluntarily from treatment may remain in the community unless their behavior brings them into contact with the police or courts; because of the severity of the problem these agents of social control channel the patients into mental hospitals where psychiatric agents gain control over

---

[5] See, for example, Jerome K. Myers and Bertram H. Roberts, *Family and Class Dynamics in Mental Illness*, Wiley, New York, 1959, Chapters 8 and 9.

their movements. Again, the evidence strongly supports this argument. Class V clinic patients delay treatment, remain in clinic treatment for shorter periods, are assigned to nonsenior staff members for treatment, and are subsequently hospitalized more frequently in a psychiatric hospital.[6]

Clinic patients in class V frequently withdraw from treatment before any manifest change occurs in their behavior. Since they never have had to present a picture of psychological health to the gatekeeper to be discharged, as in the case of class V hospital patients, the picture they present is one of extreme impairment of psychological functioning in the community. Yet, both hospital and clinic patients in class V return to the same community and face the same problems. Therefore, both are more isolated socially in the community than other patients and unable to participate effectively in marketplace activities.

Upper- and middle-class patients, on the other hand, seek psychiatric help at earlier stages in the mental illness and make greater use of outpatient facilities. No single reason can account for the more frequent and prolonged use of such facilities by higher-status patients. Certainly class I–III patients are financially better able to pay for outpatient treatment, and they are more likely, if employed, to have jobs which enable them to take time off for personal reasons or use sick-leave pay in order to secure treatment during the hours when clinic services are available. Cost, however, is only one factor involved. Upper- and middle-class patients may also possess more insight into their own problems and into the nature of the therapy; they have more favorable attitudes toward treatment and are less likely than lower-class persons to avoid it because of the stigma of being labeled mentally ill. Our earlier research also indicates the higher rates of acceptance in clinics of higher-status persons and the preferential treatment they receive which probably leads to their greater use of such facilities.[7]

In summary, social factors in the community, as well as in the treatment agency itself, operate to produce significant class differences in treatment outcome. Briefly, as social-class position decreases, psychotic patients pile up in the hospital; as class position increases, neurotic patients accumulate in outpatient facilities.

SOCIAL CLASS AND FORMER PATIENT ADJUSTMENT IN THE COMMUNITY

The findings presented so far indicate that treatment outcome—in the narrow sense of being in the community or being hospitalized 10 years

---

[6] Hollingshead and Redlich, *op. cit.;* and Myers and Roberts, *op. cit.*
[7] *Ibid.*

after the original study—is an extremely complex process. Moreover, hospital discharge and subsistence in the community do not alone provide adequate measures of treatment outcome. Substantial numbers of former patients, both hospital and clinic, have serious adjustment problems in the community. Many return to inpatient facilities for further care because of their personal and social difficulties. Unlike many physically sick persons, particularly those with acute diseases, some mental patients never recover entirely from their illness; they require treatment and support for long periods but not necessarily in inpatient agencies or solely by medical personnel.

In general, the most widespread adjustment problems are economic in nature. Mental illness seems to serve as an employment screening device which eliminates certain individuals from the labor market. Wage earners who are former mental patients, especially those who have been hospitalized, face severe employment problems. Many are unable to find regular employment; others can find jobs but only at lower levels of skill. Individual earnings are lower than those for controls. Apparently, many jobs are too demanding for persons with any significant degree of psychological impairment. In some cases, employers discriminate against former patients in the hiring process or former patients are reluctant to seek work because they fear discrimination.

Economically, the social system provides more support for patients in the middle and upper classes than at other social levels. On the job, work demands may be more flexible for the class I–III patients, fellow workers more sympathetic to problems of mental illness, and paid sick leave or leaves of absence available in cases in which psychological and personal problems require temporary withdrawal. In contrast, jobs held by skilled and semiskilled class IV workers are located in highly organized industries demanding regular working habits. Job security in these occupations is more variable, and the former patients, perhaps projecting their own beliefs, feel that employers and fellow workers are unsympathetic. In such an industrial and social climate, these patients have problems securing and holding jobs. Consequently, they may slip into marginal working situations where they suffer major reductions in income.

Similarly, class V mental patients face the problem of reemployment at discharge. Securing and holding a position is not an unusual phenomenon in the case of any class V respondent, patient or control. Finding a job, however, often requires integration into information networks composed of family and friends who are aware of job possibilities. The class V patient, returning to the community, is more isolated than patients in any other class and, therefore, lacks access to such information networks. Moreover, the actual or perceived stigma attached to mental illness, which is clearly identifiable as the result of hospitalization, evidently reduces employment opportunities. In the long run, the ability of many former patients to subsist in the community seems to depend upon support by others—family, friends, and community agencies.

In contrast, the home atmosphere appears more tolerant and flexible than that of business organizations because the female homemakers are able to function adequately. An alternate explanation, of course, is that only women who can meet rigid criteria of performance in the home are accepted back home by the family; if unable to function adequately after discharge they are returned to the hospital. Although we cannot test this alternative explanation, our interviews indicate that housework is, indeed, less demanding than employment in marketplace activities.

While economic adjustment problems are most widespread, many patients have social and psychological difficulties as well. Consequently, over half of all patients discharged from the hospital during the 10 years studied were subsequently readmitted to inpatient care. We have emphasized the career of the mental patient as a deviant one in our society. Although subsisting in the community and no longer under treatment, the former mental patient is the recipient of reactions based upon the label *mentally ill*, as well as on his psychiatric difficulties. A substantial minority of former patients and family members feel the stigma attached to mental illness is so serious that they must keep treatment for mental illness a secret. Although adjustment in the community under the impact of the mentally ill label is widespread, it differs by class: the lower the class the more handicapping the role of the mental patient. Thus, differential attitudes toward mental illness are related to class variations in posttreatment adjustment in the community. Former mental patients in classes I–III are able to function more adequately in their social roles in the community than persons at other social levels regardless of their mental status. The ability of the patients in the upper and middle classes to become effectively integrated into the community is closely related to a broad set of social conditions in the community which mitigate their psychological problems. The integration of the patient depends, in part, upon the degree to which he is tolerated by others in the community and the degree of tolerance, in turn, depends upon the values about mental illness held by individuals in the community with whom the patient has or will have contact. Apparently the values about mental illness in the upper and middle classes allow greater acceptance of the former patient. Personal idiosyncracies are more easily tolerated and understood; the patient, his family, and his friends are able to make a mutual adaptation to the patient's problems.

Even under conditions in which family and friends are less than completely understanding of the patient's problems, the upper- and middle-class patient has the advantage of access to formal and informal organizations. These patients are financially in a position to support their membership in associations, paying their own way in formal and informal organizations. Though this may or may not constitute the "buying" of friends, they are in a better position to support their associational memberships despite their psychological problems.

Lower-class families, fearing the stigma which they perceive to be attached to mental illness, apparently reject the patient when he returns to the community and hesitate to invite friends or relatives into the home when he is there. To escape the problems associated with mental illness, as they exist or are perceived, the lower-class family as well as the patient attempt to hide the history of treatment. Assuming that entry into outpatient treatment would further label the individual as "sick," the patient and his family may fail to make use of outpatient facilities. Unable to find work, the patient constitutes a drain on limited family resources, furthering the cleavage between himself and his family.

In brief, the community is better able to handle a former hospital patient in classes I–III who is psychologically impaired than a relatively well-adjusted class IV or class V individual. In classes I–III persons judged to be disturbed by any measure of mental status remain in the community and function in a relatively adequate manner. In contrast, the community cannot integrate the former patient in class V regardless of mental status. Whether a clinic patient and severely impaired psychologically or a hospital patient with a minimal degree of impairment, former patients in the lower class experience substantially more difficulty in performing their social roles than persons at other social levels. At this bottom position in society, few of the supports utilized by higher-status persons are available; yet even at this level, community support makes a difference—those few former hospital patients receiving outpatient care, no matter how minimal, are less likely to be rehospitalized than those who are not.

In class IV, the treatment agency itself makes a difference. Hospital patients, whether or not impaired psychologically, have difficulty securing employment and are relatively isolated socially. Clinic patients differ little from their matched controls. At this level, hospitalization rather than treatment *per se* makes a crucial difference.

Adjustment in the community is itself a complex process and is multidimensional in nature. Although there is a rough correlation between the various dimensions, we would question if a satisfactory single measure of total adjustment and performance or their opposite, impairment, can be developed. We have seen that class I–III persons who are severely impaired psychologically can function quite adequately in a variety of social roles. In turn, some in classes IV and V, who suffer little impairment psychologically, are unable to perform many of the social roles society expects of them. Perhaps a more meaningful approach than viewing behavior as "impaired" or "normal" would be to recognize that individuals may function well in some respects and inadequately in others.[8]

In summary, it is clear that social class is related both to the former patient's adjustment in the community and to the interrelationships between the dimensions of adjustment.

CAVEAT

The 1950 to 1960 decade has witnessed the introduction of a number of changes in the treatment of the mentally ill, although the impact of these general changes for the follow-up patient population was probably much less than for those who became ill for the first time later in the period. Recent changes in psychiatric practice may have taken place too late to influence the follow-up patient population significantly since by the time the changes were introduced many patients had deteriorated into a chronic state. Future patient populations, however, may benefit from the following observed and current changes.

First, a prominent and emerging theme in psychiatric treatment is that of flexible institutional design. Psychiatric institutions and agents are decreasingly viewed as independent, isolated facilities and seen more and more as open agencies permitting patient movement from one to the other in a process of treatment—transition from the community to and through a range of psychiatric facilities. With the development of such establishments as half-way houses, partial hospitalization facilities (day-night care), and sheltered workshops, continuity of care is becoming a unifying concept in program design.

Second, greater financial support and increased patient demands on psychiatric facilities have resulted in the expansion of services. Larger direct contributions to facilities come from federal, state, and local governments. Public and private insurance programs have been expanded to cover psychiatric treatment. Further, an increased interest in psychiatric treatment accompanied by an apparent decrease in the stigma attached to such treatment has resulted in greater demands for psychiatric services. The result has been an increase in psychiatric contacts, many of which are of a shorter duration as the patient moves from the community to a variety of integrated psychiatric services.

Finally, psychotropic drugs were not introduced on a large scale until the mid-1950's, and none of the patients we studied received them

---

[8] For a discussion of this point see, Marie Jahoda, *Current Concepts of Positive Mental Health*, Basic Books, New York, 1958.

upon their initial entry into treatment. If such drugs had been administered early, there might have been a difference in treatment outcome. Perhaps in the future the picture of adjustment in the community will will be different from the description of psychiatric treatment services affecting the Follow-Up population.

RESEARCH IMPLICATIONS AND SUGGESTIONS

Turning to problems of research, we may draw certain conclusions from the Follow-Up Study. First, the community, its institutions, and its patients—as well as the traditional mental hospital as a total institution—form an appropriate research focus for the study of mental illness today. Mental illness neither develops in a vacuum or void nor is treated within the framework of a single institution. It is important to analyze within the community relevant for the patient the social and personal mechanisms which, in a sense, single out the patient, channeling him into and between various treatment facilities, and the agencies, institutions, and persons involved in the process of the patient's readaptation to the community.

Second, changes in psychiatric treatment and the analysis of mental illness through the career of the mental patient underscore the need to deal with the illness and its treatment as a process occurring through time. While psychiatric theory pays particular attention to the developmental processes of illness, less interest has been shown in the social and psychological sequelae. The increased rates of psychiatric discharge and readmission point to the need for more longitudinal studies of mental illness. The need for long-range studies of 5, 10, 15 years or longer is apparent. Such longitudinal studies may be most productive if built in as part of a continuous or long-term evaluation process within the treatment system itself. The general pattern of economic maladjustment of former hospital patients, for example, suggests that the ability to remain in the community may depend upon the long-range support of the patient by his family, friends, community agencies, and outpatient facilities. How long the patient requires support or how long support may be offered might well determine the rate and frequency of return to treatment agencies.

Apparently, the degree and length of support which the patient receives in the community depends not only on the patient's psychological impairment but also on broad social factors acting on the patient and in turn being acted upon by the patient. The social class of the patient and the sets of values attached to illness and treatment in that class influence the acceptance of the patient as does the degree of motivation for the patient to return to the community.

The systems in the community environment capable and willing to extend assistance to the patient during the process of adjustment constitute a critical question which requires more careful study, with such factors taken into consideration as differences in types of role performance and variations in social-class demands placed on the patient. More study is needed also of community resources necessary for prolonged support of former patients in the community.

Research should be done on the long-term impact upon the family of the prolonged residence at home of a patient who requires relatively constant assistance or supervision. Does such a situation affect the family structure? What is the impact upon the children's psychological and social adjustment? Would it affect the decision of children to leave home? Or an equally interesting question—what is the relationship between mental-illness and other-illness history over a long period of time?

Third, more research is needed on the interrelationships among the dimensions of patient adjustment. The results of our study indicate clearly that patient performance following treatment differs by class for various measures of adjustment. The problem of interrelating the various aspects of behavioral adjustment, however, is complex and requires a much larger number of cases than was available for this study. We tried to examine patient and control social-class differences for one dimension of adjustment while holding constant the other, but the number of cases in the various categories resulting from the detailed multiple cross-classification is so small that it provided little basis for statistical confidence. Nevertheless, the consistency and regularity of the results indicate that while some degree of association exists among the various aspects of performance, successful adjustment in one area of behavior is not necessarily related to successful adjustment in other areas.

For example, there is a rough correlation between occupational adjustment and mental status: those persons who are poorly adjusted occupationally are also more likely to be impaired psychologically. Fifty per cent of hospital patients with poor occupational adjustment have high symptom levels, whereas only 31 per cent of those with good occupational adjustment display such psychological impairment. Among controls the corresponding percentages are 38 and 15. The same type of association between mental status and occupational adjustment is found for clinic patients and their controls.[9] However, when occupational ad-

---

[9] Seventy-seven per cent of clinic patients with poor occupational adjustment have high symptoms compared to 39 per cent with good occupational adjustment. For controls, 25 per cent with poor occupational adjustment have high symptoms compared to 15 per cent with good occupational adjustment.

TABLE 10.1

Class	Patients (%)	Controls (%)	Difference (%)
I–III	50	5	45
IV	35	15	20
V	22	19	3

justment is controlled, the same pattern of class differences in impairment of mental status is found as for all cases. Among hospital cases, patient-control differences in the proportion psychologically impaired decrease as we move from classes I–III to V whether persons have good or poor occupational adjustment. The proportion of hospital patients and controls by class, for instance, with good occupational adjustment who have high symptom levels is as shown in Table 10.1. Patient-control differences by class for those with poor occupational adjustment follow the same pattern: I–III—100, IV—20, V—11.[10] Among clinic cases the opposite relationship is found; the lower the class, the greater the patient-control differences in psychological impairment, regardless of the quality of occupational adjustment.

Similarly, there is a rough correlation between mental status and social participation and between social participation and occupational adjustment. However, the general class patterns of patient-control differences, described earlier in the chapter, continue to hold when we control for each dimension. More careful research with larger numbers of cases is necessary to determine the exact relationships between dimensions.

Finally, the research design selected in the New Haven studies demonstrates the advantage of a control group of nonpatients, for we found that class differences in the adjustment of patients merely reflect differences found in the population in some instances, whereas in other instances they do not. Previous follow-up studies have included control groups, but generally they have used as controls either another patient group or the patients, themselves, as their own control in a simple before-after research design. With the increasing rate of hospital discharges and readmission and the expanded use of outpatient facilities, it is critical to view the patient in the context of the community, comparing patient behavior not only with that of other patients but with nonpatients as well.

---

[10] The percentage of hospital patients with poor occupational adjustment who have high symptom levels is as follows by class: I–III—100, IV—20, V—57, for controls the corresponding percentages are: I–III—0, IV—0, V—46.

Our present state of knowledge does not allow us to define "normal" behavior precisely. Moreover the need to view patient behavior from several perspectives—psychologically and sociologically, for example—means that no single definition of a "normal" population will suffice when specifying an adequate control group. The control group must be selected to reflect first the difference between the study population and control group with respect to the dependent variable under examination—treated mental illness, for example, in this study—but second, the control group must reflect as closely as possible the variables indexing the psychological and sociocultural milieu of the patient. Only in this way is it possible to determine how well or poorly the patient adjusts to his meaningful environment.

COMMENTS ON AN EMERGING SYSTEM OF PSYCHIATRIC INTERVENTION

Research studies of the mentally ill will not alleviate the problem of mental illness in our society unless the results of such studies are used to modify the systems of treatment and psychiatric intervention which govern the management of the mentally ill. While certain changes are being made in the traditional system of psychiatric treatment and intervention, this study suggests that even greater change should be introduced.

Historically, the psychiatric treatment model recognized only two roles and their interrelationships—that of the psychiatrist and the patient. In large part, only the specific psychiatric problem governed the relationship. The patient's psychological problem was diagnosed and the psychiatrist's expertise was brought to bear on the patient to resolve or "cure" the particular problem. Or, if the patient could not be treated, the psychiatric hospital was empowered to deal with his deviant behavior by removing him from society. Psychiatric treatment, itself, was frequently treated as though it existed in a vacuum.

In recent years a modified treatment model has been emerging but one based on some untested assumptions. There is an increasing recognition that the patient's psychiatric problems are not independent of his social experience and that social variables clearly influence the therapist, the patient, and their relationship, as well as other institutions and agencies which affect the intervention and outcome of therapy. Psychiatric treatment can no longer be viewed as a system involving the patient and the psychiatrist only. Both patient and therapist are linked to a network of institutional and social services, including nonpsychiatric professional social agencies, the family, community agencies concerned with the welfare of the patient, and other health agencies and facilities. Nor can the treatment process itself be viewed any longer as a simple system, because it is in a state of flux, expanding to include and coordinate persons and agencies not previously involved in the treatment process. Under these conditions, continued support by others not traditionally part of the system of treatment may be necessary for long periods.

Although the psychiatric treatment system is becoming more open, the individual who is defined as mentally ill is not able to abandon the patient role completely. While moving from the hospital to the outpatient service or simply back into the community he may remain identified within his own particular subculture as an ex-patient. Particularly for the lower-class person, the stigma of having been hospitalized may mean rejection by society.

The more or less general problems of occupational adjustment of all hospital patients studied here suggest a set of negative attitudes on the part of employers regarding the outcome of mental illness which may or may not be valid. It may be that some level of disability is a residuum of psychoses and hospitalization. Perhaps such patients, their families, and the community must live with this residuum and develop better ways to handle it.

It may be incorrect to assume that patients eventually move out of the treatment system. The former patient is able to perform certain roles in the community but he apparently continues to need support over a long period: reentry to inpatient or outpatient facilities or continuous financial, social, and affectual support from family, friends, and community organizations. Certainly, the fact that two thirds of the class I–II former hospital patients received outpatient treatment during some of the 10-year Follow-Up Study suggests the need for continued treatment. Yet for certain individuals (particularly those in class V), this support is not available, and the system of management of the illness becomes more constricted. Unable to adjust to the community after discharge from the hospital, these individuals return to the hospital where they may remain for long periods.

The results of the Follow-Up Study indicate that the emerging systems of management of mental illness must clearly take into account the influence of community and social factors and the roles of various treatment agencies. Moreover, if the management of mental illness in the community is to become maximally effective, the system of treatment which appears to be emerging must move further beyond the traditional patient-physician (psychiatrist) treatment model. Intervention or therapy which begins when the patient presents himself or is presented to a treatment agency may be too late; intervention which ceases at discharge may be terminated too early. A more comprehensive system of therapy would be one which organized psychiatric and community services for: (1) the prevention of mental illness, (2) the early identification of the mentally ill in the community, (3) the use of resources beyond the traditional psychiatric facilities, and (4) the coordination of services to incorporate the patient back into the community, that is, aftercare services in the community which are not necessarily "treatment" services per se. Job counseling, for example, may be required, not only for the patient but also for employers in the community.

Training programs for mental-health workers will have to take into account the need for a coordinated set of services designed to help move the patient, wherever possible, back into a satisfying, productive role in the community. Such services present a number of problems for those traditionally involved in the care and treatment of the mentally ill. For example, in such a system can the psychiatrist limit himself to the patient in the traditional manner of the patient-therapist relationship? Probably not. The need for the psychiatrist to expand his role to coordinate services for the patient and the probability of his doing so are points which must be considered. This may not be the best utilization of the skills of the psychiatrist. Other professionals must be involved in the treatment process. Once the hospital patient moves into the community he is beyond the control of the hospital psychiatrist, yet what happens in the community determines the outcome of the therapy in many cases. Eventually, some type of coordination will be required, whether performed by the psychiatrist or by a new type of treatment agent yet to be found or developed.

Whatever form a comprehensive treatment or management program for mental illness assumes, the results of this study indicate that the emerging treatment system must recognize and interact with community and social forces. No single treatment agent or modality will ensure successful readjustment permanently, or even temporarily, for all patients nor will simple coordination of existing services and facilities necessarily provide maximum care of the mentally ill. The fewer resources available in the community for lower-class individuals who enter psychiatric treatment do not ensure the same degree of integration for them into the community as for those at higher social-class levels. The community, at present, seems unable to deal effectively with the lower-class mentally ill person. Yet in those cases where it is available, outpatient care improves the chances of both class IV and V patients remaining in the community. This suggests that if more community outpatient facilities are provided for lower-class persons there might be a reduction in some of the class differences in adjustment we have found.

Apparently, past attempts to coordinate existing community resources are inadequate to allow for the successful return of the lower-class patient to the community. Successful treatment which maximizes the productivity and freedom of all patients depends on new (perhaps experimental and, certainly, imaginative) comprehensive programs, designed to prevent mental illness, identify the mentally ill in the community, and coordinate treatment, precare and aftercare services. The community factors influencing the new system have only recently attracted interest, yet such factors are important. Social class, as an example, is an important determinant of access to and use of services and resources, since lower-class patients do not use available resources as frequently, are not aware of them, or are treated differently within them. Often lower-class persons come in contact with treatment facilities as a result of intervention by police or courts only after they are so disturbed that treatment of any type may be unsuccessful. Assuming that the community cannot deal with the lower-class patient, the hospital control agents exercise greater care in their decision to release such patients.

The next 10 years may well indicate whether the trends that we see emerging in comprehensive care for psychiatric patients will be more successful than the traditional systems of psychiatric treatment. The evaluation of treatment requires research. Such research must be planned as an integral part of the new comprehensive community mental health programs.

supplementary tables

TABLE A1.1

Comparison between Hospital and Clinic Patients of 1950 Age, Diagnosis, Social Class, Sex, and Marital Status (Per Cent)

1950	Treatment Status	
	Hospital	Clinic
A. Age Distribution		
Under 35	18	70
35–44	17	20
45–54	19	6
55–64	21	3
65 and over	25	1
B. Diagnosis		
Neuroses	4	72
Alcohol and drug addictions	4	20
Other psychoses	92	8
C. Social Class		
I–II	3	5
III	8	21
IV	40	43
V	49	31
D. Sex		
Male	48	62
Female	52	38
E. Marital Status		
Unmarried	51	44
Married	26	42
Separated, divorced, widowed	23	14

TABLE A1.2

Hospital Patients Discharged from 1950 to 1960, by Social Class

Social Class	Discharged					
	First Discharge		After First Readmission		After Second Readmission	
	n	%	n	%	n	%
I–II	46	43	10	100 [a]		
					17	82 [a]
III	121	36	24	79 [a]		
IV	559	33	106	66	53	68
V	686	20	85	67	39	67
	1412		225		109	

$\chi^2 = 38.77, df = 3,$ $\chi^2 = 4.79, df = 2,$ $\chi^2 = 1.49, df = 2,$
$p < .05$ $p < .10$ $p > .20$

[a] Classes I, II, and III are combined in the calculation of χ^2 because of the small number of cases in classes I–II.

TABLE A1.3

Readmission of Discharged Hospital Patients to a Psychiatric Hospital from 1950 to 1960, by Social Class

Social Class	First Readmission		Second Readmission		Third Readmission	
	n	%	n	%	n	%
I–II	20	50				
			29	59 [a]	14	77 [a]
III	43	56				
IV	184	58	70	76	36	72
V	135	63	57	68	26	77
	382		156		76	

$\chi^2 = 1.78, df = 3,$ $\chi^2 = 3.39, df = 2,$ $\chi^2 = .07, df = 2,$
$p > .20$ $p < .20$ $p > .20$

[a] Classes I, II, and III are combined in the calculation of χ^2 because of the small number of cases in classes I–II.

TABLE A1.4

Hospital (Worker) Patients and Controls Employed Full Time (Per Cent)

	Social Class [a]			
	I–III	IV	V	Total
Patients [b]	69	62	47	54
Controls [c]	92	92	77	83
Difference	−23 [d]	−30	−30	−29

[a] Unless otherwise stated, social-class and patient-control differences, χ^2 test, $p < .05$.
[b] Differences by social class, χ^2 test, $p < .20$.
[c] Differences by social class, χ^2 test, $p < .10$.
[d] χ^2 test inappropriate because of small expected frequencies.

TABLE A1.5

Hospital (Worker) Patients and Controls Unemployed and Without Earned Income for at Least One Week during Preceding 12-Month Period (Per Cent)

	Social Class [a]			
	I–III	IV	V	Total
Patients [b]	31	31	52	43
Controls	8	6	23	15
Difference	23 [c]	25	29	28

[a] Unless otherwise stated, social-class and patient-control differences, χ^2 test, $p < .05$.
[b] Differences by social class, χ^2 test, $p < .20$.
[c] χ^2 test inappropriate because of small expected frequencies.

TABLE A1.6

Clinic (Worker) Patients and Controls Employed Full Time (Per Cent)

	Social Class			
	I–III	IV	V	Total
Patients [a]	89	92	57	80
Controls [b]	84	85	81	83
Difference	5 [b]	7 [b]	−24 [c]	−3 [d]

[a] Differences by social class, χ^2 test, $p < .05$.
[b] χ^2 test inappropriate because of small expected frequencies.
[c] Patient-control difference, χ^2 test, $p < .10$.
[d] Patient-control difference, χ^2 test, $p > .20$.

TABLE A1.7

Clinic (Worker) Patients and Controls Unemployed and Without Earned Income for at Least One Week during Preceding 12-Month Period (Per Cent) [a]

	Social Class			
	I–III	IV	V	Total
Patients	22	29	76	43
Controls [b]	6	21	24	17
Difference	16 [b]	8 [c]	52	26

[a] Unless otherwise stated, social-class and patient-control differences, χ^2 test, $p < .05$.
[b] χ^2 test inappropriate because of small expected frequencies.
[c] Patient-control difference, χ^2 test, $p > .20$.

TABLE A1.8

Summary Table of Social Participation for Hospital Cases: Patient-Control Differences

	Social Class (Level of Significance)		
	I–III	IV	V
No visits exchanged with neighbors	.20	.05	.05
No neighbors regarded as close friend	>.20	.05	.05
No close friends	a	.05	.05
Does not receive visits from friends	.10	.05	.05
Does not visit friends	>.20	.20	.05
Participates socially with friends or relatives less than once a month	>.20	.20	.10
Not affiliated with church or synagogue	.20	>.20	.05
Does not attend religious services	.20	.05	.05
Does not belong to church organizations	>.20	.20	.05
No membership in formal organizations	>.20	.05	.05
Although affiliated, does not attend meetings	>.20	>.20	.05
Visits less frequently	>.20	>.20	.05
Has fewer friends	.10	.05	.05
Participates less in formal organizations	>.20	>.20	.05
Attends fewer religious services	.05	.10	.05

[a] χ^2 test inappropriate because of small expected frequencies.

TABLE A1.9

Informal Social Interaction and Lack of Participation in Formal Organizations for Clinic Patients and Controls (Per Cent) [a]

	Social Class			
	I–III	IV	V	Total
INFORMAL				
A. No Visits Exchanged with Neighbors				
Patients	9	33	52	29
Controls [b]	18	20	22	20
Difference	−9 [b]	13 [b]	30	9 [c]
B. No Neighbors Regarded as Close Friends				
Patients [b]	55	44	67	53
Controls [b]	48	37	29	39
Difference	7 [b]	7 [b]	38	14
C. No Close Friends				
Patients	3	20	41	19
Controls [d]	3	5	9	5
Difference	0 [d]	15	32	14

(*Continued*)

227

TABLE A1.9 (Continued)

	Social Class			
	I–III	IV	V	Total
INFORMAL				
D. Does Not Receive Visits from Friends				
Patients [c]	16	33	39	28
Controls [c]	9	30	22	21
Difference	7 [b]	3 [b]	17 [c]	7 [b]
E. Does Not Visit Friends				
Patients	3	30	39	23
Controls [b]	13	28	26	22
Difference	−10 [d]	2 [b]	13 [b]	1 [b]
F. Participates Socially with Friends or Relatives Less than Once a Month				
Patients	3	14	29	14
Controls [d]	6	12	8	9
Difference	−3 [d]	2 [b]	21 [e]	5 [b]
FORMAL				
G. Not Affiliated with Church or Synagogue				
Patients [b]	39	33	46	38
Controls [b]	42	28	25	32
Difference	−3 [b]	5 [b]	21 [c]	6 [b]
H. Does Not Attend Religious Services				
Patients [b]	24	18	29	23
Controls [b]	18	8	13	12
Difference	6 [b]	10 [b]	16 [c]	11 [e]
I. Does Not Belong to Church Organizations				
Patients [c]	60	85	85	77
Controls	74	52	89	68
Difference	−14 [b]	33	−4 [b]	9 [b]
J. No Membership in Formal Organizations				
Patients	24	55	79	51
Controls [e]	36	48	67	48
Difference	−12 [b]	7 [b]	12 [b]	3 [b]
K. Although Affiliated, Does Not Attend Meetings				
Patients [b]	24	33	60	31
Controls [b]	24	29	25	26
Difference	0 [b]	4 [b]	35 [d]	5 [b]

[a] Unless otherwise stated, social-class and patient-control differences, χ^2 test, $p < .05$.
[b] Social-class and patient-control differences, χ^2 test, $p > .20$.
[c] Social-class and patient-control differences, χ^2 test, $p < .20$.
[d] χ^2 test inappropriate because of small expected frequencies.
[e] Social-class and patient-control differences, χ^2 test, $p < .10$.

228

TABLE A1.10

Changes in Social Participation of Clinic Patients and Controls
(Per Cent) [a]

	Social Class			
	I–III	IV	V	Total
A. Visits Less Frequently				
Patients [b]	20	23	35	25
Controls [b]	23	41	27	32
Difference	−3 [b]	−18 [c]	8 [b]	−7 [b]
B. Has Fewer Friends				
Patients	7	15	36	18
Controls [b]	21	21	16	19
Difference	−14 [b]	−6 [b]	20 [d]	−1 [b]
C. Participates Less in Formal Organizations				
Patients [e]	4	17	40	13
Controls [b]	33	24	13	26
Difference	−29 [e]	−7 [e]	27 [e]	−13 [c]
D. Attends Fewer Religious Services				
Patients [b]	38	41	28	37
Controls [b]	17	21	16	18
Difference	21 [c]	20	12 [b]	19

[a] Unless otherwise stated, social-class and patient-control differences, χ^2 test, $p < .05$.
[b] Social-class and patient-control differences, χ^2 test, $p > .20$.
[c] Social-class and patient-control differences, χ^2 test, $p < .10$.
[d] Patient-control difference, χ^2 test, $p < .20$.
[e] χ^2 test inappropriate because of small expected frequencies.

TABLE A1.11

Patient-Control Differences in Social Participation of Hospital and Clinic Patients, by Social Class (Per Cent)

	Social Class					
	I–III		IV		V	
	Hospital	Clinic	Hospital	Clinic	Hospital	Clinic
No visits exchanged with neighbors	16	−9 [a]	20	13 [a]	20	30
No neighbors regarded as close friends	13 [a]	7 [a]	18	7 [a]	23	38
No close friends	9 [b]	0 [b]	18	15	22	32
Does not receive visits from friends	16	7 [a]	29	3 [a]	33	17
Does not visit friends	12 [a]	−10 [b]	14	2 [a]	28	13 [a]
Participates socially with friends or relatives less than once a month	6 [a]	−3 [b]	10	2 [a]	12	21
Not affiliated with church or synagogue	15	−3 [a]	9 [a]	5 [a]	20	21
Does not attend religious services	12	6 [a]	15	10 [a]	24	16
Does not belong to church organizations	−16 [a]	−14 [a]	16	33	16	−4 [a]
No membership in formal organizations	7 [a]	−12 [a]	17	7 [a]	14	12 [a]
Although affiliated, does not attend meetings	3 [a]	0 [a]	0 [a]	4 [a]	29	35 [b]

[a] $p > .20$; unless otherwise indicated, $p < .20$.
[b] χ^2 test inappropriate because of small expected frequencies.

numerical
comparison of
patients and controls

The numerical distribution is given below for the tables in the text where patients and controls are compared by class. Since patients are compared with their matched controls, the numbers are the same for both except as noted below. The numbers presented are total cases in a cell and represent 100 per cent. The actual numbers may vary from table to table because data are not always available for all cases. The total number of hospital patients and matched controls by social class is as follows: I–III–34, IV–68, V–102, total–204. The corresponding figures for clinic patients and controls are: I–III–33, IV–44, V–29, total–106.

At times, numbers may be smaller because the materials in a given table are not applicable to all patients and controls. For example, data on employment are relevant only for "workers"; only members of organizations can attend meetings; and only church members can belong to organizations within the church.

At times, when only portions of the total sample are included, such as persons who belong to organizations within the church, the number of patients and controls differs. For example, 140 hospital controls but only 111 hospital patients are affiliated with a church or synagogue. Obviously, only these persons can belong to an organization within the church and only a percentage of them actually do. Because of the great reduction in numbers in such instances, we have used all patients and controls instead of matching individually, in order to have enough cases for statistical analyses. These exceptions are noted with an asterisk (*) and the number of patients and controls are listed separately.

Table		Social Class			Total
		I–III	IV	V	
7.2	Hospital patients and controls with mental-status scores in the impaired range	34	66	93	193
7.3	Clinic patients and controls with mental-status scores in the impaired range	32	39	28	99
8.1	Hospital (worker) patients and controls with good occupational-adjustment scores	12	35	62	109
8.2	Clinic (worker) patients and controls with good occupational-adjustment scores	18	20	21	59
8.3	Hospital patients and controls with savings	33	65	91	189
8.4	Clinic patients and controls with savings	33	40	25	98
8.5	Mean annual income for hospital (worker) patients and controls	12	35	62	109
8.6	Mean annual income for clinic (worker) patients and controls	19	23	21	63
9.1(A)	No visits exchanged with neighbors (hospital)	31	66	92	189
9.1(B)	No neighbors regarded as close friends (hospital)	31	66	91	188
9.2(A)	No close friends (hospital)	33	66	89	188
9.2(B)	Does not receive visits from friends (hospital)	32	65	91	188
9.2(C)	Does not visit friends (hospital)	32	66	90	188
9.2(D)	Participates socially with friends or relatives less than once a month (hospital)	34	66	92	192

Table		Social Class			
		I–III	IV	V	Total
9.3(A)	Not affiliated with church or synagogue (hospital)	33	66	92	191
9.3(B)	Does not attend religious services (hospital)	33	65	92	190
9.3(C)	Does not belong to church organizations (hospital)*				
	Patients	23	42	46	111
	Controls	28	48	64	140
9.4(A)	No membership in formal organizations (hospital)	32	66	92	190
9.4(B)	Although affiliated, does not attend meetings (hospital) *				
	Patients	20	22	18	60
	Controls	22	33	31	86
9.5(A)	Visits less frequently (hospital)	32	66	91	189
9.5(B)	Has fewer friends (hospital)	33	66	90	189
9.5(C)	Participates less in formal organizations (hospital) *				
	Patients	20	22	18	60
	Controls	22	33	31	86
9.5(D)	Attends fewer religious services (hospital)	33	66	89	188
A1.4	Hospital (worker) patients and controls employed full time	13	37	64	114
A1.5	Hospital (worker) patients and controls unemployed and without earned income	13	35	62	110
A1.6	Clinic (worker) patients and controls employed full time	19	26	21	66
A1.7	Clinic (worker) patients and controls unemployed without earned income	18	24	21	63
A1.9(A)	No visits exchanged with neighbors (clinic)	33	40	23	96
A1.9(B)	No neighbors regarded as close friends (clinic)	33	41	24	98

Table		Social Class			Total
		I–III	IV	V	
A1.9(C)	No close friends (clinic)	32	41	22	95
A1.9(D)	Does not receive visits from friends (clinic)	32	40	23	95
A1.9(E)	Does not visit friends (clinic)	32	40	23	95
A1.9(F)	Participates socially with friends or relatives less than once a month (clinic)	32	42	24	98
A1.9(G)	Not affiliated with church or synagogue (clinic)	33	40	24	97
A1.9(H)	Does not attend religious services (clinic)	33	40	24	97
A1.9(I)	Does not belong to church organizations (clinic) *				
	Patients	20	27	13	60
	Controls	19	29	18	66
A1.9(J)	No membership in formal organizations (clinic)	33	40	24	97
A1.9(K)	Although affiliated does not attend meetings (clinic) *				
	Patients	25	18	5	48
	Controls	21	21	8	50
A1.10(A)	Visits less frequently (clinic)	30	39	26	95
A1.10(B)	Has fewer friends	29	39	25	93
A1.10(C)	Participates less in formal organizations (clinic) *				
	Patients	25	18	5	48
	Controls	21	21	8	50
A1.10(D)	Attends fewer religious services (clinic)	29	39	25	93

two-factor
index of
social position

The occupational scale used in the *Two Factor Index of Social Position* is a modification of the Alba Edwards' system of classifying occupations into socioeconomic groups employed by the U.S. Bureau of the Census. The essential differences between the original system and its modification is that Edwards does not differentiate among the kinds of professionals or the sizes and economic strengths of the businesses. The scale used in the Index of Social Position ranks professions into different groups and businesses according to their size and value. The seven positions on the modified scale are: (1) executives and proprietors of large concerns and major professionals; (2) managers and proprietors of medium concerns and minor professionals; (3) administrative personnel of large concerns, owners of small independent businesses, and semiprofessionals; (4) owners of little businesses, clerical and sales workers, and technicians; (5) skilled workers; (6) semiskilled workers; and (7) unskilled workers. This scale is premised upon the assumption that different occupations are valued differently by the members of our society. The hierarchy ranges from the low evaluation of unskilled physical labor toward the more prestigeful use of skill, through the creative talents, ideas, and management of men. The ranking of occupational functions implies that some men exercise control over the occupational pursuits of other men. Normally, a person who possesses skills has control over several other people.

This is exemplified in a highly developed form by an executive in a large business enterprise who may be responsible for decisions affecting thousands of employees.

The educational scale is premised upon the assumption that men and women who possess similar educations tend to have similar tastes and attitudes and tend to exhibit similar behavior patterns. The educational scale is divided into seven positions: (1) graduate professional training (persons who completed a recognized course which led to the receipt of a graduate degree); (2) standard college or university graduation (individuals who had completed a four-year college or university course leading to a recognized college degree); (3) partial college training (individuals who had completed at least one year but not a full college course); (4) high-school graduation (all secondary-school graduates, whether from a private preparatory school, public high school, trade school, or parochial high school); (5) partial high school (individuals who had completed the tenth or eleventh grades but not the high-school course); (6) junior high school (individuals who had completed the seventh, eighth, or ninth grades); (7) less than seven years of school (individuals who had completed less than seven grades irrespective of the amount of education received).

To calculate the Index of Social Position score for an individual, the scale value for occupation is multiplied by the factor weight for occupation, and the scale value for education is multiplied by the factor weight for education. For example, John Smith is the manager of a chain supermarket. He completed high school and one year of business college. His Index of Social Position score is computed as follows:

Factor	Scale Score	Factor Weight	Score × Weight
Occupation	3	7	21
Education	3	4	12
Index of Social Position score			33

The *Two Factor Index of Social Position* scores may be arranged on a continuum or divided into groups of scores. The range of scores on the continuum is from a low of 11 to a high of 77. For some purposes a researcher may desire to work with a continuum of scores, while for other purposes he may desire to break the continuum into a hierarchy of score groups. We have found that the most meaningful breaks for the purpose of predicting the social-class position of an individual or of a nuclear family are as follows:

Range of Computed Scores	Social Class
11–17	I
18–27	II
28–43	III
44–60	IV
61–77	V

A detailed description of the Two Factor Index and its determination can be obtained from August B. Hollingshead, *Two Factor Index of Social Position* (copyrighted 1957), privately printed, 1965 Yale Station, New Haven, Connecticut.

mental status index

The mental status scale used in this study is presented in Table A4.1. For the background to the development of this scale and similar scales, as well as the scoring method used, see Chapter 7. The scale is essentially the same as the one used by Gurin and his associates in their nationwide study of mental health. Only two slight modifications in wording were made to clarify certain terms, and these are noted in the footnote to Table A4.1.

TABLE A4.1
Mental Status Scale Items, Response Categories, and Scores

Question	Response and Score
1. How often are you bothered by having an upset (sour, acid) stomach? *	1. Nearly all the time 2. Pretty often 3. Not very much 4. Never
2. Have you ever been bothered by nervousness, feeling fidgety and tense?	1. Nearly all the time 2. Pretty often 3. Not very much 4. Never

* Items marked by an asterisk differ from the wording of the original Gurin scale as follows: (1) (sour, acid) added to clarify "upset stomach," (15) "Dreams which frighten or upset you" added to clarify "nightmares."

Question	Response and Score
3. Do you feel that you are bothered by all sorts of pains and ailments in different parts of your body?	2. Yes 4. No
4. Are you ever troubled by headaches or pains in the head?	1. Nearly all the time 2. Pretty often 3. Not very much 4. Never
5. Do you have loss of appetite?	1. Nearly all the time 2. Pretty often 3. Not very much 4. Never
6. Do you ever have any trouble in getting to sleep or staying asleep?	1. Nearly all the time 2. Pretty often 3. Not very much 4. Never
7. Do you find it difficult to get up in the morning?	1. Nearly all the time 2. Pretty often 3. Not very much 4. Never
8. Are you ever troubled by your hands or feet sweating so that they feel damp and clammy?	1. Many times 2. Sometimes 3. Hardly ever 4. Never
9. Has any ill health affected the amount of work you do?	1. Many times 2. Sometimes 3. Hardly ever 4. Never
10. Have you ever been bothered by shortness of breath when you were not exercising or working hard?	1. Many times 2. Sometimes 3. Not very much 4. Never
11. Have you ever felt that you were going to have a nervous breakdown?	2. Yes 4. No
12. Have you ever been bothered by your heart beating hard?	1. Many times 2. Sometimes 3. Hardly ever 4. Never

(Continued)

TABLE A4.1 (Continued)

Question	Response and Score
13. Do your hands ever tremble enough to bother you?	1. Many times 2. Sometimes 3. Hardly ever 4. Never
14. Do you ever drink more than you should?	1. Many times 2. Sometimes 3. Hardly ever 4. Never
15. Are you ever bothered by nightmares? (dreams which frighten or upset you?) *	1. Many times 2. Sometimes 3. Hardly ever 4. Never
16. Have you ever had spells of dizziness?	1. Many times 2. Sometimes 3. Hardly ever 4. Never
17. Do you tend to lose weight when you have something important bothering you	1. Many times 2. Sometimes 3. Hardly ever 4. Never
18. Have there ever been times when you couldn't take care of things because you just couldn't get going?	1. Many times 2. Sometimes 3. Hardly ever 4. Never
19. For the most part, do you feel healthy enough to carry out the things you would like to do?	4. Yes 2. No
20. Do you have any particular physical or health trouble at present?	2. Yes 4. No

occupational-
adjustment
index

The occupational-adjustment index used in this study is a modified form of the Adler Scale of Occupational Adjustment. The need to modify the Adler Scale arises from the design of the study which contrasts the occupational adjustment of a group of former patients who have been in the community for varying periods of time with a group of control individuals who have not been in treatment. The occupational history collected for the patients covers the period since return to the community for the hospitalized patients or the entire period of tenure in the community for clinic patients following the original 1950 observation period. Since there are variations in the length of time the patients were in the community, a five-year job history was collected for the control respondents to minimize recall errors and average this time variation. In addition, since our study emphasizes current performance in the community, slightly greater weight was given to stable employment during the past year. The Adler Scale and our modification of it follow:

ADLER OCCUPATIONAL-ADJUSTMENT SCALE

1. Regularly self-employed since release.
2. Regularly employed or farming since release.
3. Employed or farming; worked more than half time last six months and some, but not all, of the time since release.

4. Employed or farming; worked some of the time since release and less than half time last six months.

5. Not working at time of interview; had been employed within last six months and some of the time since release.

6. Not employed in last six months but had been employed since release.

7. Not employed since release.

OCCUPATIONAL-ADJUSTMENT INDEX AND INDEX SCORES

Description of Index	*Index Score*
Regularly self-employed past five years or since discharge	1
Regularly employed since discharge or past five years	2
Employed: worked more than half time past 12 months and all of preceding four years or since discharge	3
Employed: worked more than half time past 12 months and some but not all of preceding four years or since discharge	4
Employed: worked less than half time in past year, and all of time in preceding four years or since discharge	5
Employed: worked less than half time in past year; and some but not all of time in preceding four years or since discharge	6
Not employed in past year but had been employed during all of preceding four years or since discharge	7
Not employed in past year; employed some but not all of the preceding four years or since discharge	8
Not employed in past five years or since discharge	9

author index

243

subject index ▮

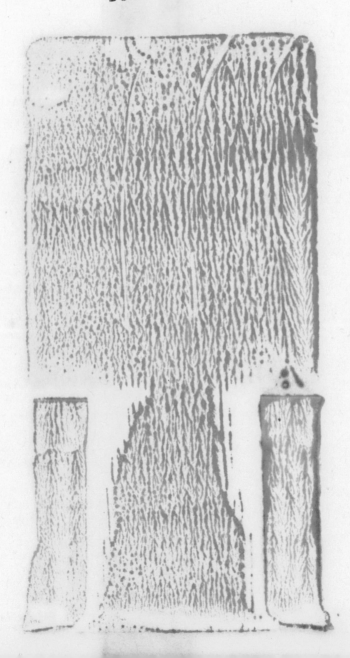